SOCIALIST ALTERNATIVE

This work was published by Red Flag Books – a project of Socialist Alternative, Australia's largest Marxist organisation.

We produce and distribute texts like this in order to help build a radical left armed with the knowledge of history, politics and revolutionary theory necessary to challenge the capitalist system, and all the barbaric forms of oppression that come with it.

All proceeds from this book's sale support our work.

At the back of this book, learn about some of our other projects.

INDIGENOUS LIBERATION & SOCIALISM

Jordan Humphreys

Indigenous Liberation & Socialism
by Jordan Humphreys

ISBN 978-1-922927-05-7

© Jordan Humphreys

Published by Red Flag Books
Melbourne, August 2023

Red Flag Books is an imprint of Socialist Alternative
redflag.org.au // sa.org.au
books@redflag.org.au

Cover
Vinil Kumar

Subediting and proofing
Ben Hillier
Tess Lee Ack
Oscar Sterner

Cover photo: 1972 Black Moratorium march in Sydney.
Courtesy of Mitchell Library, the State Library of New South Wales and the SEARCH Foundation.

Layout and production by Oscar Sterner
Printed by IngramSpark

Contents

Acknowledgements 7

Introduction 9

I. Indigenous oppression and capitalism

1. The origins of Indigenous oppression 21
2. Indigenous oppression today 35
3. Pitfalls of settler colonial theory 53

II. A history of struggle

4. Indigenous resistance and the early workers' movement 77
5. The Communist Party of Australia and Indigenous liberation 93
6. Post-war struggles: from civil rights to land rights 135
7. Black Power 169

III. Marxism and the fight for liberation

8. Racial, national or colonial oppression? 195
9. The new Indigenous middle class and Australian capitalism 209
10. Indigenous liberation, class struggle and socialist revolution 245

References 261

Acknowledgements

This book developed out of a series of articles I wrote for *Marxist Left Review*, so a particular thanks to the other members of the editorial committee: Omar Hassan, Mick Armstrong, Sandra Bloodworth and Louise O'Shea. Tess Lee Ack and Oscar Sterner edited the entire text at short notice. Ben Hillier also put a lot of work into making much of the text more readable and logical, while Nick Everett, Kim Bullimore, Gavin Stanbrook, Will Simms, Diane Fieldes and Oskar Martin read drafts of the book in full or in part, and I discussed many of the ideas in the book with Chloe Rafferty. Bob Boughton provided very useful information on the CPA and Indigenous politics, although we have divergent views on the usefulness of the Voice to Parliament. Evan Te Ahu Poata-Smith's thesis on Māori politics and Samuel Rose's writing on class and Indigenous communities in North America were both revelations and helped enormously with my own research.

Introduction

GORDON COPELAND FELL INTO THE FREEZING GWYDIR RIVER in northern New South Wales in the early hours of 10 July 2021. He was fleeing police officers who mistakenly thought that the car he had been travelling in was stolen. The police called out to the 22-year-old Gomeroi man, but after 30 minutes of searching they left the area. Returning at 3:45am to collect evidence, the officers heard Copeland calling from the river. They failed to locate him. He disappeared shortly afterwards, never to be seen alive again.

Copeland's body was found three months later, thanks to sustained pressure from his family and the local community when Moree police ended the search after three days. The delay in finding the body, and the police conduct that led to Copeland's death, triggered a coroner's inquest. This found that police had shown a lack of "respect" to his family, and revealed video footage of officers laughing about Copeland's disappearance during their initial search.

The episode is part of a longer history of racism, police harassment and disrespect in the northern NSW town. In the 1965 Freedom Ride, students from Sydney University arrived in Moree to protest racist discrimination. When escorting six Aboriginal children into the segregated pool, they were surrounded by 500 racist locals who jeered and spat at them. A fistfight broke out between a white woman and an Aboriginal woman, while a former Alderman known for his support for Aboriginal rights was "picked up on the street by hoodlums and dumped in the gutter".[1]

Racism remained a feature of Moree long after the Freedom Riders departed. In the 1980s, there were repeated clashes and racism-fuelled riots at the Post Office Hotel. When Aboriginal men entered the establishment in 1980, with a television camera crew in tow, and protested when they were

---

1. *Sydney Mirror*, 21 February 1965, p.1.

refused a drink, police arrested 12 and flogged them with batons. A few days later, someone fired a shotgun at the home of a prominent local Aboriginal activist involved in the protest. Then, in 1982, Ronald "Cheeky" McIntosh, a 19-year-old Aboriginal man, was shot dead after a clash between white racists and Aboriginal men at the Imperial Hotel, on the town's main street.[2] Left-wing newspaper *Tribune* argued at the time:

> Cheeky's murder and the wounding of three other Moree Aborigines last week was the end result of decades of racism. Moree, since the time of the Freedom Ride in 1965 has been a symbol of Australian racism. The town has seen changes since 1965, but too many of them have been superficial. The apartheid bans on Aborigines entering Moree's baths, cafes and pubs have gone. But what remains are the miserable living conditions of the town's 3,000 Aborigines (out of a total population of 10,500), the near-total unemployment, the lack of land rights and, above all, the racism of police and courts.[3]

From 1965 to today, many things have changed – but the racism that Aboriginal people face in Moree has endured. And while the town might be a "symbol of Australian racism", it is not an aberration.

Australia is often portrayed as a vibrant multicultural democracy committed to human rights, but the treatment of Indigenous people reveals a different picture. The Aboriginal and Torres Strait Islander population, numbering more than 900,000, is one of the most oppressed sections of our society. From the tens of thousands who live in remote and town-based communities in the north-west and centre of the continent, to those who live in rural towns – often not far from the old "missions" – across the eastern states, the hundreds of thousands who live in the major coastal cities, and those living on the islands of the Torres Strait or in Queensland's far north, Indigenous experiences vary greatly. However, there are some common themes of oppression.

Despite making up less than 4 percent of the Australian population, Indigenous people comprise almost 30 percent of prisoners. In the Northern

---

2. *Tribune*, 10 December 1980, p.7.
3. *Tribune*, 10 November 1982, p.1.

Territory, they are 83 percent of adult prisoners. The punitive logic of the "justice" system traps many from a shockingly young age. Nearly two-thirds of children under the age of 14 in detention are Indigenous; 94 percent of those detainees aged between 10 and 12 end up in adult prison before they turn 18.[4] Once in the system, recidivism is rife: 78 percent of Indigenous prisoners in 2021 had previously been jailed, compared to 49 percent of non-indigenous prisoners. One of the most horrific aspects of this mass incarceration is the Indigenous deaths in prisons, cells and police vans across the country.[5]

There has been much international and Australian coverage of the appalling levels of African-American incarceration in the United States. Yet as criminal defence lawyer and academic Russell Marks explains, the situation is worse here:

> [T]he discrepancies between black and white incarceration in the United States pale against those in Australia. Black Americans are imprisoned at five times the rate of white Americans, but Indigenous people are *twelve times* more likely to go to prison than non-indigenous people in Australia.[6]

Those who avoid becoming trapped in the incarceration system still face many other challenges. There is the pervasive economic inequality that endures despite endless policy papers and government announcements. In the decade from 2008 to 2018, the Indigenous adult employment rate increased only slightly from 48 percent to 49 percent, compared to 75 percent for non-indigenous people. Even in the major cities, where there are substantially more work opportunities, the Indigenous adult employment rate was only 59 percent in 2018.[7]

Indigenous people and their supporters, through decades of activism and defiance, have overturned a series of racially discriminatory laws and practices. However, behind formal "equality" before the law, the old mechanisms of oppression – economic, social and political – continue despite surface-level modifications. Deaths in custody keep occuring, poverty endures, land rights

---

4. AIHW 2020.
5. ABS 2021.
6. Marks 2022, p.9.
7. Closing the Gap 2020.

are respected only if they don't impinge on lucrative commercial activities, and Indigenous identity, culture and history remain politically contested.

Polite society now acknowledges that there have been historic crimes against the Indigenous population. There is even the admission that such crimes continue to affect Indigenous people and that further cultural recognition of past and present injustices is desirable. However, genuine restitution for both past injustices and continuing oppression remains elusive.

There is a growing desire for a transformation in the relationship between Indigenous people and the rest of society. Among progressive Indigenous and non-indigenous people, this is often expressed as support for a project of "decolonisation" that would end what is described as an exploitative, colonial, relationship between Australian settler society and Indigenous people, and open a path towards equality. As Marcus Stewart, co-chair of the First Peoples' Assembly of Victoria, has said: "[W]e don't believe that the solutions lie within the colonial system".[8]

For many, "decolonisation" simply means greater respect for Indigenous self-reliance and agency, support for Indigenous businesses, the promotion and revival of Indigenous culture free from paternalism or exploitation by non-indigenous people, and greater levels of education and understanding of Indigenous history and culture by non-indigenous people.

Decolonisation has also been expressed in various political projects. The most modest has been for constitutional changes to recognise the existence of Indigenous people. It was on this basis that the Recognise campaign was established in 2012. The multi-million-dollar advertising campaign was overseen by the NGO Reconciliation Australia and received widespread support from major businesses such as BHP and Qantas, as well as right-wing politicians like former Liberal prime ministers John Howard and Tony Abbott. While only a minority of conservative Indigenous figures supported the campaign, it fell apart in the face of strident grassroots opposition by many Indigenous people who recognised that it was a political PR exercise which would change little.

The inadequate symbolism of constitutional recognition fuelled interest in an alternative proposal: a constitutionally enshrined Indigenous Voice to Parliament created through a national referendum. This would be an advisory

---

8. Cosoleto 2022.

body for government Indigenous policies. A Voice to Parliament was one of the main proposals in the Uluru Statement from the Heart, endorsed at the Referendum Council's Regional Dialogues and the National Constitutional Convention, held at the Ayers Rock Resort near Uluru in May 2017. Advocates of the Uluru Statement present the Indigenous Voice to Parliament as the first step in a process that will deal with the structural dimensions of Indigenous oppression, end the powerlessness that plagues Indigenous communities and, along with a Makarrata Commission of truth-telling and agreement-making, lead to genuine Indigenous self-determination for the first time since colonisation.

Yet, while the Voice goes beyond merely constitutional recognition of Indigenous people, it too is an almost entirely symbolic gesture. The proposed body would have an advisory role only, and no power over government policy. Parliament would have to listen to its views, which it could then freely ignore.

While the Voice proposal was developed by a layer of Indigenous academics and lawyers, it has gained broad support among corporate Australia and within the federal Labor Party. It was strongly endorsed by 86 percent of the public submissions to the Joint Select Committee on Constitutional Recognition Relating to Aboriginal and Torres Strait Islander Peoples. These included submissions by most of the key sections of the Australian capitalist class. The submission from the Business Council of Australia, for instance, stated:

> The Business Council and its members are committed to the empowerment of Aboriginal and Torres Strait Islander peoples (in this report referred to as Indigenous Australians) and the creation of opportunities for full participation in the Australian economy and accordingly supports meaningful constitutional recognition of a Voice to the Parliament for Indigenous Australians. Without recognition of Australia's First Peoples, the Australian Constitution cannot be complete…
>
> The Business Council believes this issue is too important to be kicked into the weeds as we approach an election year. Equally, we do not support the politicisation of constitutional recognition and would not want to see a question put alongside next year's federal election. The Business Council

believes the question should be agreed, formulated and put to the Australian people via referendum within 12 months of the next federal election.[9]

As for the Labor government, the Voice is part of Prime Minister Anthony Albanese's strategy of presenting a progressive face to the public while pursuing a right-wing alliance with big business, the corporate media and wealthy but socially liberal Australians. The Labor Party hopes to be re-elected in part by portraying the Liberals and Nationals as dinosaurs out of touch with urban middle-class voters and corporate Australia, who have embraced cultural recognition for Indigenous people in recent years. In the process, Labor also hopes to neutralise the growing anti-racist sentiment in society by folding it into a tame cat institution unlikely to upset the status quo. This approach is hardly unique to Indigenous issues – on everything from climate change to trade union rights, foreign policy and LGBTI+ issues, hollow progressive symbolism dominates current government practice.

Support for the Voice from mining bosses, the Labor government and Liberal moderates reflects that the proposal can hardly be described as a reform. It will have no control over funding, legislation or communities. It will not make any difference to the lives of most Indigenous people, but it will further the social and political capital of a small section of the Indigenous middle class. Importantly, a victory for the Voice in the referendum will provide progressive cover to an insipid Labor government that refuses to address either the specific issues that Indigenous communities face or the cost-of-living crisis affecting the whole working class.

The Voice is a balancing act by the dominant parts of the Australian ruling class, who recognise the need to appear modern and anti-racist, but who don't want to concede any real power to Indigenous people and communities.

This approach has nevertheless faced strident opposition from the conservative right of Australian politics, who have used the Voice referendum to mobilise the most significant campaign against Indigenous rights in decades. The Liberals, the Nationals, One Nation and right-wing media outlets have worked together on the No vote campaign, drawing on longstanding racist hostility to Indigenous rights.

---

9. BCA 2018.

These right-wingers argue that while many Indigenous people may be disadvantaged, they are not deserving of the "special treatment" the Voice will confer – be it in "unearned privileges" or, in the minds of the more far-right sections of the campaign, some kind of "apartheid" system of reverse racism against white people. Underpinning the modern right, then, is an outlook not that different from the old racist assimilationism of decades past: that there should be no recognition of Indigenous oppression and that they should instead be considered socially and economically disadvantaged by their own illogical desire to continue cultural connections. As the former conservative Prime Minister Tony Abbott put it: "[T]his assumption that Indigenous people are 'different' and need to be treated differently – this separatist mindset – is at the heart of the problem".[10] Liberal opposition leader Peter Dutton has described the Voice as "the most significant change to the constitution proposed since federation". He says that it would "disrupt our government" and "re-racialise" Australian society.

The right-wing movement against the Voice has been coupled with revived campaigning about the need for more policing and government control over Indigenous communities – particularly those in Alice Springs – and even calls for another Northern Territory Intervention. The emergence of this campaign is a reminder that there is still an openly racist minority of Australian society connected to powerful conservative political institutions opposed even to symbolic advances for Indigenous people.

The embrace of constitutional recognition and cultural acknowledgment of Indigenous peoples by the rest of the political establishment and much of corporate Australia has also opened a space for a progressive critique of the endurance of Indigenous oppression.

The 2017 Constitutional Convention that gave birth to the Voice proposal faced dissenting progressive perspectives, which at the time were dismissed. A breakaway group of seven delegates and their supporters from Victoria, Canberra and New South Wales, including longstanding Indigenous activists Jenny Munro, Lyall Munro Jr. and future senator Lidia Thorpe, walked out of the convention in protest at what they viewed as a charade stitched up by conservative Indigenous leaders such as Noel Pearson before the

---

10. *The Australian*, 8 April 2023.

meeting. These concerns dovetail with the broader – and healthy – suspicion of anything that smacks of co-opting the Indigenous rights campaign in order to put it to bed without transforming the situation for Indigenous people. Many remember how, in the aftermath of Labor Prime Minister Kevin Rudd's 2008 apology to the Stolen Generations, little changed in terms of Indigenous oppression, epitomised by Rudd's continuation of the racist Northern Territory Intervention.

This experience has led a layer of more radical-minded Indigenous and non-indigenous people towards the politics of Indigenous nationalism, drawing from the history of the Black Power movement in Australia and similar movements overseas. This is often connected to the demand for a treaty – or more often, treaties – between the Australian state and Indigenous peoples, which are often now viewed as sovereign Indigenous nations. Among those who consider themselves anti-capitalists, this is sometimes connected to the need for some kind of anti-colonial revolution that breaks the racist logic of the Australian settler colonial state.

The perspective of decolonising Australia raises a series of important questions about the nature of Indigenous oppression and how it can be confronted, and ultimately done away with. Are Indigenous people oppressed today by colonialism? If Indigenous people are being oppressed by colonialism, then are they engaged in an anti-colonial struggle? How does this fit with the economically "advanced" and modern political structure of Australian society? And how does the struggle for Indigenous rights relate to other campaigns for economic and social justice?

This book offers a socialist perspective on these issues. It seeks to explain how Indigenous oppression is a result of capitalist society, and why the struggle for Indigenous liberation is bound up with challenging capitalism and, therefore, with the fight for socialism.

Often, scholarly analysis of the internal development of Indigenous politics is isolated from a broader analysis of Australian capitalism, or its relationship to the social classes whose interests and struggles shape the Indigenous population in an endless variety of ways. A key argument of this book is that we require an understanding, firstly, of the evolving nature of Australian capitalism and, secondly, of the development of the working-class movement and the socialist left in Australia. These two elements are vital to grasping both the relationship between the struggle for Indigenous justice and broader society, as well as the development of Indigenous politics and its own characteristics.

A key motivation for writing the book is the presence of a significant contradiction within the issue of Indigenous rights.

The ongoing oppression of Indigenous people is one of the most morally compelling issues of our time. Hundreds of thousands of Indigenous and non-indigenous people are horrified by the lack of progress and are willing to protest against the celebration of Australia Day, the closure of remote Indigenous communities and the seemingly never-ending Indigenous deaths in custody. Alongside climate change, LGBTI+ rights and economic inequality, support for Indigenous justice is one of the dominant themes of contemporary left politics in this country.

And yet the expression of this support has for the most part been confined to a general social mood and the occasional large protest. It has not led to the emergence of a mass movement drawing hundreds of people into sustained activism. Instead, most activist bodies remain relatively small and are primarily made up of those who have been campaigning for years, or decades, rather than significant layers of new younger forces. Political discussions around Indigenous issues are still dominated by either paternalistic symbolism or traditional conservatism, with little space for a more radical examination of both the causes of Indigenous oppression and the strategies that might be necessary to end it. Even among those on the radical left, there is surprisingly little written analysis of Indigenous politics beyond some historical studies and impressionistic journalistic works on contemporary issues.

This book seeks to make a modest contribution to closing the gap between the potential for a serious fight against Indigenous oppression and the limited nature of current struggles, by exploring how the revolutionary politics of Marxism can illuminate the causes of Indigenous oppression and outline a strategy to end it.

The first part of the book, "Indigenous oppression and capitalism", argues that understanding the nature of capitalism is key to grasping why Indigenous oppression continues. It explores how the initial invasion of the continent was driven by the expansionist logic of capitalism and how that system structured the oppression of Indigenous people after they were dispossessed of control over their own land. It then discusses why Indigenous oppression is reproduced in the modern capitalist system and the implications this presents for the influential argument that Indigenous people are oppressed today by colonialism.

"A history of struggle", the second part of the book, explores the historical relationship between struggles for Indigenous rights, the workers' movement and the socialist left. In the process, it examines the attitudes, theories and strategies that different currents on the left developed through the late 19th century and into the 20th, including the early shearers' unions and socialist organisations, as well as the Australian Labor Party, the Industrial Workers of the World, the Communist Party of Australia and its various offshoots, and the New Left of the 1960s and 1970s. It also examines the politics and history of major Indigenous organisations that often had relationships with the socialist left, such as the Australian Aboriginal Progressive Association founded in 1924, the campaign organisations of the 1930s that organised the 1938 Day of Mourning and Protest, the post-war civil rights organisations, and the land rights and Black Power campaigns of the 1960s and 1970s.

The final part of the book, "Marxism and the fight for liberation", begins by drawing up a balance sheet of the strengths and weaknesses of the different left-wing currents and their approaches to the struggle for Indigenous liberation, before examining how that struggle can be integrated into a broader Marxist strategy for confronting Australian capitalism. The emergence of an Indigenous middle class is explored from this perspective. The final chapter outlines how revolutionary socialist politics can contribute to renewing the struggle for Indigenous justice in the future.

The core arguments of this book are simple enough: capitalism is the root of Indigenous oppression; a revival of working-class struggle and the socialist left would profoundly benefit the fight for Indigenous justice; and genuine liberation for the vast majority of Indigenous people is impossible without a socialist revolution.

PART ONE

Indigenous oppression and capitalism

Chapter one

The origins of Indigenous oppression

> The discovery of gold and silver in America, the extirpation, enslavement and entombment in mines of the indigenous population of that continent, the beginnings of the conquest and plunder of India, and the conversion of Africa into a preserve for the commercial hunting of blackskins, are all things which characterise the dawn of the era of capitalist production.
>
> — Karl Marx, *Capital*.[11]

THE ORIGINS OF INDIGENOUS OPPRESSION IN AUSTRALIA lie in the colonisation of the continent, the dispossession of the Indigenous population and the establishment of a settler colonial state. This process of dispossession, which involved acts of genocidal violence, radically transformed the lives of Indigenous people, forcing them into the lowest positions within the new social structure. This process of colonisation and dispossession was itself part of the development of capitalism in the 18th and 19th centuries.

Capitalism and colonialism

While there are some examples of empires replacing Indigenous populations with settlers before the emergence of the capitalist system, the origins of modern settler colonies lie in the global expansion of the European empires from the late 15th century onwards.[12]

The Spanish and Portuguese feudal monarchies began this colonial expansion. Fresh from their reconquest of the Iberian territories and the

---

11. Marx 1990 [1867], p.915.
12. For examples of pre-capitalist settler colonial projects see the first four chapters of Cavanagh and Veracini (eds.) 2017.

expulsion of the Muslims and the Jews in the late 1400s, conquistadors unleashed a catastrophic wave of violence against the Indigenous peoples of the Americas following Christopher Columbus' voyage to Haiti. They were quickly followed by the Dutch, the French and the English. Many Indigenous people who avoided being murdered, or killed through forced labour, died as a consequence of the destruction of the socio-economic basis of their societies, as the Europeans ravaged the land in pursuit of gold and other riches.

The destruction of Indigenous American societies created a problem for the European powers. They needed lots of labourers to extract the vast amounts of wealth now open for plunder. But in many of the new colonies, the decimation of the Indigenous population reduced the potential labour force considerably. So the European ruling classes looked to two other sources: European settlers and African slaves.

Initially, the conquest of the Americas primarily benefited the feudal monarchies and their close supporters. However, as the wealth poured into Europe, it strengthened the social position of a rising layer of merchants who used it to fund the growth of early capitalist industry. As Karl Marx and Friedrich Engels noted in the *Communist Manifesto*:

> The discovery of America, the rounding of the Cape, opened up fresh ground for the rising capitalist class. The East-Indian and Chinese markets, the colonisation of America, trade with the colonies, the increase in the means of exchange and in commodities generally, gave to commerce, to navigation, to industry, an impulse never before known.[13]

European colonial exploitation intensified as the Industrial Revolution began. A horrific relationship was established between the burgeoning factory system of Europe, the enslavement of Africans and the growing European populations in the colonies of the so-called New World. This also intensified the geopolitical competition between the large European states, spurring on further colonial expansion.

Great Britain, the most developed capitalist country of its time, emerged as the most dynamic colonial force. During the 15th and 16th centuries, it

---
13. Marx and Engels 1848.

pioneered a new form of colonialism in Ireland, which involved driving the Irish population from certain areas and replacing them with tens of thousands of English and Scottish settlers. Many of the British administrators in Ireland used their "experiences" in later colonisation schemes. It was also in Ireland that an Anglo version of proto-racist theories about the inferiority of certain groups, in this case the Irish Catholics, was developed. Those ideas mixed with others developed during the reconquest of Portugal and Spain and the beginning of the slave trade in Africa, taking on an expanded meaning as colonial empires spread across the globe.[14]

British colonialism didn't go unchallenged by its rivals, or even its own colonial subjects. Defeat for the British in the American War of Independence decisively shaped the decision to establish a colonial settlement in Sydney. The British ruling class needed a new territory to dump its surging convict population, and by pivoting towards Asia and the Pacific it also hoped to counter the influence of the Spanish, Dutch and Portuguese in the region. The British feared that if they didn't set up a permanent presence in New South Wales, perhaps one of their imperial rivals would.

But what kind of colony was to be established? European colonial expansion had founded a variety of new societies. Some were little more than militarised trading outposts. Others involved the subjection and exploitation of millions of native people by a layer of white settlers. Others established colonial rule indirectly, through a subservient class of collaborating native elites backed by a smaller layer of colonial functionaries, merchants and soldiers.

While Sydney initially was established as a penal colony, within a few years it developed on a similar basis to the former British colonies in North America and the Spanish colonies in Argentina and Uruguay. These were primarily based on the extreme marginalisation of Indigenous people, rather than their incorporation as a mass exploited workforce. In the aftermath of the Napoleonic Wars, the British Treasury was burdened with an enormous debt; the government had a strong interest in promoting economic self-sufficiency for, and even a return on investment from, its colonies. This provided further impetus for Indigenous people in Australia to be driven from their land to make way for capitalist economic development.

---

14. Allen 2012.

Patterns of colonisation and the frontier wars

The establishment and expansion of a European colony in Australia required the destruction of the socio-economic basis of Indigenous society. Prior to the British invasion, Indigenous communities had collectively owned their lands and there was no separate class of exploitative rulers. For capitalist private property relations to be established, this communal system had to be smashed, and any Indigenous land claims denied.

To justify this criminality, the British used the racist theories of European supremacy that already underpinned the enslavement and colonisation of Africa, the wars of conquest in Asia, the occupation of Ireland and the extermination of Indigenous peoples in the Americas. While the Indigenous peoples of the Australian continent heroically resisted colonisation for many decades, the balance of forces was strongly stacked against them.

Unlike in North America and New Zealand, the British government would not sign any treaties here. This was due to a range of factors. The initial colonisation was under the direct control of the British state, and there weren't many free settlers – there were the convicts, the garrison and few others. European settlers couldn't establish trade relations or sign private treaties with Indigenous people until representatives of the British government established their authority. Also, while the British originally feared that other European powers might occupy the continent, this didn't happen. So the British didn't need treaties with Aboriginal or Torres Strait Islander people to create military alliances against rivals – this had been a strong motivation for many of the treaties in North America and even in New Zealand.[15] The lack of any treaty with Indigenous people increased their marginalisation within colonial society, because they lacked even the limited legal and political recognition afforded to the Māori in New Zealand.

Initially, the genocidal offensive against the local population was confined to the areas surrounding the colonies. But as these outposts grew and became centres of capitalist expansion in the 1820s, the war against Indigenous people spread throughout the continent.

These frontier wars were not primarily the result of the actions of paranoid

---
15. Attwood 2020.

small-farming settlers on the fringes of the colony. They were driven by the expansionist logic of the capitalist economy, which grew ever greater as the profitable potential of the land beyond the Blue Mountains became more obvious. The expansion of the colony, and therefore the dispossession of the surrounding Indigenous people, was achieved by a relatively small military force in alliance with the wealthiest and most powerful capitalists in the colony.

For example, William Cox, a magistrate, landowner and former paymaster for the New South Wales Corps (the British garrison) was employed by Governor Macquarie to build the road through the Blue Mountains to what would become Bathurst. On finishing the project, Cox was paid £300 and appointed the civilian commandant of the town. While Macquarie and the British government discussed how the land around the outpost would be divided, Cox was using convict labour to build structures and yards for his own future stations and was moving his cattle and sheep into the area before the government herds arrived. Unsurprisingly, Cox became one of the major landowners in the area.[16]

When Macquarie pushed for colonial settlement on the Wiradyuri land that Cox was already helping himself to, there were 16,000 British in and around Sydney. But originally, just 10 settlers were granted land west of Bathurst, under the protection of nine soldiers. As historian Stephen Gapps has explained:

> The initial occupation of Wiradyuri lands was never a great rush of so-called explorers and settlers, military and convict workers – and accompanying vast flocks of sheep and cattle – along Cox's road across the mountains. In fact it was a long process, which took another seven years. The initial westward expansion of the colony was very much what historian David Roberts has called a "government frontier".[17]

A "government frontier" contains few free settlers and is under the control of military personnel, whose needs are met by a small number of convicts. The few settlers who did live on the frontier were often deeply connected to

---

16. Gapps 2021.
17. Gapps 2021, pp.41–2.

the colonial government and as such were part of the colonial ruling class, or were quickly being integrated into it.

When the landowners and the military pushed their way deeper into Indigenous lands, they came into greater conflict with local Indigenous groups, who might raid the squatters' supplies, take cattle and sheep, and occasionally attack the invaders. The powerful landowning families then demanded protection for their cattle and sheep runs as they expanded across New South Wales. The governors and colonial security forces were only too happy to defend the interests of the nascent Australian capitalist class.

The Bathurst War of 1822–24, for instance, was instigated by absentee graziers and pastoral capitalists living in Sydney. In response to raids and attacks on their properties by the Wiradyuri people, the landowners convinced Governor Brisbane to declare martial law in the region west of the Blue Mountains and to send reinforcements to the Bathurst garrison. In September 1824, a battle took place between Wiradyuri warriors and a group of colonists led by Theophilus Chamberlain. Chamberlain was an overseer, notorious for his cruelty towards convict workers, and was employed by the powerful Cox family to manage their cattle and sheep stations. The colonisation of the New England region from 1830 was similarly driven by the graziers and pastoralists, as Ambēyaŋ historian Callum Clayton Dixon has explored.[18]

The capitalist state and the capitalists themselves were behind most of the massacres of Indigenous people throughout the 18th, 19th and early 20th centuries. Of the 415 massacres identified by the Colonial Frontier Massacres Digital Map Project, 207, or 50 percent, directly involved "agents of the state" – that is, police, soldiers or government officials. Most of the other 208 massacres were carried out by employees of pastoralists or miners, often organised by the bosses or their representatives, with the tacit approval of the police or local state officials.[19] Professor Lyndall Ryan, who led the Digital Map Project, explained in a 2022 *Guardian* interview:

> Particularly after 1860, it is becoming clear that most of the massacres are being conducted by employees of major companies who are bankrolling these big

---

18. Clayton-Dixon 2019.
19. Colonial Frontier Massacres Digital Map Project 2022.

pastoral leases, or mining leases. These companies have more money to arm their employees with good firearms to go out and do their work. It's not the small selector who's killing Aboriginal people, it's these big companies who have experienced overseers, experienced stockmen, to patrol and contain the Aboriginal people.[20]

The Australian colonial frontier is often understood and written about as a clash between a homogeneous white settler society and the Indigenous population. To the extent that social class is introduced into the picture, the lower classes are generally blamed for the violence, letting the colonial elites off the hook. For example, Richard Broome, in the fifth edition of his popular book *Aboriginal Australians,* writes: "[T]hose with convict backgrounds toughened by abject poverty and the lash were probably more inclined to use violence to solve problems".[21] This ignores the reality that the expansionist drive of capitalism *inevitably* led to conflict with the Indigenous population. That conflict could only end in violence.

It is also important to understand that the capitalist state and ruling class overseeing the dispossession of the Indigenous population were also cruelly exploiting both convict and free labourers, and could react with extreme brutality towards both when they rebelled. The same colonial landowners, convict overseers and military officers who fought the Wiradyuri in the 1820s also crushed the Ribbon Boys' Rebellion of Bathurst convicts in 1830. As historians Connell and Irving have argued, "force was applied on two fronts, against convicts and blacks – controlling the white workforce by the lash and the gallows, and creating the space within which the settlement could grow".[22]

The colonisation process greatly enriched the nascent Australian capitalist class and its British financiers. By the 1820s, "practically all the usable land in the Sydney region had passed into private hands". The overwhelming majority of this land was in the hands of the already wealthy.[23]

20. Allam and Evershed 2022.
21. Broome 2019, p.41.
22. Connell and Irving 1980, p.32.
23. Connell and Irving 1980, p.35.

In 1821, about 80 men controlled 60 percent of all alienated land in New South Wales. By the 1830s, there were around 400 gentry estates in New South Wales and 250 in Van Diemen's Land (the future Tasmania). From 1830 onwards, colonial policy shifted towards the sale of Crown land to private persons rather than the granting of land primarily by political patronage. However, this still excluded most people from land ownership. Ex-convicts or free settlers who enriched themselves through the colonial economy could buy land, but they were only a small minority of the population.[24]

By 1860, 4,000 European landowners were in control of over 400 million hectares of stolen Aboriginal land. The British government's decision in 1822 to favour wool from Australia and other British colonies over wool from continental Europe resulted in massive profits for these squatters, who by that time owned 20 million sheep.[25]

In contrast, the quarter of a million European immigrants who had arrived in the Australian colonies by 1860 were overwhelmingly propertyless wage labourers. Only a small minority were involved in violent attacks on Indigenous people or were able to own any of the land that was taken from them. Most ended up in the six colonial capitals or the large country towns. Left-wing historian Humphrey McQueen notes that, while the dream of being a small landowner played an important ideological role in the colonial working class, in reality, "Australia had a greater percentage of its population in towns than almost any other country". Rural workers remained an important section of the Australian labour force into the early 20th century. One study estimates that as late as 1915, 60 percent of the NSW population still lived in "country districts". However, the trajectory of the country was towards greater levels of urbanisation.[26]

Also, the rural population in the colonial era had specific features. There was never a significant small farmer class like that of the United States, let alone a peasantry such as that which existed in the older Latin American colonies. The bulk of the rural population was made up of migratory, unskilled, landless labourers. This shaped their relationship with the Indigenous population, as

---
24. Connell and Irving 1980, pp.51–2.
25. Broome 2019, pp.37–8.
26. McQueen 1976, p.151, quoted in Rowse 2017, p.7. Statistics on NSW population from Day and Cottle 2015, p.43.

we will see in more detail in chapter four. Unlike the American pioneer small farmers, the vast majority of Australia's rural working class was not involved in extended periods of armed conflict with the Indigenous population in order to seize land for their own small holdings. Most owned no land at all, or had a home closer to the coast or perhaps in one of the towns or cities.

The origins of the structures of Indigenous oppression

The colonisation of Australia was a product of the growth of global capitalism, and the frontier wars were driven by capitalism's expansionist logic. But this doesn't, by itself, explain the roots of Indigenous oppression. We also have to explain why it continued after the population was dispossessed. Some colonial officials believed that the differences between Indigenous and non-indigenous people would disappear as the former were absorbed into white society. But as we know, this did not happen.

The effects of colonisation varied across the country and resulted in long-lasting legacies for the various Indigenous identities and struggles in different areas. In the east and the south, the colonisation process was rapid and extensive. In central and northern Australia, some Indigenous groups maintained more of their traditional pre-invasion lifestyles and cultures, even though these were steadily undermined by the expansion of capitalism. The uneven effects in different areas created the material basis for divisions to emerge between so-called "tribal" and "detribalised", and "full-blooded" and "half-caste" Indigenous people – divisions reinforced by government policy and discrimination.

Until the 1840s, the general view of the colonial authorities was that, once Indigenous people had accepted their dispossession, they would be incorporated relatively easily into the colonial economy as wage labourers. Governor Macquarie thought that they could be useful "as labourers in agricultural employ or among the lower class of mechanics", while Governor Gipps believed that it was through wage labour that "the civilization of the Aborigines…must be worked out".[27]

---

27. Reynolds 1983, p.124.

There was, however, significant Indigenous resistance to the discipline that came with wage labour. While colonial authorities at the time took this as proof of the inherently backward nature of Indigenous people, historian Henry Reynolds notes that this "paralleled the situation in many parts of the world where capitalism penetrated traditional peasant and hunter-gatherer societies". At least one colonial administrator recognised the similarities, writing in 1842: "I find generally that the Blacks are lazy on the Monday like English Cobblers. I fear they will keep St. Monday [a traditional peasant holiday carried over by workers into the industrial revolution —JH]".[28]

A key issue was that Indigenous societies did not have the rigid class divisions of European capitalism (or feudalism, for that matter), so Indigenous people had not been conditioned to have the sense that some people had the right to exploit others for individual gain, or the associated deference to bosses and managers that is so vital in the capitalist workforce. The missionary James Gunther, for instance, explained that among the Aboriginal people he met, "no man has an idea of serving another".

> This idea of their own dignity and importance is carried so far that they hesitate long before they apply the term Mr. to any European even when they know full well the distinction we make between master and servant.[29]

He illustrated the point by recounting a time when he asked one of the Aboriginal men living on the mission to plough a field. The man refused, saying that "he was a master too".[30]

Another issue was the relationship between the Indigenous and non-indigenous workforce. One aspect of this was that the promotion of racist ideas by the colonial elite could lead to racial conflict between Indigenous and non-indigenous workers. However, the opposite concern was also expressed by colonial authorities: if Indigenous workers were integrated into the labour force, they might embrace the rebelliousness of the convicts and free labourers. As Reynolds explains, in the eyes of the authorities, Indigenous workers were

---

28. Quoted in Reynolds 1983, p.126.
29. Quoted in Reynolds 1983, p.127.
30. Reynolds 1983, p.127.

to "behave according to an idealised pattern of deference and loyalty rather than take their cue from the actual workforce".[31]

Many Indigenous people did become integrated into the early capitalist economy, whether through necessity, desire or force. Often, they worked as trackers, stockmen, shearers and labourers. A few worked as sailors, and during the gold rushes some took up small-scale mining. In the sparsely populated region of north-western Australia, there was a greater need for Aboriginal workers than in the south-east, due to a prohibition on the use of convicts in that region and the difficulty in attracting free labourers to such remote areas. By the end of the 1870s, "northern colonisation accounted for less than three hundred white settlers whose economic survival depended on the work of over one thousand Aboriginal people on sheep stations and pearling boats".[32] In the Pilbara and Kimberly regions, Aboriginal labour was essential to the development of vast pastoral estates. Similarly, in the Northern Territory and parts of Queensland, Indigenous workers formed an important part of the rural workforce.

However, Indigenous people didn't just dissolve into the rest of colonial society through wage labour. Many had only a sporadic connection to employment at any rate, and many others had none at all. They were often employed to cover labour shortages; when recessions hit, they were the first to be fired. Only a relatively small number of Indigenous workers, such as skilled shearers in particular regions, were considered indispensable by bosses.

In the remote areas where Aboriginal people formed the bulk of the workforce, a more intense racism was required to assert control over their labour. The bosses made significant profits by refusing to pay Aboriginal workers money wages and by overseeing a brutally exploitative system of near-slavery. To justify and enforce these racist practices, hardline racist ideas and institutions were required.

For Indigenous workers unable to be fully incorporated into the labour market, the alternative was the "mission". Missions were first established in the 1830s and 1840s in New South Wales and Port Phillip. At first, they were

---
31. Reynolds 1983, p.130.
32. Pedersen and Woorunmurra 1995, p.19.

simply a place to dump Indigenous people who had been pushed off their land by pastoralists.

The mission system was organised segregation. The missionaries looked on Indigenous people with the pity appropriate in their eyes to a proud but "primitive" people. Church authorities argued that contact between Indigenous people and white society had to be regulated as much as possible. While they acknowledged that Indigenous people might one day be safely assimilated into "Western civilisation", they believed that this would be possible only after a long period of "development" under the benevolent eye of the church. In the meantime, segregation was needed for the missionaries to enforce their control and discipline. Even when they approved the employment of Indigenous labour by private capitalists, they did so "only in ways that did not jeopardise the mission's moral and industrial project".[33]

This brought the mission system into periodic conflict with capitalists who did want to employ Indigenous workers, and whose main concern was figuring out how to make money from this otherwise unwanted and unassimilated section of the population.

Many Indigenous people were caught between the segregation of the missions and the exploitation of the white bosses, navigating between the two spheres, trying to gain the greatest amount of autonomy in the ambiguities between them. Some adapted aspects of pre-colonial life to these new conditions or worked out ways to sustain as much of their traditional culture as possible despite the challenges.

However, no one could ultimately escape the continent-wide transformation. As colonisation reached even the furthest fringes of the land, and the colonies federated and became self-governing, control over Indigenous people became more and more overseen by the capitalist state.

Victoria was the first to pass laws specifically controlling the Indigenous population, starting with the Aboriginal Protection Act (1869), which replaced a more ad hoc body with the Victorian Central Board for the Protection of Aborigines and introduced various regulations about where people could live and work, what kinds of jobs they could hold and who they could marry. This was followed by a suite of laws in other colonies and, after federation,

---
33. Rowse 2017, p.50.

state governments, which established Aborigines Protection Boards, defined who was and wasn't Indigenous, prohibited the sale of alcohol to Indigenous people, and empowered government "protectors" to commit Indigenous children to be raised in state institutions. This developed into the so-called protection system that dominated Indigenous politics for the first half of the 20th century.

The police played an increasingly important role as well. Historian Chris Owen has extensively documented how policing in the Kimberley frontier was deeply aligned with the interests of station owners who needed a force to discipline Aboriginal labour. In the eastern states, police often served as the local "protectors" of Aboriginal people and police commissioners sat on the Aborigines Protection Boards. When rural communities called for stricter segregation, when government officials decided to institutionalise Indigenous children, or when Aboriginal people bucked the authority of white bosses, the police were called to enforce the racist rules of Australian society.[34]

With the entrenchment of the missions, the stations, the police and the Aborigines Protection Boards as ongoing capitalist institutions, Indigenous oppression was transformed from a consequence of dispossession into something that would endure.

Understanding the capitalist origins of Indigenous oppression is vital, then, for explaining both its origins and its continuation. As we have seen, the colonisation of Australia was bound up with the development of global capitalism. And the growth of the colonies and the subsequent frontier wars were driven by the expanding needs of domestic capitalism, which was tied to the industrial expansion in Britain. Once the Indigenous population had been dispossessed, oppression was structured through institutions designed to deal with what now appeared to be an "alien" section of the population which would not easily be integrated into the labour force of the new economic system.

While this was the outcome of a brutal process, it wasn't entirely unique. The European peasantry had also been dispossessed and forced to become a new class of landless workers to staff the factories of industrialising Europe. They suffered brutal treatment at the hands of various institutions that were

---

34. Owen 2016.

established to control them socially and economically, such as the poor houses and the prisons – as well as the system of convict transportation itself, which forcibly removed hundreds of thousands from their homes and families.

The key difference between that situation and the one Indigenous people in Australia faced was that the latter became a linguistic, cultural and racial minority that could be pushed to the fringes of society because, in most cases, their labour wasn't necessary for Australian capitalism to flourish. Whereas the landless workers of Europe were the majority of the population and the essential source of labour for the emerging capitalist system, Indigenous people in Australia were to a much greater degree viewed as an obstacle to economic development.

Chapter two
Indigenous oppression today

FOR WELL OVER 150 YEARS, the Australian establishment ridiculed Indigenous people as biologically inferior and subjected them to horrendous cruelties: the frontier massacres, economic exploitation, the removal of children and social segregation. In the second half of the 20th century, things started to shift as the struggles of Indigenous people and non-indigenous activists overturned discriminatory laws and racist practices, challenging public attitudes, exploitative bosses and state bureaucrats. Ruling-class attitudes towards Indigenous people also shifted – not to sincerely embrace them and seek a real end to their oppression, but to cynically shape the growing anti-racist sentiment in a way that wouldn't challenge the status quo. The old racist ideology of assimilation was replaced by the idea of multiculturalism, which imagined Australia as a pluralistic society based on the tolerance of different ethnic groups. Yet this was also the era in which Liberal Prime Minister John Howard refused to apologise to the Stolen Generations and railed against the "black armband" view of history, which purportedly was too critical of the crimes committed against Aboriginal people.

This dichotomy between the promises of multiculturalism and the reality of racism continues. The ABC can air footage of smiling kids singing "I am Australian" in Indigenous languages, while it can also report that 100 percent of the children in detention in the Northern Territory are Indigenous. Albanese's government can be hailed for beginning a process of decolonisation with its support for an Indigenous Voice to Parliament, while leaving in place the key pillars of the inherently racist Northern Territory Intervention. The mining industry bosses, the Business Council of Australia and the Murdoch media can shake their heads at the failure to close the income, health and education gaps between Indigenous and non-indigenous people, while overseeing the system of exploitation, privatisation and corporate greed that makes this inevitable.

In this chapter, we trace how Indigenous oppression endured and changed throughout the 20th and into the 21st century.

From "protection" to assimilation

The Indigenous population was dispossessed as capitalism spread across the continent. In the process, Indigenous people were transformed into a racially oppressed minority living mainly on the margins of Australian capitalist society.

This racist oppression was embedded in the "protection" system that emerged in the late 19th and early 20th century out of the various Protection Acts of state and territory governments. These acts gave a chief protector or a Protection Board extensive powers over almost all aspects of Indigenous people's lives, including the ability to force them to live on, or leave, reserves and to move Indigenous children into boarding houses away from their families. "Protection" was justified within government circles on the basis that Indigenous people were a "dying race" – only by placing them under government control could there be any hope of staving off total extinction. However, from the 1920s, the Indigenous population stabilised and then started to increase. Despite this, the idea of a "dying race" lingered until the 1970s and the protection system remained entrenched, even as Indigenous people revealed their determination to survive and their opposition to government control.[35]

Those living outside of the reserves and the protection system in this period also faced segregation and discrimination, products of a society drenched in racist ideology, as the historian Richard Broome has explained:

> The customary practices of the caste barrier meant exclusion from many shops and businesses, churches, community organisations, social and sport clubs and the town's swimming pools. Hairdressers excluded Aboriginal customers lest their white clientele raise health concerns. Town housing was often made unavailable to Aboriginal people by estate agents to keep white areas "safe" and "pure". Work opportunities were confined to domestic service for

---
35. On the changing demographics of the Indigenous population during the protection period see Rowse 2017, pp.134–68.

women, and for men to rural manual work on properties, the local council, and the railways.[36]

This racist treatment ensured that most employed Indigenous people congregated at the bottom rungs of the working class in low-paid, seasonal and unskilled jobs. At late as the 1960s, 81 percent of Aboriginal workers in New South Wales were unskilled, 18 percent were semi-skilled and only 1 percent were skilled. The resulting low wages, combined with racist discrimination, underpinned poor health and a lack of education and housing opportunities. Poverty was then used as evidence of the supposed biological inferiority of Indigenous people.[37]

At first, assimilation was presented as an advance from the faults of the protection system. Academics and public servants interested in Indigenous welfare raised various concerns about the fate of Indigenous peoples – both those still living a more or less traditional way of life in distant parts of the continent and those under government authority. In 1937, a conference was held that brought together Commonwealth and state authorities. Attendees were forced to acknowledge the significant growth in what they called the "detribalised" and "semi-civilised" sections of the Indigenous population, which undermined the thesis that they were simply a "dying race". The conference passed resolutions indicating that the goal of government policy should be to assimilate them into white society (apart from those still living in a "tribal nomadic state"). "The destiny of the natives of aboriginal origin, but not of full blood, lies in their ultimate absorption by the people of the Commonwealth and it therefore recommends that all efforts should be directed towards that end," read one of the resolutions.[38]

While the conference criticised prejudice against "half-castes", it argued the only way to end it was for the Indigenous population to be liquidated into the rest of society. "Are we going to have 1,000,000 blacks in the Commonwealth or are we going to merge them into our white community

---

36. Broome 2019, p.179.
37. Broome 2019, p.181.
38. Rowse 2017, pp.195–97.

and eventually forget that there were any Aborigines in Australia?", asked Auber Neville, the chief protector in Western Australia.[39]

While first outlined in the 1930s, assimilation became official governmental policy following a 1951 Native Welfare conference sponsored by Paul Hasluck, the Liberal minister for territories from 1951 to 1963. At first, Hasluck tried to give the new policy a more progressive veneer by claiming that it didn't mean the end of Aboriginal cultural practices or languages. However, as the reality became clear, left-wing critics emerged who became increasingly suspicious of the policy and preferred "integration", in which Indigenous people could still keep aspects of their cultural heritage, instead of outright assimilation. In response to these critics, Hasluck became more conservative and opposed any preservation of Aboriginal culture among those not living a traditional way of life. Assimilation became a part of the broader vision of a "classless, monocultural, unified Australia" promoted by the Menzies Liberal government, in which the issue of Aboriginal people was seen as a welfare problem, not an issue of racism.[40]

The era of assimilation resulted in even more Indigenous people being placed under government control. While children had long been taken from their families and raised in institutions, there was now a significant increase in child removals, in line with assimilation's declared aims of "merging" Indigenous people into white society. More and more communities in the Northern Territory and Western Australia were moved onto missions and overseen by government officials.

Even on its own racist terms, assimilation proved to be a failure. By the early 1960s at the latest, it was clear that the bulk of "detribalised" people were not going to assimilate into white society. The fastest growing section of Indigenous people by the late 1960s was those living outside of the reserves, in shanty encampments on the outskirts of large country towns and in urban slums such as Redfern in Sydney. While some Indigenous people had taken the road towards assimilation, many either refused or were unable to do so. The whole assimilationist framework with its model of "advancement" from "tribalised" to "semi-civilised" to "civilised" had failed as the number of people

---

39. Broome 2019, p.211.
40. Broome 2019, p.212.

caught between the two worlds steadily expanded. Just as the previous idea of a "dying race" had been undermined by reality, the idea of an assimilated Indigenous population failed to materialise.

By the 1960s, it was clear that assimilation was facing serious structural challenges. But it took resistance by Indigenous people and their allies for a full-blown crisis of the assimilation system to develop. In the 1950s, there had been a flowering of activist groups, many of which united under the Federal Council for the Advancement of Aborigines in 1958. These groups, influenced by the civil rights movement in the United States, campaigned against racist segregation and criticised the government's assimilationist policies. From the mid-1960s, this movement intertwined with an emerging student radicalisation in universities, and later in workplaces, around opposition to the Vietnam War and to the general conservatism of Australian society. The idea that the issue of Indigenous people was a welfare problem that would be solved through assimilation, rather than a problem of racism, was fast becoming totally untenable.

The brief promise of self-determination

In the late 1960s and early 1970s, two elements pushed the assimilation strategy into total crisis. The first was the land rights issue, which was brought to the fore during the Gurindji strike that started in 1966 and spread across many rural and even some urban Aboriginal communities. The Liberal government was hostile to land rights and tried to dismiss their importance. But public support for struggles like those of the Gurindji threw the government on the defensive; it appeared rudderless and confused about the issue. The second element was the radicalisation of Indigenous activists in the cities with the emergence of the Black Power movement. All this took place in a broader context of industrial strikes, street protests and a sharp shift to the left in society.

So when the Whitlam Labor government was elected in 1972, ending 23 years of conservative rule, space opened up in new directions. The new prime minister announced that his government would pursue "self-determination" for Indigenous people and that there would be an

Aboriginal-elected committee to advise the government, an inquiry to establish land rights legislation and a six-fold increase in funding for Aboriginal affairs.

Despite these promises, the newly named Department of Aboriginal Affairs viewed the National Aboriginal Consultative Committee not as an independent body to present the views of Indigenous people, but as a body that should be subservient to government policy. Whitlam began the Woodward Commission of Inquiry into land rights. But there was no Indigenous representation, it was limited to the Northern Territory, mineral rights remained with the government and compensation for Aboriginal communities was ruled out of consideration. The increase in funding for programs to alleviate Indigenous poverty and discrimination was welcome, but not enough to overcome, or even seriously challenge, decades of oppression. At any rate, the government started to cut the funding as soon as the global economy turned towards recession.

Whitlam's government was dismissed in 1975 and Malcolm Fraser's Liberal government moved away from Whitlam's limited reforms. Self-determination was rebranded as "self-management", and more cuts were made to, and bureaucratic controls placed over, government-funded Indigenous programs.

The following year, Fraser passed the Aboriginal Land Rights (NT) Act, which was even more limited than that proposed by the Woodward inquiry. The Act "established a mechanism for granting land rights, but only in the Northern Territory, and only to Aboriginal reserves or vacant Crown lands to which traditional and ongoing attachment could be proven". Indigenous people alienated from their traditional lands or in urban environments got nothing. A "veto" clause was embedded in the Act, giving the government the ability to override claims that conflicted with the "national interest". And if mining companies and Indigenous communities couldn't come to an agreement, the government had the right to appoint a meditator whose decision was final.[41] This was land rights in name only. Aboriginal groups could negotiate for mining royalties. Some hoped that these might provide the economic basis for communities

---

41. Broome 2019, p.285.

to escape white control and gain independence. But as Richard Broome has explained:

> [M]ining royalties need to be seen in perspective. They did not produce great wealth, despite Queensland premier Joh Bjelke-Peterson's claim that Aboriginal people would become "very wealthy people – like the sheiks of the Middle East". It was estimated in the mid-1980s that, by the year 2000, Aboriginal people whose land was mined would earn $3,413 per annum and those in other parts of the Territory, $750 yearly. While royalties could provide some capital for development, royalties at the rate then awarded were insufficient to provide economic independence.[42]

The election of the Hawke Labor government in 1983 once again raised expectations that there would be a significant change in approach. However, under Hawke and then Paul Keating, Indigenous people continued to face shocking levels of inequality. This was largely because these Labor governments aggressively pursued a series of economic measures that had a devastating impact on the conditions of working-class communities: financial deregulation, privatisation of public assets, a shift from a formal commitment to full employment towards the idea of "fighting inflation", a market-oriented restructuring of welfare and public spending, and a Prices and Income Accord which resulted in trade union strength being eroded over time.

For Indigenous workers in rural areas, this period resulted in the increased automation of production, the casualisation of labour, the deregulation of wages and a radical reduction in the number of jobs. The result of this was the "collapse of small rural centres, the increase in migration to urban and regional cities, and the fragmentation and dispersal of working populations that had been reliant on local industry". In the "wake of the new economic order", it was the "most marginal populations that carried the burden of the inequalities".[43]

A similar process took place in urban Indigenous communities, as the impact of the new policies as well as the recessions of 1982–83 and 1991–92

---

42. Broome 2019, p.285.
43. Morris 2014, p.6.

entrenched economic inequality in general and Indigenous poverty in particular. Indigenous unemployment skyrocketed from 5 percent in the 1950s to 35 percent by 1986 – four times the Australian average. Indigenous incomes stagnated throughout the 1980s, despite increased access to welfare payments. Those payments made up an increasingly large portion of Indigenous incomes – 50 percent by 1986, compared to 23 percent for the rest of the population.[44]

All of this was facilitated by the Labor Party. As academic Michael Morrissey has explained:

> The brute fact is that the gap between Indigenous Australians and the rest either remained static or actually widened in terms of the key indicators of health, labour force and education participation, as well as income levels and incarceration rates during the period of Australian Labor Party (ALP) government: and a fundamental reason for this was the fact that a sweeping rhetoric of reconciliation, atonement and social justice was never, at any point, underpinned by anything near the appropriate commitment of resources.[45]

While Keating could make grand speeches, like the one at Redfern in 1992, the unfolding offensive against working conditions, social welfare, public education, public health and government projects, in general resulted in most Indigenous people being locked into structural racial and economic discrimination – a position in which they remain to this day.

Hawke and Keating were more interested in words than deeds when it came to Indigenous issues. Hawke had been elected promising a commitment to national land rights legislation. But faced with substantial opposition from mining companies, and undermined by his own commitment to working with corporate Australia, Hawke quickly buckled and said that states should just decide their own laws. In a joint press statement, Joh Ah Kit, director of the Northern Land Council, and Pat Dodson, co-coordinator of the Federation of Land Councils, accused the Hawke government of "crumbling in the

---

44. These statistics from Broome 2019, pp.261–62.
45. Morrissey 2006.

face of a spiteful campaign waged by the mining industry".[46] This led to tensions with the National Aboriginal Conference (NAC), which had been established under the Fraser government. Some members wanted to work with the Labor government; others were more critical. In June 1985, angered by criticism from the NAC over the backdown on land rights, Hawke dissolved the organisation.

During the 26 January 1988 bicentenary celebrations, tens of thousands took part in a protest in Sydney organised by the National Coalition of Aboriginal Organisations around the issues of sovereignty, land rights and deaths in custody. Under pressure, Hawke announced a royal commission into Aboriginal deaths in custody and the creation of the Aboriginal and Torres Straits Islander Commission (ATSIC). Many of the 339 recommendations from the royal commission were never implemented. While ATSIC had a broader mandate than previous bodies, a substantial part of the organisation was composed of unelected bureaucrats beholden to the government.

Paul Keating became prime minister in 1991 and came under pressure over the land rights issue in the wake of the 1992 Mabo High Court decision. The resulting government policy, the Native Title Act 1993, was primarily concerned with ensuring that mining and pastoral interests were protected. It established a very high benchmark for the recognition of native title and confined applications to Crown land.

Recent Labor and Liberal governments

The election of arch-conservative John Howard in 1996 marked the start of a new offensive against Indigenous rights. The Howard Liberal government is often presented as the political polar opposite of the previous Labor governments; after all, Keating embraced reconciliation and gave impassioned speeches about genocide and the frontier wars, while Howard derided that "black armband" view of history, refused to apologise to the Stolen Generations and shut down the Aboriginal and Torres Strait Islander Commission. Yet in many ways, the Hawke and Keating governments laid the groundwork for Howard's more aggressive attacks, by granting only meagre reforms that

---
46. Quoted in *Trade Union Committee on Aboriginal Rights Newsletter*, March 1985, p.3.

could be undermined and backing down in the face of campaigns by mining companies, which emboldened the racist political right.

The culmination of Howard's more aggressive approach was the Northern Territory Intervention, launched on the eve of the 2007 federal election. Howard manipulated concerns about the abuse of children to introduce extremely authoritarian and racist controls over Aboriginal communities in the Northern Territory. Demeaning signs banning alcohol and pornography were placed at community entrances, welfare "quarantining" was introduced, regulations on government access to remote communities were suspended and the government compulsorily acquired 65 communities, granting them only five-year leases to Crown land. To avoid legal issues, the government suspended the Racial Discrimination Act.

Labor was nevertheless elected under leader Kevin Rudd. Once again, the party positioned itself as sympathetic to the concerns of Indigenous people – epitomised by the apology to the Stolen Generations. However, Rudd ruled out compensation even though it had been recommended in the 1997 *Bringing Them Home* report, the published outcome of the National Inquiry into the Separation of Aboriginal and Torres Strait Islander Children from their Families. Leading Aboriginal activist Gary Foley commented that the apology was "yet another fraud in the long line of historically fraudulent acts and dishonest gestures that typify the indigenous experience of all governments in Australian history".[47]

Rudd's government continued the Northern Territory Intervention with minor changes, as did the Gillard Labor government. Progress on land rights, Black deaths in custody or economic inequality was ruled out by the Labor government's commitment to balanced budgets, tax cuts for the rich and a centrist political agenda.

The election of the Abbott Liberal government in 2013 set off another more aggressive attack on Indigenous rights, this time with the 2015 decision to cut federal funding to 150 so-called "economically unviable" remote Aboriginal communities, which came alongside a racist campaign decrying taxpayer funding for Aboriginal "lifestyle choices". Abbott's successor, Liberal moderate Malcolm Turnbull, took a less antagonistic approach. But he

---
47. As quoted in McKinnon 2008.

also dismissed calls for a constitutionally enshrined representative body for Indigenous people and for changing the date of Australia Day, as did the more conservative Liberal Prime Minister Scott Morrison. Throughout this period, Indigenous deaths in custody continued and the annual *Closing the Gap* reports recorded little to no progress on income, health and educational outcomes for Indigenous people.

The Labor Party's 2022 election victory under Anthony Albanese once again raised expectations in some quarters that there would be significant changes in government Indigenous policy – particularly with Albanese's support for a referendum around yet another Indigenous representative body, the Indigenous Voice to Parliament. As with the previous Labor governments, though, there is a huge gulf between the government's rhetoric and its practice.

The aspects of Indigenous oppression today

There has always been an economic dimension to Indigenous oppression. Whether it was those forced into the pearling trade in the 1800s, or the stockmen used in the pastoral and cattle industries in the west and north of Australia, there is a long history of exploitation. The other side of this is the poverty that many Indigenous people have been forced to endure due to a lack of access to employment on the reserves and in the rural and urban slums.

There is still an important economic aspect to Indigenous oppression, but it is not because Indigenous people are brought together as a super-exploited section of the workforce (like in the pastoral industries of old). The changing nature of Indigenous economic exploitation can be seen in the example of the Ngarrdangarli people who live in the Pilbara region of Western Australia. In the 1860s, settlers dispossessed the Ngarrdangarli. While some were able to find "refuge" in more remote parts of the Pilbara, most were "herded onto cattle stations, or worked in competing mining and pearling industries".[48] The pastoral industry's control over the land and access to Aboriginal labour was ensured by the Western Australian government, police and local magistrates.

This control was challenged in the post-war period by the activism of Aboriginal station workers and a broader push for wage equality by left-wing

---

48. Cleary 2021, pp.9–10.

trade unions. This eventually led to the Federal Pastoral Industry Award in 1967, which effectively granted equal pay for Indigenous workers in the industry. When the Award came into force in 1968, it led to the mass sackings of hundreds of Ngarrdangarli workers by the pastoral bosses. They were then evicted from the stations and lived in slum conditions on the reserve on the outskirts of Roebourne.

In the early 1970s, the lives of the Ngarrdangarli were transformed once again, this time by the emergence of large-scale iron ore mining in the region. Overnight, hundreds of white workers inundated Roebourne to work on new mining projects like the Robe River development. Poor health, entrenched poverty and very low levels of formal education meant that there were very limited employment opportunities for the local Aboriginal population. On top of this, journalist Paul Cleary explains that "Roebourne's new status as a staging post for the mining boom led to a raft of social problems for the Aboriginal population still living on the reserve" – including a significant increase in alcoholism and interpersonal violence.[49]

While the mining companies and the state government made enormous fortunes out of the stolen Ngarrdangarli land, they moved the services for the mining workforce (including the Roebourne Shire Council offices but, unsurprisingly, not the prison) to three newly created towns: Karratha, Dampier and Wickham. The result was "like something out of apartheid South Africa, the white workforce lived in air-conditioned comfort while the Aboriginal population of Roebourne lived in overcrowded and squalid conditions".

> This disparity is now even more pronounced... There are yawning gaps in the employment participation of the population. Only 36 percent of Indigenous people in Roebourne work full-time, a full 20 percentage points below the average for Western Australia and Australia as a whole. Only 20 percent work part-time, 10 percentage points below the WA and Australian average... While one-third of the 11,000 Aboriginal people residing in the Pilbara are better off as a result of employment in mining, the two-thirds made worse off "bear all the hallmarks of the so-called resource curse".[50]

---

49. Cleary 2021, p.11.
50. Cleary 2021, pp.11–12.

For an increasing majority of Indigenous people, the key site of exploitation is not in the remote communities but in the industrial heartlands of Australian capitalism. During the 19th and most of the 20th centuries, most of the Indigenous population was confined to the fringes of capitalist society, whether that was on the missions, in urban slums or in remote communities. While important differences remain, today most Indigenous people are part of the working class, and a significant section is far more integrated into the urbanised blue- and white-collar working class than ever before.

Fewer than 100,000 Indigenous people now live in "remote or very remote" communities in the Northern Territory and Western Australia. The vast majority of the other 800,000 live in coastal cities and large rural towns, particularly in New South Wales and Queensland. The 2021 census revealed that 37 percent of Aboriginal and Torres Strait Islander people (more than 300,000) live in capital cities, and that the fastest growing populations are in the more urbanised states of NSW, Queensland and Victoria, while Western Australia and the Northern Territory, which are home to larger Indigenous populations living in remote areas, have recorded very little population growth.[51]

As Australia once again enters a period marked by a cost-of-living crisis, stagnant wages, unaffordable housing and ruling-class concerns about government debt, the whole working class is suffering. But those concentrated at the bottom rungs of the class, such as Indigenous people, are suffering the most. As Russell Marks notes:

> [G]overnments have...done just about everything they could have to destroy the social safety net which people who can't compete in the employment market depend on. They've sold off public housing and created waiting lists in some places – like the Northern Territory – as long as *ten years*. They've abandoned the economic policy goal of full employment. They've created hurdle upon hurdle for people who need to access social security. They've refused to ensure the paltry dole amounts keep pace even with inflation. They've pursued policies which have created a multigenerational underclass. These policy decisions have had an enormous impact upon Indigenous people living the legacy of dispossession. It's not middle-class people – Indigenous or settler – who are

---

51. ABS 2022.

feeding Australia's prisons. Australia's prisons have become twenty-first century warehouses for First Nations poverty and disempowerment.[52]

While poverty and inequality provide the material underpinnings of the situation many Aboriginal and Torres Strait Islander people face, Indigenous oppression can't be reduced to an economic phenomenon. Issues such as land rights, the policing of Indigenous communities, historical and ongoing discrimination and debates around reconciliation, Indigenous representation and culture have repeatedly become political battlefields on which the nature of contemporary oppression is laid bare.

The decades of racist lies promoted about Indigenous people have become embedded in many rural or more socially conservative sections of the middle class and a minority of more right-wing workers. They have been more resistant to shifts in mainstream consciousness and form the base of the conservative right's anti-Indigenous campaigns. The Liberal and National parties and right-wing politicians like Pauline Hanson have periodically managed to tap into this racist audience, which has also been strengthened by the international development of far-right attitudes, often influenced by the movement around Donald Trump in the United States. Right-wing politicians can tap into pre-existing racist ideas but also galvanise and mobilise those attitudes to suit their electoral purposes.

Similarly, many contemporary racist ideas about Indigenous people are related to crime and policing. Indigenous people are both overpoliced and endure greater levels of poverty, which results in a section of them committing "crimes" of poverty. This reality creates the social basis for racist ideas to flourish because it can *appear* that Indigenous people are more prone to crime. Why, asks the political conservative, would they be so over-represented in the prison system? Why would the police constantly be called on them if they weren't doing something wrong?

The racist logic of this law-and-order campaigning, and the role of the conservative right, was on display in the Queensland city of Rockhampton in 2023 when local One Nation activist Torin O'Brien whipped up a mob of 30 people to surround the home of two Aboriginal youths accused by

---
52. Marks 2022, p.182.

Torin of being responsible for a spate of criminal acts. The Facebook group that O'Brien used to organise the protest was filled with vile racist posts, including one that claimed a "race war" was unfolding and said: "Bring it on that would mean we could legally go and get these dogs". Another post included a photograph of the home of an Aboriginal family with the comment: "[W]ho's got about 14 body bags for these little cunts?" A week later, O'Brien organised an intimidation convoy of cars to drive past the homes of Aboriginal families.[53]

This came after a wave of racist social media and mainstream media campaigns. In one incident, media reports falsely claimed that a residential care home was a halfway house for young people accused of crimes. According to a report in the *Guardian*, this led to a flurry of death threats against the Aboriginal children staying in the care home, "including calls for neighbours to 'storm the house' and 'hang whoever is inside'". Notably, this occurred as the Liberal Party was launching a series of attacks on the ALP for not doing enough to combat crime in Indigenous communities and as the Queensland Labor government was tightening laws aimed at criminalising Indigenous youth.[54]

The right denies that there is any political aspect to Indigenous oppression. For example, conservative figures argue that the over-representation of Indigenous people in prison is not due to racism in the police force or the judicial system, but is the result of "Indigenous disadvantage" manifested in widespread unemployment and alcoholism.

In books such as Noel Pearson's *Our Right to Take Responsibility* and Sutton's *The Politics of Suffering*, the argument is that high rates of Indigenous incarceration are due to the high rates of Indigenous criminality. In the eyes of these conservative commentators, this is the unintended side effect of the movements for Indigenous rights in the 1960s and 1970s. According to this theory, the winning of equal pay for Indigenous workers in the 1960s and the subsequent mass sackings of rural Indigenous workers, the discrediting of assimilation and the overturning of restrictive laws preventing Indigenous people from accessing alcohol led to the breakdown of Indigenous communities

---

53. Smee 2023a.
54. Smee 2023b.

in the second half of the 20th century in a wave of rising unemployment, alcoholism and violence.

For these commentators, high rates of incarceration have little to do with racism *per se*, but result from Indigenous people failing to integrate into mainstream Australian society. The solution, then, is the same as the one Pearson proposes for solving Indigenous poverty: Indigenous people just need to get off welfare and embrace the "real economy". Then poverty rates will fall, then crime rates, and finally incarceration rates.

Removing racism from the picture renders incomprehensible the 2004 murder of Cameron Doomadgee on Palm Island by police officer Chris Hurley, or the acquittal of Zachary Rolfe for the 2019 murder of Kumanjayi Walker in the Northern Territory. And while Palm Island and the Northern Territory might be explained away as particularly racist areas, this theory also can't explain the day-to-day racist policing in Redfern or western Sydney.

The denial of any political dimension to Indigenous oppression is important for the conservative right. They know that if they can reframe the discussion away from racism and towards "disadvantage", they will create a formidable barrier to any serious proposals for combating Indigenous oppression.

Liberal centrists on the other hand do acknowledge that there is a political aspect to the treatment of Indigenous people. The Labor Party, many corporate media outlets, cultural and educational institutions, boardrooms and government departments accept that Indigenous people have been treated terribly by governments and bosses. They can even admit that this history has an ongoing legacy, which requires a change in how Indigenous culture and history are understood by non-indigenous people and how Indigenous people are represented in the political system.

However, socially liberal centrists have a very narrow understanding of Indigenous oppression. They often divorce the socio-economic aspects of oppression from its political manifestations; the inequality that Indigenous people face is often presented as an outcome of a lack of political and cultural representation, rather than having anything to do with the structures of society. It is easier for centrists to accept the need for constitutional recognition, Indigenous political bodies, and even potentially a change to the date of Australia Day than it is to challenge the neoliberal setup of the economy or the power of mining companies to veto land rights claims. Centrists are also deeply invested in the idea that some grand gesture of reconciliation, in which Indigenous people are finally acknowledged appropriately within the nation-state, will resolve or at least begin to resolve the racism that Indigenous people suffer from.

The political oppression that Indigenous people face, then, is not simply that of the openly racist right-wingers. Centrists also end up reinforcing the political oppression of Indigenous people, because they oppose any movement or proposal that seeks to alleviate the conditions of Indigenous people by looking outside of the structures of liberal democracy and the capitalist market. They seek to convince people, Indigenous and non-indigenous, that no radical challenge to the nature of society is necessary to defeat racism.

As Yellowknives Dene First Nation activist and writer Glen Coulthard has explained in his book *Red Skin, White Masks: Rejecting the Colonial Politics of Recognition*:

> [I]nstead of ushering in an era of peaceful coexistence grounded on the ideal of reciprocity or mutual recognition, the politics of recognition in its contemporary liberal form promises to reproduce the very configurations of colonialist, racist, patriarchal state power that Indigenous peoples' demands for recognition have historically sought to transcend.[55]

If conservatives need to downplay the fact that Indigenous people are oppressed as a race, then centrists need to explain how the existence of this racism doesn't raise any fundamental criticisms of the capitalist system.

Aspirations of Indigenous people in this country for an end to all manifestations of racism are simply not compatible with the setup of Australian capitalism. Poverty and economic exploitation are rooted in the nature of the capitalist labour market, which is structured to generate profits for bosses rather than satisfy the needs of workers. And the capitalist state ensures that the welfare system is geared towards disciplining the poor.

The political aspects of Indigenous oppression are also connected to capitalism. Take the issue of self-determination. The long history of racist

---

55. Coulthard 2014, p.3.

state controls over the lives of Indigenous people has made the issue of self-determination a central one for Indigenous politics. Yet capitalism is inherently antagonistic to any form of genuine democratic control over society. This is because it is a system in which a small minority controls the means of producing wealth, and can only maintain that wealth through the exploitation of the labour of the majority of the population. The top-down bureaucratic structure of all the institutions in our society – the parliament, the public service, the police, the courts, the media, the education system – is determined by the fact that we live in a society dominated by the capitalist class.

While liberal democratic capitalism has created various structures which help promote the idea that it depends on the will of the people, this is a charade. Underneath it all, the dictatorship of capitalism reigns and the democratic will of the working class is stifled. It is not impossible for workers, or sections of the oppressed such as Indigenous people, to win some narrow democratic control over their own lives. However, this will always be limited by the overall undemocratic nature of the capitalist system. Genuine self-determination and sovereignty will always remain illusory in a society dominated by a wealthy elite controlling the vast majority of resources.

Instead of genuine self-determination, liberal centrists promote a dramatically restricted conception of Indigenous sovereignty, embodied in the creation of new bureaucracies, NGOs and private businesses. Rather than challenging the undemocratic power of state bureaucracies, corporate giants and corrupt political parties, such a narrow idea of self-determination is about promoting the interests of a small layer of Indigenous elites within these very institutions, while leaving the vast majority of Indigenous people disempowered. This is the only form of Indigenous "self-determination" compatible with capitalist society.

For left-wing people appalled at the racism of the right and disillusioned with the inadequacy of the mainstream liberal approach, there is an apparent alternative in the politics of settler colonial theory, which is the subject of the next chapter.

Chapter three
Pitfalls of settler colonial theory

THE COLONISATION OF THE CONTINENT and the resulting dispossession, violence and exploitation ensured that Indigenous people would become one of the most oppressed sections of Australian society. As the Black Power activist Roberta Sykes put it: "Blacks were thrown to the bottom of Australia's social and economic ladder by the theft of their land and usurpation of their status as owners of the country".[56] Yet an acknowledgement that the roots of Indigenous oppression lie in colonisation doesn't necessarily tell us why that oppression continues, or how it has changed. As Sykes also argues, there is both a "historical basis and a contemporary manner of maintenance" of Indigenous oppression.[57] This chapter explores the popular argument that the contemporary maintenance of Aboriginal and Torres Strait Islander oppression is due to the settler colonial nature of Australian society, as well as the idea that there is an ongoing process of colonisation.

Settler colonial theory

The theory was first popularised in left-wing circles by Australian academic Patrick Wolfe, who argued that there are fundamental differences between specific forms of colonial societies. Wolfe drew a distinction between colonial societies in which most inhabitants were ruled by a foreign power – one often dependent on the labour of the colonial population – and settler colonial societies in which the Indigenous population was violently forced to the margins to make way for an influx of settlers. Wolfe argued that the Indigenous peoples of North America and Australia are "people whose territorial expropriation was foundational", and that therefore "their relationship with their colonizers…

---

56. Sykes 1989, p.22.
57. Sykes 1989, p.18.

centred on land", while the relationship of African Americans, for instance, to their rulers "centred on labour".[58] Wolfe also argued that a core dynamic within settler colonialism is a "logic of elimination" and that "settler colonialism has both negative and positive dimensions".

> Negatively, it strives for the dissolution of native societies. Positively, it erects a new colonial society on the expropriated land base – as I put it, settler colonizers come to stay: invasion is a structure not an event. In its positive aspect, elimination is an organizing principle of settler-colonial society rather than a one-off (and superseded) occurrence. The positive outcomes of the logic of elimination can include officially encouraged miscegenation, the breaking-down of native title into alienable individual freeholds, native citizenship, child abduction, religious conversion, resocialization in total institutions such as missions or boarding schools, and a whole range of cognate biocultural assimilations. All these strategies, including frontier homicide, are characteristic of settler colonialism.[59]

As Lorenzo Veracini puts it, settler colonialism should be seen as a "distinct mode of domination" in which "colonialism supersedes rather than reproduces the colonial rule of difference; settlers win by discontinuing unequal relationships rather than maintaining them". So land and dispossession, rather than labour and exploitation, are considered central to the oppression of the Indigenous population.[60]

This framework is not confined to academic journals. On the Australian left, the dominant explanation for Indigenous oppression is that we are still living in a settler colonial society. In activist circles, Clare Land, with her book *Decolonizing Solidarity*, and the self-described "Aboriginal nationalist" group Warriors of the Aboriginal Resistance are prominent advocates of the settler colonial argument. For many left-wing people, the idea that colonialism persists is taken in a vague and general way. Primarily it serves as an acknowledgement that anti-Indigenous racism is linked to the continent's

---

58. Wolfe 2001, p.867.
59. Wolfe 2006, p.388.
60. Veracini and Cavanagh 2017, p.3.

invasion in 1788 and as a rebuttal to right-wing commentators who argue that Australia has resolved – or should resolve – Indigenous disadvantage by progressing to a post-racial society. Yet, as a serious analysis, settler colonial theory offers both an inaccurate portrayal of the present nature of Indigenous oppression and a disorienting impact on attempts to develop a strategy for liberation.

Australia and settler colonialism

Is the situation of Indigenous people in Australia marked by an ongoing colonial process of elimination? Does the Australian state oppress Indigenous people by "discontinuing unequal relationships rather than maintaining them"? Is Indigenous oppression primarily about the question of land rather than labour and exploitation?

The origins of Indigenous oppression in Australia undoubtedly lie in the colonisation of the continent. As noted in chapter one, the dispossession that resulted transformed Indigenous people into a racially oppressed section of Australian society. However, this initial process of colonisation was completed a long time ago. The Australian state gained total control of the continent more than 100 years ago. The state's territorial integrity has not been seriously challenged since federation. Indigenous people face terrible discrimination and inequality, and they have repeatedly resisted racist oppression. But this has not taken the form of an ongoing colonial war between colonisers and colonised since at least the end of the 19th century, some occasional rhetoric and isolated frontier skirmishes aside.

Compare the situation in Australia to that in Palestine, where there is an ongoing process of colonisation. Israel's expansionist desire to claim more Palestinian land constantly comes up against the resistance of the Palestinians, which breaks out into open military conflict on a semi-regular basis. Sections of territory remain under at least the formal political control of Palestinian authorities.

Settler colonial theorists often argue that the colonisers' need for more land lies behind the oppression of Indigenous populations. Sai Englert goes further, arguing that an important feature of settler societies is that intense economic or political crises can be resolved within them "by intensifying the dispossession of indigenous populations in order to improve the material conditions of settler workers".[61]

This is not a dynamic operating in modern Australian history. No government has ever seriously attempted to resolve a political or economic crisis by increasing the dispossession of Indigenous people and somehow passing on the spoils to the rest of society – not during the great strikes of the 1890s or the 1917 general strike, not during the militancy of the immediate post-war years or of the 1960s and 1970s, and not during the recessions of the 1980s and early 1990s. This shouldn't be surprising. After all, Indigenous people *don't* have serious control over substantial amounts of resources or land that could otherwise be transferred to the rest of the population. This is precisely because the process of colonisation was completed with the total dispossession of the Indigenous population.

The main factors shaping attacks on Indigenous people have been the changing interests of Australian capitalism and the dynamics of Australian politics. For example, the intensified assault on land rights throughout the 1990s wasn't an attempt to resolve class conflict by doling out benefits to the working class. It was shaped by the needs of mining capitalists to stop any expansion of Indigenous land control in a period of expanding markets for raw minerals. And it was bolstered by a conservative cultural offensive by a new generation of right-wing politicians in the Liberal and National parties.

It is true that land rights have been a recurring and important issue. However, reducing contemporary Indigenous oppression to the land question creates a highly distorted picture of contemporary Indigenous political life. As the previous chapter explored, most Indigenous people now live in either urban industrial or large rural cities. They are oppressed and exploited by racist capitalist institutions such as the police, the courts, the welfare system, the labour market and the workplace. While the question of land rights and, in some cases, a connection to traditional lands are still important issues for urban Indigenous people, land theft is not driving their oppression.

Settler colonial theorists argue that there is a "logic of elimination" at work in settler colonial societies like Australia, which endeavours not to reproduce

---

61. Englert 2020, p.1658.

the racist oppression of Indigenous people, but to marginalise and exclude them from society altogether. To some extent, this could usefully describe the situation in the 19th century and early 20th centuries, when 90 percent of the Indigenous population had been wiped out and they were forced to live overwhelmingly on the margins of society. Even then, however, sections of the dispossessed Indigenous population were drawn into the working class, in some cases as a highly exploited workforce concentrated in certain industries – on the cattle stations, for example, or in casualised labouring jobs such as pea picking on the NSW South Coast – or otherwise dispersed among the rest of the non-indigenous workforce, usually in blue-collar jobs.

At any rate, throughout the 20th century, the situation changed as Indigenous peoples neither ceased to exist nor remained purely on the margins. Instead, they slowly, hesitantly and through great effort carved out a space for themselves within a hostile racist society. The 1967 referendum was an expression of this and opened the space for further advances. Of course, even once it became clear that Aboriginal and Torres Strait Islander peoples could not and would not allow themselves to be confined to the margins of society, they still had to confront all sorts of racist challenges. However, many of the obstacles were strikingly similar to, rather than fundamentally distinct from, those faced by non-indigenous racially oppressed groups around the world: segregation in public areas, exploitation in the workplace, discrimination in government policy, and racism in general.

This is not to say that there are no differences in how Indigenous people are treated compared to other oppressed groups in Australian society. Often, they can be treated far worse. It's just that these differences, at least in Australia today, are not so great as to justify settler colonial theorists' assertion that the idea of "discontinuing unequal relationships rather than maintaining them" is the key to understanding Indigenous oppression, as opposed to the ways in which we understand other forms of racism or oppression.

Most settler colonial theorists acknowledge that the situation today has changed in some ways for Indigenous people. Wolfe, for example, argued that while settler colonialism "is inherently eliminatory", it is "not invariably genocidal".[62] However, because these theorists hold on to the logic of

---

62. Wolfe 2006, p.387.

elimination and the overall settler colonial framework, they cannot accurately explain why these changes have occurred.

For instance, when discussing Indigenous labour relations, they often refer to them as "colonial" labour relations, even well into the 20th century.[63] This can appear justified, because historical Indigenous labour often had specific features such as the non-payment of wages, or the payment of goods or welfare instead of wages, and it was utilised in systems of extreme exploitation or even slavery. For example, the practice of "blackbirding" involved the use of Aboriginal workers as enslaved labourers for the early pearling industry in Western Australia, and of Pacific Islanders in Queensland. However, as Marxist historians have demonstrated, the persistence of "unfree" labour is not incompatible with a capitalist society. It doesn't constitute a separate structure within the capitalist mode of production, but is one of the forms that capitalist labour relations can take.[64] At any rate, today the vast majority of employed Indigenous people work in modern workplaces alongside non-indigenous people. These workplaces might be relatively more or less exploitative or racist, but there isn't anything "colonial" about them.

A significant aspect of Indigenous oppression is the public political campaigning that denigrates and scapegoats minority populations. These campaigns are a constant feature of Australian political life. Their purpose is to divide working-class people, to create a multi-tiered labour market, to divert attention away from the crimes of the ruling class, to entrench the subjugation of disadvantaged and oppressed groups, and to strengthen conservative ideas in society more generally. These vile campaigns develop out of the racist logic of modern conservative capitalist politics, not from a colonial process or from the endurance of a colonial frontier war mindset in society.

Mining companies have used racism in their campaigns to limit land rights. For example, they have attempted to win broader support for such campaigns by implying that any extension of land rights would result in Aboriginal people taking over the "backyards" of people living in the cities. However, most racist campaigns are not motivated by a desire to take more land – the Australian government and the pastoral and mining industries

---

63. Beckett 1977.
64. See Banaji 2010, in particular chapter five.

already control or have access to the land that matters most to them. This is why the racist campaigns against Indigenous people are so very similar to those against non-indigenous racially oppressed groups such as certain migrant communities (Africans, Middle Easterners, Jewish people historically) or other oppressed groups such as LGBTI+ people. The conservative right's hostility to Indigenous rights is part and parcel of its broader opposition to progressive gains for any section of society that faces discrimination.

Settler colonial theorists also find it difficult to understand the emergence of class divisions within the Indigenous population, and why ruling classes and state institutions have embraced recognition for Indigenous people in recent years. After all, if the driving force behind Indigenous oppression is a logic of elimination that seeks either the physical destruction of Indigenous people or the repression of their culture, identity and history – the persistence of which challenges the legitimacy of the colonial mission – then the current state of Indigenous oppression is incomprehensible. How can the "settler state" of Australia celebrate Indigenous culture, identity, and even the history of resistance and struggle? How can it incorporate and in fact promote the emergence of an Indigenous middle class?

Some settler colonial theorists have attempted to explain these developments within their existing framework. Yet their answers are unsatisfactory. For example, Wolfe argued that the Australian state has been more easily able to adopt aspects of Indigenous culture into Australian national identity because of the absence of a pre-1788 white culture here, and the need for societies to base themselves on a long-established historical tradition. By contrast, the Israeli state can draw on traditional Zionist mythologies.[65] But this doesn't explain why the use of aspects of Indigenous culture in Australian national identity was marginal until the late 20th century, nor why another settler colonial state, New Zealand, embraced Māori culture more easily and quickly.

The comparison with Israel ignores the central differences: that there is an ongoing military struggle over control of some of the historic land of Palestine, and that the question of what to do with the Palestinians is the central issue of Israeli politics. Any serious attempt to embrace Palestinian culture would

---

65. Wolfe 2006, p.389.

undermine the Zionist project and is therefore stridently rejected. In Australia, by contrast, there can be an accommodation with Indigenous culture without the same effect. That there is an ongoing colonial process in Palestine, and not in Australia, is the major factor explaining this difference. The different tempo of development in countries which are historically rooted in settler colonialism but have completed their colonial processes – Australia, New Zealand, the United States, Canada etc. – is shaped by a series of domestic factors: the relative social weight of Indigenous groups, the level of struggle they have been able to organise and the reaction to that struggle by different classes within those societies.

Sarah Maddison describes the shifts between government policies of protection, assimilation, self-determination and intervention, as well as the recent embrace of the discourse of recognition. She argues that underneath the apparent policy differences, there is "an eliminatory logic that has attempted to erase Indigenous alterity through a range of techniques".[66]

Here settler colonial theorists are on stronger ground, because there certainly has been an enduring thread of racism and oppression running through all the years of changing policies. However, we ought to be careful about a one-sided stress on continuity. Australian capitalism has adapted to shifts in culture and popular consciousness. This has led it to embrace not just symbolic acts like recognition, but also the cultural diversification of capitalist institutions in order to facilitate the integration of a layer of middle-class Indigenous people, and their cultural values and identities, into the framework of Australian capitalism.

Adaptation within a capitalist society doesn't at all mean a break with racism. Take the example of the United States: a substantial Black middle class and capitalist class, even a recent Black president, coexist with endless poverty, racism and police brutality.

Yet the reality is that the oppression of Indigenous people in Australia today is different from the specific ways that they were oppressed in the eras of protection or assimilation, when it was presumed that governments could eliminate the Indigenous population. This is no longer the aim of the Australian state, or a realistic possibility.

---

66. Veracini and Cavanagh 2017, p.435.

There are two dangers present in the suggestion that Australian capitalism is incapable of incorporating Indigenous identity into the status quo. Either you deny reality by trying to pretend that nothing has changed in Indigenous politics in the 21st century, or you can end up thinking that the Australian ruling class is actually carrying out the very decolonial transformation that you wish for. This is reinforced by the often highly ambiguous usage of the term "decolonisation", under which any number of strategies for social change can be included, including stock standard moderate liberal ones. Either way, the danger, to borrow words of radical theorist Michel Foucault used in a different context, is thinking that by saying yes to the celebration of Indigenous identity, one says no to power.

To say that Indigenous oppression today is rooted in Australian capitalism doesn't mean that the origins of that oppression in the settler colonial period are irrelevant. Quite the contrary. If the Indigenous population had been entirely wiped out, as happened in parts of the Caribbean, or if there had been no Indigenous population to begin with, then there would be no Indigenous political question in Australia today. Many Marxists have fruitfully explored how the context of Australian capitalism developing as a settler colony shaped, and continues to shape the politics of race, immigration and imperialism. However, the point is to explain why Indigenous oppression endured even after the colonisation of the continent was completed.

As we have explored in the previous chapter, all the major economic, social, political and ideological aspects of Indigenous oppression are rooted in capitalist society. While the origins of Indigenous oppression lie in the colonisation of the continent – a process that at any rate developed out of the global expansion of capitalism – and their dispossession transformed Indigenous people into a racially oppressed section of the new society, the situation continues because of capitalism, not colonialism. This is not a trivial point: if it is true, then only by challenging the racist logic of capitalist society will we ultimately end Indigenous oppression.

The lack of any serious exploration of the dynamics of capitalist society and the role racism plays within capitalism is a core weakness of settler colonial theory. Jack Davies argues that, ultimately, settler colonial theory is based on an academic and moral critique of society, rather than a materialist or political one. Instead of a rigorous critique of the actual workings of modern capitalism and racial oppression, we find an abstract model into which settler colonial theorists try to force the complexities of actual history and politics. As Davies argues, settler colonial theory "uprooted and untethered, quietly leaves behind the materialist considerations of the earth and fascinates itself with the phenomenological density of the moment that Settler met Native, and merely implores us to take a side".[67]

Part of the confusion on this issue is that it is popular to see capitalism as a purely economic system. It is then supposed that Marxist analysis is concerned only with exploitation in the workplace and can be dismissed as having little to say about Indigenous oppression. While it is true that Marxists view the exploitative relationship between bosses and workers as the backbone of capitalist society, we understand too that a body is made up of more than a spine. Capitalism depends on the economic exploitation of workers and the legal defence of private property, but it is so much more than this. The sexism that women face in the home due to the role played by the family in class society, the oppression that LGBTI+ people face because of the challenge they present to the family norm, the discrimination against migrants due to the restrictive borders of nation-states, the racism that many suffer for all sorts of economic, political and geopolitical reasons – all are expressions of the deeply unjust nature of capitalist society, rather than some addendum to it.

Settlers?

One of the most problematic aspects of settler colonial theory is the idea that the key division in Australia is between settlers and Indigenous people, and that "settler society" as a whole – migrants of all backgrounds, non-indigenous workers, in fact pretty much everyone else – gains material privileges from the dispossession of the Indigenous population. As Sarah Maddison explains in her book *The Colonial Fantasy: Why white Australia can't solve black problems*:

> I use the terms "settler" and "non-indigenous" in relation to any individual or group of people who came to Australia at any time after the first invasion

---
67. Davies 2023.

in 1788. The term "settler" is intended to be discomforting, deliberately underscoring the nature of non-indigenous people's relation to this territory and its peoples as a further impetus towards decolonial transformation.[68]

Maddison does acknowledge that "the extent to which settlers benefit from colonisation is modified to varying degrees by their skin colour and cultural background (not all settlers are white or Anglo), and by class, gender, sexuality and physical ability". However, she also claims that settlers "are all complicit in sustaining colonial relationships… We are none of us outside or above these relationships. Migrants are still settlers, white progressives are still settlers". This analysis is shared by most left-wing writers on Indigenous issues. Sai Englert is more explicit, arguing that "even if working-class settlers are exploited by their ruling classes, overthrowing the settler state would mean overthrowing a system in which they share, however unequally, in the distribution of the colonial loot".[69]

Academic Nandita Sharma has drawn attention to how it has become quite common in left-wing activist and academic circles to argue that migrants are "settlers" or even "colonisers", that immigration is "conquest" and that Indigenous people need to be "centred" at the expense of migrants. Migrant populations, including those that have suffered and continue to suffer from racism and oppression, are often portrayed as a privileged layer who benefit from the racism directed towards Indigenous people.[70] This is a profoundly conservative worldview that expresses some of the worst, most self-defeating aspects of privilege theory politics. To start with, as Sharma writes, it downplays the racist treatment of migrants:

> Portraying all non-indigenous people as "settlers" assumes that no clear distinction was made between Whites and non-Whites in the "White Settler" colonial projects, nor that any distinction is made between those racialized as White and those racialized as not White in today's White National-Native projects. Instead, those whom imperial states (and later nation-states) clearly

---

68. Maddison 2019, p.xii.
69. Maddison 2019, p.xiii and Englert 2020, p.1659.
70. Sharma 2020.

racialized as undesirable and inferior (e.g., Trask's "Asians'" in Hawai'i) are now represented as having been a party to the very projects they were expressly – and juridically – excluded from. Indeed, in the effort to render the experiences of Indigenous National-Natives and Migrants as incommensurable, the violence done to those who were made into Migrants is rendered as politically unimportant.[71]

One particularly terrible example that Sharma cites are the arguments of Bonita Lawrence, a Métis scholar, and Enakshi Dua, a self-identified "Asian settler colonist". Lawrence and Dua argue that, in Canada, all "people of color are settlers".

> Broad differences exist between those brought as slaves, currently working as migrant labourers, refugees without legal documentation, or émigrés who have obtained citizenship. Yet people of color live on land that is appropriated and contested, where Aboriginal peoples are denied nationhood and access to their own lands.[72]

Lawrence and Dua also assert that anti-racist campaigns by migrants contribute "to the active colonization of Aboriginal peoples" and that "anti-racism is premised on an ongoing colonial project" and accepts "a colonizing social formation".[73] Settler colonial theory doesn't just downplay the discriminatory treatment of migrants (whether non-white or white, such as oppressed European migrant groups in Australian history). One of the central arguments of settler colonial theorists is that most exploited workers are "settlers" who benefit from Indigenous oppression. Sai Englert puts forward this view:

> If settler workers are exploited as workers within the settler colony, they remain settlers. As such they participate in the processes of accumulation by dispossession through the occupation of lands, the elimination or exploitation

---

71. Sharma 2020, p.254.
72. Sharma 2020, p.252.
73. Sharma 2020, p.252.

of indigenous peoples, and the extraction of expropriated resources. For example, at a very basic level, their houses, workplaces, and basic infrastructure such as roads, railways, etc., are all premised on the capture and control of indigenous land. Settler workers are both exploited by settler bosses and their co-conspirators in the dispossession of indigenous peoples. As such, class struggle within a settler society has a dual character: it is waged over the distribution of wealth extracted from their labour as well as over the colonial booty.[74]

By starting from the perspective that all Indigenous people are being exploited by "settler society", you end up obscuring the fact that Indigenous oppression is in the interests of the Australian ruling class and is enforced by capitalist institutions. The working class, who make up most of the population, do not benefit from mining bosses being able to exploit Indigenous land, from Black deaths in custody, or from the crippling poverty and inequality that Indigenous people suffer.

While rarely acknowledged today – particularly by liberal academics who make a living out of writing about other people's oppression – the story of the workers' movement and the socialist left, and the history of the struggle for Indigenous rights, are deeply intertwined in this country. From the Day of Mourning and Protest in 1938 and the post-World War Two strikes of Aboriginal workers in the Pilbara and Darwin to the land rights and Black Power struggles of the 1960s and 1970s, thousands of Indigenous and non-indigenous working-class activists have found themselves drawn together into common struggles against our class-divided, profoundly racist, capitalist society.

The reasons behind this aren't hard to fathom. The workers' movement and at least the majority of working-class Indigenous people face many of the same enemies and should share the same goals.

The capitalists who drove Indigenous people off their lands in the 1800s and who exploit the mineral riches of those lands today are the same bosses that workers fought and organised against for more than 200 years. The police who murder Aboriginal men and women are the same oppressors who have

---

74. Englert 2020, p.1658.

frequently broken picket lines, arrested strike leaders and harassed socialist and union activists. The economic system of capitalism, which prioritises profits and exploits millions of Australian workers, is the same system that creates the poverty and discrimination in which most Indigenous people find themselves trapped.

This doesn't mean that Indigenous and non-indigenous working-class people are treated the same. Clearly, Indigenous people are oppressed in specific ways because of the racism directed towards them. The creation of Indigenous missions, the stealing of children by government officials, the huge levels of incarceration and police violence, the denigration of Indigenous identities and cultures, and the vicious discrimination and lies about Indigenous peoples – all of this, while being an expression of the deeply unjust nature of the capitalist system, affects Indigenous people in a particularly heinous way.

Despite this, members of the non-indigenous and Indigenous working class share common material interests rooted in their subordinate place within capitalist society. This makes it possible for them to unite in common struggles, and to support each other in their own struggles. However, common interest, while essential, is in and of itself not enough for solidarity to emerge. The reason why non-indigenous workers were both able and willing to fight for Indigenous rights was because they themselves had a history of struggle out of which they built formidable organisations. From the colossal 1890s strikes and the mass movement against conscription during the First World War, to the post-war industrial upsurge and then the radical class struggles of the 1960s and 1970s, Australian workers have fought against bosses and governments and in the process gained a sense of their own power to impact society more broadly. This is what gave them the confidence and the capacity to stand against injustices such as Indigenous oppression throughout much of the 20th century.

A key role was played, both in these struggles and in promoting an anti-racist consciousness around Indigenous issues, by militant socialist activists, who tried to broaden and deepen the movement for working-class emancipation, and who could see how combating Indigenous oppression fitted into that perspective.

It could be argued that non-indigenous workers in Australia benefit not because they are directly involved in the colonisation of land, but because without the dispossession of Indigenous people, the whole economy and society in which they live wouldn't exist. This is the implication of the arguments of many settler colonial theorists. It also bears some similarities to the theory of the labour aristocracy that is popular among some sections of the Marxist left. In fact, it shares much with the most extreme versions of the theory of the labour aristocracy, such as that espoused by Japanese-American Maoist J Sakai, who argues that the white working class in the US is a privileged and reactionary social layer incapable of uniting with any section of the oppressed.[75] The problem with this argument is that it can't explain why non-indigenous workers have supported Indigenous struggles. In fact, it generally suffers from a lack of historical analysis or one-sided comparisons between very different situations.

For instance, settler colonial theorists often compare the relationship between the non-indigenous working class and Indigenous workers in Australia with the relationship between the Israeli and Palestinian working classes to argue that the Australian working class benefits from Indigenous oppression. However, there are significant differences between the two cases. In Israel, there is compulsory military service. So significant sections of the Israeli working class have some direct experience in oppressing Palestinians. There is also a sizeable minority of Zionist settlers who are involved in recurring violent struggles with the Palestinians over land control. The question of the expansion of the Zionist project and the subjection of the Palestinians is the major question of Israeli politics. Even most of what passes as the left and the socialist movement in Israel supports the continued oppression of the Palestinians.

By contrast, there is no real equivalent to the Zionist settler population among the Australian working class. While some racist workers have acted in appalling ways towards Indigenous people and many others are indifferent to the plight of Indigenous people, the vast majority of the working class has never been involved in violent conflicts with Indigenous people over control over their land. The battle over Indigenous rights in Australia is still very much

---

75. Sakai 2014. For a critique of the theory of the labour aristocracy in the context of Australian history, see Bramble 2012.

politically contested, but hegemonic support for oppressing the Indigenous population does not exist in Australia. Mass demonstrations in Australia, like those held on Invasion Day, generally support Aboriginal rights. In Israel, mass demonstrations call for the expulsion of Palestinians.

The settler colonial argument that non-indigenous workers and their bosses are simply fighting over the spoils they have stolen from Indigenous people also doesn't capture the actual dynamics of class struggle and exploitation in Australia. The capitalist society that has been created on the dispossessed lands of Indigenous peoples is filled with exploitation, oppression and cruelty. It is not in the material interests of the non-indigenous working class that this society continues as it currently exists. Rather, it is in its interests to build a radically different one based upon workers' democracy, economic planning and genuine equality.

Indeed, when working-class struggle has been more intense and more generalised, the tendency has been for more solidarity and joint action with oppressed groups. If workers' struggle was about gaining more at the expense of Indigenous people, then the opposite would be the case: the conditions for Indigenous people would deteriorate the more workers won. History shows such a proposition to be utterly preposterous. In fact, the strongest argument against the assertions of settler colonial theory is the history of the relationship between the Indigenous and non-indigenous working class and the socialist left, which is discussed at length in part two of this book.

Settler colonial theory and anti-racist strategy

Ambiguity surrounds the entire political strategy of "decolonisation". Originally, decolonisation referred to the processes by which colonised nations of the so-called Global South achieved independence. Today, it is a more amorphous term that refers to the process of deracialising oppressive structures, societies and cultures. It can encapsulate any number of mutually contradictory political practices and strategies. One account argues:

> Decolonisation includes actively dismantling systems of inequity (sharing power and resources) and dismantling white supremacy in thought (redressing

the mistaken belief that the western canon of knowledge and knowledge production is the only valid system of science). Decolonisation includes critical processes of situating Aboriginal and Torres Strait Islander ways of knowing (epistemology), being (ontology) and doing (axiology) in the front and centre, and embedded within systems, that work with Aboriginal and Torres Strait Islander peoples.

While decolonisation is in everybody's interests (think about the benefits of Aboriginal management of country in preventing bushfires and blocked waterways), decolonisation in the workplace for Aboriginal and Torres Strait Islander Peoples centres on issues like poor recruitment and retention processes, limited supports and vague procedures for dealing with interpersonal and institutional racism, ways of managing lateral violence and performance measures only being based on mainstream values and definitions of success. Decolonising an organisation must be intentional, resourced and based on ethical, moral and legal motivations for workplaces to learn and apply respectful ways of ensuring Indigenous self-determination and institution-wide responsibility.[76]

Fighting against racism in the workplace and in society is vital, of course. But what this account leaves out is any idea of *how* we are to dismantle "systems of inequity" and "white supremacy in thought". Often, talk about decolonisation is a cover for standard moderate liberal approaches to challenging racism. So the Indigenous Voice to Parliament can be presented as the first step in a process of decolonisation, even though it will do little to change the balance of power between Indigenous people and the Australian state. The flourishing of Indigenous businesses and the growth in Indigenous representation in the media, academia, politics and public life more generally is also sometimes touted as decolonisation in practice. Yet most of this is simply about increasing the representation of mainly middle-class Indigenous people in the structures of Australian capitalism, not challenging structural racism.

Radical-sounding rhetoric can amount to much the same thing. Sarah Maddison, for instance, argues that the contemporary "failures" – of the

---

76. Philips and Hirvonen 2021.

Northern Territory Intervention, the attempts to reduce Indigenous incarceration rates and the Closing the Gap strategy – are due to the ideological dominance of the "colonial fantasy" among policymakers. On this basis, she argues: "Australia may yet be capable of decentring colonial power and making space for Indigenous resurgence in the justice system, but first it must relinquish the colonial fantasy".[77]

But does "decentring colonial power" mean confronting and ultimately overthrowing the racist institutions of our society? Or simply reforming them? The classic left-right divides within movement activism – grassroots organising or bureaucratic lobbying; struggle against institutions or working within them; solidarity and protest or deference and accommodation – often end up blurred, rather than clarified, by settler colonial theory.

Some proponents of settler colonial theory may want to transform the racist structures of society. However, without clarifying the relationship between Indigenous oppression and capitalism, let alone the question of solidarity between Indigenous and non-indigenous workers, it is difficult for them to develop a strategy for defeating racism. The more left-wing supporters of the theory often point to the failures of paternalistic approaches, but their correct criticisms of middle-class liberal racism often spill over into scepticism about genuine displays of popular support for Indigenous justice by non-indigenous people. It often seems that the central point for these theorists is to aim their fire at those seeking to show solidarity with Indigenous struggles or at those engaging in their own struggles against injustice, rather than the exploitative system that oppresses both Indigenous people and non-indigenous workers.

In Australia, there have been several examples of figures on the progressive left dismissing the struggles of racially oppressed non-indigenous groups on the basis that they are somehow less legitimate than the struggles of Indigenous people.

In 2020, for instance, a group of Sudanese high school students, inspired by the Black Lives Matter rebellion in the US, tried to organise a solidarity rally in Melbourne. They were instantly denounced on the internet as "settler" Africans. They were told that they had no right to organise such

---
77. Maddison 2019, p.153.

a rally because their experience of racism was, supposedly, fundamentally different from that of both Indigenous people and African Americans. This totally ignored the fact that Sudanese people in Melbourne had been the target of racist police harassment and hysterical right-wing media campaigns for years.

Similarly, during the campaign against the proto-fascist Reclaim Australia movement, significant sections of the Sydney left argued that unless Indigenous issues were the dominant theme of the rallies, they were essentially reinforcing racism. This was despite Reclaim Australia's central focus being opposition to a supposed Islamic takeover of Australian society. In fact, Reclaim Australia raised no racist demands about Indigenous people (although undoubtedly there were people in it who had racist ideas about Indigenous rights) and even flew the Aboriginal flag at their rallies. The idea was never raised that Muslims should play a central role in combating a movement that wanted to prohibit Halal certification and deport Muslims from the country.

These are examples of a totally self-defeating political approach that undermines any attempts to build a strong, united and radical movement against racism.

The pitfalls of settler colonial theory's strategic perspectives reflect the absence of any orientation towards a social force that can challenge and ultimately overcome Indigenous oppression. This is the result of its commitment to the idea that in countries with minority Indigenous populations, politics are defined by a relationship between settlers and natives.

Jack Davies argues that settler colonial theory's "naked disinterest in the exploitation of workers, except where they are legally 'unfree'" is not only a product of a decades-long shift by left-leaning academia away from Marxism and political economy, but also "a symptom of the dramatic economic upheaval since the 1970s, where the traditional critical standpoint of the industrial worker all but vanishes from the Global North amid technological developments, outsourcing, and financialisation…"

> All this ultimately achieves, however, is a simple reversal of the formerly positive valence, such that the "worker", automatic hero of a vulgar traditional Marxism, becomes a backward worker, a "settler" almost in J. Sakai's meaning,

thus displacing a thin notion of the "revolutionary subject" from the "worker" to the "native".[78]

If this is the case, it is based on an extremely superficial grasp of the historical relationship between Indigenous and non-indigenous workers, and of the contemporary possibilities of anti-racist class struggle.

There is a double problem. The first is that settler colonial theory promotes the idea that there is a class struggle "over there" – somewhere independent of Indigenous people and having little to do with them. Yet Indigenous people have played a role in the labour movement at various points in Australian history, and at various times they have conceived of their own struggles as taking place on the general terrain of class struggle and anti-capitalist politics – a conception that is hard to square with the dogmas of settler colonial theory.

Even today, when it is less likely that Indigenous activists would associate their actions so closely with the workers' movement and the socialist left, or might even express hostility to such an association, it would be misleading to construct a picture of a super radical Indigenous militant at war with the entirety of settler society. Any movement of Indigenous people aiming to advance their interests, let alone abolish the basis of their oppression entirely, will take place within the broader context of Australian capitalism and will have to confront a series of questions: what power do Indigenous people have? What social forces can they form alliances with, and how? Which strategies are likely to succeed, and which ones will lead away from liberation? None of the answers to these problems will be forthcoming without an analysis of the class structure of Australian society.

An example of how the abstractions of settler colonial theory lead to dead-end strategies is provided in Patrick Wolfe's writings. Logically following from the analysis that Indigenous people are irrelevant to settler colonial societies that only want to eliminate them, Wolfe argues:

> In the settler-colonial economy, it is not the colonist but the native who is superfluous. This means that the sanctions practically available to the native

---

78. Davies 2023.

are ideological ones. In settler-colonial formations, in other words, ideology has a higher systemic weighting – it looms larger, as it were – than in other colonial formations.[79]

In the theory of Wolfe, it is only on ideological terrain that Indigenous people can hope to perhaps disrupt settler colonialism, presumably by exploiting the contradiction between the public endorsements of human rights, equality etc. with the reality of Indigenous dispossession.

This offers no real path forward for Indigenous struggles, which of course have an ideological aspect, but must nonetheless have a firm basis to actually challenge the structures of oppression. That Indigenous people are a minority of the population, with limited socio-economic power, means that questions related to overcoming oppression can't be solved just by looking at them independent of their relationship to society, in which at any rate they are deeply enmeshed.

It is of course true that the political strategies Indigenous people can feasibly use to advance their own interests are limited by their numbers and small socio-economic weight. To assess which options are viable for Indigenous people to pursue – whether a civil-rights-style movement of protest marches, or a project to create sovereign Indigenous nations, or the growth of an enclave of Indigenous capitalism, or the formation of an Indigenous political party to contest elections, or any combination thereof – we require an assessment based on some kind of analysis of Australian society more broadly. Yet settler colonial theory, as an analysis, obscures rather than illuminates the dynamics of class society.

The second problem is that, at important moments in its history, significant sections of the workers' movement have taken up the question of Indigenous oppression, with varying degrees of success. This phenomenon is inexplicable from the point of view of settler colonial theory. Sarah Maddison argues that contemporary progressive thought on Indigenous oppression remains trapped within the "Australian colonial fantasy", in particular the belief that "colonialism was something sad but inevitable" and would be resolved by it being "supplanted by a modern, unified nation", backed "by the misplaced

---

79. Wolfe 1999, p.3. Davies 2023 also discusses this problem with Wolfe's theory.

belief that public policy would provide the means of resolving the colonial problem".[80] While this is an accurate criticism of much middle-class liberal thinking on racism in Australia, there is a very different tradition within the radical wing of the workers' movement and the Australian socialist left.

The second part of this book attempts to provide a more substantial basis for rejecting the arguments of the settler colonial theorists by creating a more detailed picture of the changing relationships between Indigenous and non-indigenous workers, and of how the socialist left has understood and responded to these changes.

---

80. Maddison 2019, pp.218–19.

PART TWO

A history of struggle

Chapter four
Indigenous resistance and the early workers' movement

Sir, — I was a member of the Shearers' Union from the time of its organisation until I was too old to work. I am now 78 years old. I was a subscriber to "The Worker" all this time. I have now retired, about 24 years, and for the last 10 years of my life I have devoted my energies to the emancipation of my people, the aborigines... I was active in the Union in the year of the call-out, 1890, on the Darling River, and in the big shearers strike in 1892. In the strike of 1894 I was on picket duty. I mention this and the fact that many others of my people have been loyal members of the Union, as many are still, to show that the appeal I am about to make is to our brother unionists.

— Letter from Aboriginal activist William Cooper to *The Australian Worker*, 1939.[81]

Like most aboriginals he was a good Unionist. Bundaburra was always one of the first to nominate for his ticket when an organiser called.

— Obituary for "Bundaburra Jack" in *The Worker*, 1909.[82]

THE DEFEAT OF THE INITIAL INDIGENOUS ARMED RESISTANCE to colonisation did not end the opposition to oppression. However, it took place in a vastly different context once capitalist society was firmly established throughout the continent. Forms of resistance were shaped by the relationship between the Indigenous population and other social groups, in particular the workers' movement and the socialist left.

During the 1800s, a labour movement developed within the working class. In the 1890s, it exploded in a series of often violent confrontations between

---
81. *The Australian Worker*, 10 May 1939, p.15.
82. *The Worker* (Wagga), 3 February 1909, p.7.

workers and bosses, the military and the police, particularly during the 1894 shearers' strike. In the aftermath of these mass confrontations, the Australian Labor Party emerged as one of the most electorally successful working-class political parties in the world, forming the first social democratic state and federal governments. The election of Labor governments, however, left many workers unsatisfied. From 1907, there was a significant revival of class struggle, expressed as a series of spectacular strikes and struggles such as the Broken Hill lockout of 1909, the Queensland general strike of 1912, the mass anti-conscription campaign during the First World War and the New South Wales general strike of 1917, the latter of which involved more than 100,000 workers and spread interstate.

These confrontations cemented trade unions as a central actor in Australian society and left a decades-long legacy. Union membership rose from 5 percent of the workforce in 1900 to 20 percent in 1910. In 1927, union density reached 47 percent, one of the highest in the world, and remained around this level until the 1980s. In the late 19th and early 20th century, the working class was a major social force that all political parties and institutions had to respond to. The strength of the working-class movement also shaped the struggles of Indigenous people against oppression and the responses of white workers to them.

While Indigenous people formed a small minority of the overall workforce, their involvement in the labour movement goes back to the 1800s, with Aboriginal miners present at protest meetings in the lead-up to the Red Ribbon and Eureka rebellions on the Victorian goldfields.[83] One of the Eureka stockaders, the Italian radical Raffaello Carboni, spent time with local Aboriginal people and apparently learned some of their language. In his account of the Eureka Stockade, Carboni said that one of the questions that entered the mind of a supporter of the miners was: "Is there not plenty of Victorian land for every white man or black man that intends to grow his potatoes?"[84]

AM Fernando, an Indigenous man who gained international fame as an activist in Europe, claimed to have been a union member (possibly in the

---

83. Howitt 1855, p.406 and Clark 2005.
84. Carboni 2004, p.37.

maritime industry) prior to leaving Australia in 1903. Fernando's biographer argues that along "with his experiences of settler colonialism and his Catholicism, Fernando's views about humanism were informed by his notion of the nobility of the working life", an idea he learned from the Australian labour movement, despite apparently being excluded from union membership at some point.[85]

The first substantial numbers of Aboriginal workers involved in union campaigning seem to have been in the shearing industry, where the issue of Aboriginal membership was seriously discussed for the first time. Indigenous workers were involved in the shearers' unions from very early on. In a series of articles in the *Worker*, an early leader of the shearers, AJ Sullivan, recalled being asked to speak at a massive 1885 union meeting in Wagga, run by an Aboriginal shearer named Tommy. Tommy had been paid to organise the meeting by mostly white shearers at Binya station. The meeting ended in a brawl between Tommy and some others, but it laid the basis for the future Wagga branch of the shearers' union.[86] In early 1887, a newspaper reported that on a station in the Victorian town of Framlingham all the Aboriginal shearers except for two were members of the shearers' union, and even the two non-unionists demanded, and were paid, union rates.[87]

Andrew Stuart Stepney was another of the early Aboriginal shearing unionists and a representative of the strike camp in Cobar during the 1894 strike. He led hundreds of horse-riding shearers in battles with scabs and police, both in Cobar and later in Queensland. He had been a member of the shearers' union since 1886, the year of its formation, and had also played a role in a strike in Hay in 1890. Tommy and Stepney were just two of the hundreds of Aboriginal workers who were members of the shearers' unions in the late 1800s.[88]

An early experience that would have shaped the leaders of the shearers' unions was an organising tour of New Zealand at the end of 1886. The goal

---

85. Paisley 2012, pp.12–13.
86. Sullivan 2005 [1916].
87. *Warwick Examiner and Times*, 3 December 1887, p.2.
88. For more detail on Stepney, see Humphreys 2021 and Cunneen 2022.

of the trip was to win New Zealand shearers to trade unionism, so that they wouldn't be used as scabs in the Australian colonies. While they initially focused on recruiting white shearers on the South Island, union leader David Temple contacted Māori workers, who did most of the shearing on the North Island, and found them enthusiastic about the idea of unionising. Temple believed that they would be open to joining en masse once the union's rules were translated into their own language.[89]

Throughout the late 1880s, the Amalgamated Shearers' Union (ASU) brought together several shearers' unions and fought a running battle with the pastoralists, rapidly gaining thousands of members. The issue of Aboriginal workers was discussed in some detail at the 1891 ASU conference, at which a motion was moved by the Creswick, Victoria branch to allow all Aboriginal workers admission as life members of the union, without paying any union fees if they, like other ASU members, refused to work in non-union sheds.

Temple supported this motion, arguing: "It is a graceful act to those from whom the country has been taken. No liberal minded man could surely object to this concession to the original owners of the soil". Cook, a delegate from South Australia, concurred, making the point that Aboriginal workers shouldn't have to pay union fees considering that "their circumstances were not the same as white men, and their earnings were not the same".

Some delegates objected to the motion, arguing that Aboriginal workers were less committed to unionism and shouldn't get special treatment for their lack of interest, that "they were not altogether to be depended upon", and that if "poverty was a justification for free membership, there were numbers of white men who deserved similar consideration". These arguments were rebutted by delegates who drew upon their experiences organising Aboriginal shearers. Cook stated there were "60 or 70 in South Australia, all good unionists". McInerney, from Young, NSW, "wished all the white men were as good as the Australian darkies – they were fine fellows as far as he saw. He knew a number who had cleared out of the shed when it was found 'non-union'". Percy, from Cobar, was "in favour of enrolling all the

---
89. Merritt 1986, p.96.

Aboriginals". "In one shed in Cobar an aboriginal was the only one of twenty who walked away for unionism", he said.[90]

In the end, a compromise was reached, waiving the entrance fee for "pure bred aborigines" only. Whatever one thinks about this debate, the significance lies in the fact that it was about whether special measures were needed to recruit more Aboriginal workers to the union, *not* about whether they should be members in the first place. At least some of the unionists displayed an awareness of the dispossession of Indigenous people and its consequences. These attitudes weren't limited to shearers in Victoria, New South Wales and South Australia. The Queensland Shearers' Union (QSU), despite complaining that the ASU was too soft on the "coloured question", also refused to exclude Aboriginal workers in the union rules. Even a short-lived right-wing split from the QSU, the National Union of Labour, based at the Wolfang station, supported employment for Aboriginal workers.[91]

While the shearers' unions weren't free of paternalistic or racist ideas, many unionists expressed sympathy for the plight of Aboriginal people and at least some understanding that their dispossession was morally wrong and had disadvantaged them. So an 1892 article printed in the *Worker* (Brisbane) argued:

> I've yet to learn, don't you know, that the immortal British Empire or any other speck of country owns by sheer right divine all the land it can get its clutches on. There's no more natural sense in a bleary-eyed officer with gold lace and a taste for rum, sticking a few feet of stick, with a few square inches of painted calico attached, into the ground and saying "I annex this 'ere country", than there is in you or me taking a trip across to Europe and going through the same pantomime at Brighton or Monte Carlo. You or I've got exactly the same "right" as the gold laced gentleman who appreciates rum. The only thing is that he has a title deed in the shape of a few thousand tons of men of war, with guns enough to blow the unfortunate natives to little small bits if they object. Wonderful justice, isn't it?... The aboriginals had more right to be in Australia than we had, looking at things justly.[92]

---

90. All quotes from the record of the conference were published in *Shearers' & General Labourers' Record*, 15 June 1891, p.2.
91. Merritt 1986, p.189.
92. *The Worker* (Brisbane), 16 July 1892, p.4.

Other articles repeat the same point: "In the long ago a Christian nation crossed the seas and took from a happy race who had never wronged them, their country, out of which they afterwards made many millions of pounds".[93] "A great deal of nonsense is talked about the benefits white men confer on native races when they conquer them and annex their country. In many cases the whites make the blacks, to all intents and purposes, their slaves."[94] Another states that the squatters "pushed their civilisation…by the crack of the rifle and flour mixed with arsenic".[95] A long article about an inquiry into the mass killings of Aboriginal people in Queensland prompted the writer to "remember, in bygone years, men having the mission to 'disperse' myalls for the convenience of white settlers, or in plain English, a licence to shoot, kill, or frighten away from the path of the white man the lawful owner of the soil". The writer recommended that the inquiry use as evidence a white settler's rifle that he claimed had notches in it for each Aboriginal person he had killed.[96]

There are several positive accounts of Aboriginal workers standing up to bosses and demanding better pay or conditions. There are also accounts of white unionists intervening in disputes between Aboriginal workers and bosses to demand that the Aboriginal workers were paid the correct amount. At Bundarra station in 1900, white shearers refused to work until Aboriginal shed hands were given a fair wage. Union organiser reports published in the *Worker* made constant reference to the recruitment of Aboriginal shearers and station hands, and a summary of the labour movement's gains in 1906 noted that "even the Aborigines were taking it up".[97]

In some situations, Aboriginal shearers played a vital role. In August 1902, strikes broke out at stations around Condobolin, a town in western NSW. The first shed to stop work was at Booberoi station, where workers faced off against a particularly tough station owner, Alexander Haley. Haley had the support of the pro-boss Machine Shearers' Union, an organiser of which had threatened striking workers with a revolver. Most of the shearers at Booberoi,

---

93. *The Worker* (Brisbane), 26 January 1895, p.1
94. *The Worker* (Wagga), 22 April 1899, p.2.
95. *The Worker* (Brisbane), 28 May 1892, p.4.
96. *The Worker* (Brisbane), 9 May 1896, p.10.
97. *The Worker* (Brisbane), 17 July 1897, p.6; *The Worker* (Wagga), 20 October 1900, p.7; 6 December 1906, p.2.

on being offered poor wages at the start of shearing season, walked off the job and set up a strike camp at Euabalong, leaving the station with only two shearers to work on around 30,000 sheep. A significant number of the 40 shearers on strike and living at the camp were Aboriginal, possibly from the local Wiradjuri community. The *Worker* reported positively on their role in the strike:

> At Booberoi, the aborigines who refused M.S.U. terms were employed on the run up to roll call. Am I not a Man and a Brother? asks the Dark. The white creature who takes what master cares to throw him snivels out: "I am neither a Man nor a Brother – only a tool!"[98]

In this article, Aboriginal workers are portrayed as brothers, while white workers who scab on their fellow workers are merely tools to be pitied or hated. William Johnson, chairman of the Australian Workers' Union (AWU) Central Branch and future Labor mayor of Auburn, visited the strike camp and argued:

> The knock-out to Haley was the unanimous roll up of the aborigines, who are staunch Unionists; and deserve our assistance in other ways. If the whites had been as true to their fellows as the dark skins, Booberoi would be Union today.[99]

This doesn't mean that there are no examples of hostility towards Aboriginal workers. There were concerns raised about the use of Aboriginal workers as scabs during the 1894 strike in Queensland, particularly at the North Yanko station, and condemnation of the government giving them temporary free train passes to get to the stations. However, the same paper also reported positively on the Aboriginal shearers at the Weilmoringle strike camp, who refused to work under a non-union agreement even when the struggle was clearly lost. Another article noted that, during the 1894 strike, there was a shed in which all the white shearers scabbed, while the two Aboriginal shearers refused to work under a non-union contract. When the two walked out of

---

98. *The Worker* (Wagga), 30 August 1902, p.6.
99. *The Worker* (Wagga), 30 August 1902, p.6.

the shed, the *Worker* reported that one yelled: "Well, the only thing I'm sorry for is that I have one drop of white blood in me".[100]

In response to the daily newspapers criticising the shearers' union for discriminating against Aboriginal workers, David Temple wrote a widely republished reply that exposed his racist opposition to migrant groups yet revealed a different attitude towards Aboriginal workers:

> The bush unionist objects to Chinese, Cingalese, Polynese, Malayese and such, not to the harmless and much injured aboriginal whom if an occasional unionist insults – there are blackguards everywhere – an occasional squatter still more frequently shoots on sight like a dingo. In many of the strike camps were aboriginals who had knocked off with the rest from various stations. At Warri Warri there were thirty-two whites and as many blacks.[101]

There were even sympathetic articles that made more general statements about Aboriginal dispossession. One noted a "well received" speech by Mr Breston, an Aboriginal man, who condemned the government for its treatment of his people and demanded that it "give the aboriginals half the land they had been robbed of". Another explained that a group of Aboriginal people were demanding the right to attend the Victorian parliament, because "as their country had been stolen from them by the white fellows they deserved some consideration".[102] An American journalist who spent time among shearers at the end of the 1800s reported that "some fast shearers are black men, and they are the only shearers whom the true shearer bears no grudge".[103]

It would be misleading to think that sympathy for Aboriginal workers was guaranteed or automatic. Militant unionists had to formulate a political attitude to Aboriginal workers and make arguments to the rest of the shearers about how they should relate to Aboriginal people. At the 1891 ASU conference, the most pro-Aboriginal statements were made by left-wing delegates from the most militant branches of the union, such as W Percy

---

100. See *The Worker* (Wagga), 15 September 1894, p.3; 18 May 1895, p.1; 5 October 1901, p.6.
101. *The Worker* (Brisbane), 27 June 1891, p.3.
102. *The Worker* (Brisbane), 14 December 1895, p.4; 19 February 1898, p.11.
103. *Australian Town and Country Journal*, 14 April 1900, p.33.

from Cobar, and H Langwell and Robert Stevenson from Bourke (who moved the original motion on behalf of the Creswick branch). These branches were in the far-flung western New South Wales division. The membership of the union here was dominated by propertyless workers from outside the area, unlike the central and eastern divisions which had a larger number of shearers who were also small farmers.

The fact that sympathetic attitudes weren't automatic is also revealed by the later history of the union in Western Australia. In the north-west of the country, there were pastoral stations on which a significant section of the workforce was Aboriginal. The AWU failed to organise them and was criticised by Mick Sawtell, a rank-and-file AWU activist, socialist and future stalwart of the militant Industrial Workers of the World, who in 1910 wrote a series of letters and articles arguing that the union should launch an organising campaign among the Aboriginal workers on the Pilbara stations. This was discussed at the 1910 AWU conference. Members from the eastern states raised positive examples from their own experiences organising Aboriginal workers. But under pressure from more conservative members from Western Australia, some of whom wanted Aboriginal workers replaced by white workers, the conference passed a vague motion criticising the exploitation of Aboriginal workers in north-western Australia and praising the work of the WA branch. No organising effort seems to have been initiated, a failure which would have lasting consequences. When the Aboriginal workers in the Pilbara did start to organise themselves in the 1940s, it led to significant conflict with AWU officials.[104]

Aboriginal involvement in the shearers' unions shows that, even at the end of the 1800s, there were possibilities for developing solidarity between Indigenous and non-indigenous workers, at least in some circumstances. The high levels of working-class organisation and activity from the late 19th and into the early 20th century also encouraged Aboriginal workers to use the strike weapon in order to advance their own interests directly. In 1892, the *Northern Territory Times and Gazette* reported that Aboriginal seafarers were threatening to strike for higher wages. The newspaper believed that

---

104. For the 1910 AWU conference discussion see *The Worker* (Wagga), 2 February 1910, p.5 – for Sawtell's articles see 16 March 1910, p.5; 4 May 1910, p.5; 5 January 1911, p.3.

they had been influenced by white workers on the pearling ships who had "been sowing the germs of unionism".[105] In 1898, an Aboriginal man named Solomon, who was employed in haymaking, refused to work for rations and wrote a letter to the Aborigines Protection Board outlining his demands.[106] In 1913, the *Dubbo Dispatch and Wellington Independent* reported on a strike of the entire Aboriginal workforce at La Grange Bay in Western Australia. The strikers appointed as spokesperson one of their own, whom the paper described as a "rather intelligent fellow". Aboriginal women joined in the strike as picketers and as scouts on the lookout for scabs.[107] The mainstream press blamed the Aboriginal strike on the widespread industrial unrest in the rest of the country, and the rise of the Australian Labor Party. The strike led the muckraking independent Perth newspaper *Truth* to speculate that Aboriginal people would soon "arise in his might", demand the right to vote "and make his mark on the ballot box".[108]

The *Bundaberg Mail and Burnett Advertiser*, reporting on a strike by Aboriginal workers at Yarrabah in 1917, commented: "Even the mission aboriginal has been unable to escape the prevalent epidemic of 'strikitis'".[109] The strike broke out a month after the NSW general strike. In 1919, an Aboriginal man, Fred Cameron, was brought to court by the manager of the Ulgundahi Island mission in NSW for insulting behaviour, encouraging the other Aboriginal workers to go on strike and being a "coloured recalcitrant".[110] Fortunately for Cameron, the judge was unable to move him to a different mission due to the quarantine in place to stop the spread of the Spanish flu. In 1918, Aboriginal workers at the Dunwich Benevolent Asylum on North Stradbroke Island struck to demand equal pay. In 1927, Aboriginal workers at the Nowa Nowa station went on strike over poor food. In the same month, another group of Aboriginal people at the Lake Tyers mission went on strike over the removal of a sympathetic station manager.[111]

---

105. *Northern Territory Times and Gazette*, 14 October 1892, p.2.
106. *The Clarence River Advocate*, 1 February 1898, p.4.
107. *The Dubbo Dispatch and Wellington Independent*, 29 August 1913, p.1.
108. *Truth*, 16 August 1913, p.2.
109. *The Bundaberg Mail and Burnett Advertiser*, 17 October 1917, p.3.
110. *The Armidale Chronicle*, 19 July 1919, p.8.
111. *Recorder*, 28 September 1927, p.1; *Advocate*, 10 September 1927, p.5.

It is not hard to see why Aboriginal workers would use the strike weapon. After all, they could see that all around them white workers were using it to great effect.

The socialist groups that emerged in the early 20th century wrote sporadically about the living and working conditions of Indigenous people. Many of the articles concerned "slavery" in Western Australia and the exploitation, abuse and murder of Aboriginal workers by station masters, the police and government officials.[112] Others were concerned with the hypocrisy of religious missions interested only in profits.[113] Most of the articles didn't advance much beyond what had been published in the shearers' union newspapers. However, some articles did start to draw links between the exploitation of Aboriginal workers, the nature of capitalism and the need for socialism. As an article in the *People*, the newspaper of the Australian Socialist League, put it:

> It may, indeed, be doubted whether any case of brutal ill treatment of aboriginals has ever been punished except when public opinion has been so aroused that it had become unsafe to disregard it. Had the "People" the circulation amongst Australian working men and women that it deserves such verdicts would be less possible, for the real working-class movement knows neither race nor color and detests and opposes oppression and injustice everywhere. The cause of this poor maltreated half-caste girl is the cause of every worker, and their cause is hers. Only when the Social Revolution shall have accomplished itself, and Christian capitalist "civilisation" shall have been relegated to the rubbish destructor, will the rule of justice and equity, untrammelled by class interests and free from the sordid debasement of character germinated in the capitalist muck-heap, be possible.[114]

Some articles described pre-invasion Aboriginal society as a form of primitive communism.[115] The IWW took an anti-racist, internationalist stance and published a few short articles referencing Aboriginal issues.[116] In Darwin,

---
112. *The People*, 10 August 1901, p.4.
113. *The International Socialist*, 25 March 1911, p.3; *The People*, 20 August 1910, p.2.
114. *The People*, 28 August 1909, p.3.
115. *The People*, 3 January 1918, p.3.
116. *Direct Action*, 25 December 1915 p.3; 7 April 1917, p.2.

Filipino IWW activist Antonio Cubillo, who was married to an Aboriginal woman, fought against racist discrimination on the wharves in 1912.[117] It is unclear how many Indigenous members the IWW recruited, or if there are other examples of them participating in actions against Indigenous discrimination. But at least one Aboriginal worker, Ted O'Reilly, was a prominent IWW orator, and Lucy Eatock joined the IWW while participating in the anti-conscription struggles during the First World War.[118]

Despite this, working-class consciousness about Indigenous oppression was still quite limited, and often intertwined with paternalistic or racist views. As the Indigenous population was small and marginalised in a profoundly racist society, Indigenous oppression during the early 1900s did not necessarily present itself as a pressing strategic question for the Australian workers' movement in the way that, for example, the oppresson of African Americans did for the workers' movement in the United States. This was reinforced by the fact that, except for the large shearers' strikes of 1916 in western NSW, most important union conflicts of the early 20th century were either urban-based or in tightly knit coal mining communities, whereas the vast majority of Indigenous people lived in rural areas until later in the century.

Following the federation of Australia, Indigenous communities came under increased attack from governments. State parliaments passed a series of new laws giving sweeping powers to Aborigines Protection Boards, which then demanded even greater powers to control Indigenous communities. Rural communities and state officials increased the pressure to break up Indigenous landholdings or reserves that had been established on valuable land, and segregation and exploitation were further entrenched. Indigenous communities resisted these attacks in various ways – the basis for the Aboriginal activist organisations of the 1920s and 1930s was being laid.

As the number of attacks was increasing, significant sections of the leadership of the labour movement were becoming more incorporated into the running of Australian capitalism. The AWU, which had united Indigenous and non-indigenous workers earlier in the century, became the backbone of many state Labor governments. While some Labor MPs from rural

---

117. Townsend 2009, p.9.
118. Townsend 2009, p.15.

backgrounds, and often from the AWU, criticised aspects of the treatment of Aboriginal communities, most Labor politicians willingly took over the state machinery that oppressed Indigenous people, making few changes to what had been established by previous conservative administrations. When the Holman NSW Labor government debated giving the Aborigines Protection Board greater powers to control communities in 1915, only four MPs, all from Labor, opposed the proposed amendment. George Black, the minister for agriculture, withdrew his opposition in a sign of cabinet solidarity.[119]

Labor governments came to power at the state and federal levels repeatedly throughout the early 1900s. They either changed little for Indigenous people, or actually increased the attacks on their rights. For example, in 1904, when the ALP first came to power in Western Australia, the *Westralian Worker* urged the new government to stop the exploitation of Aboriginal workers in the north-west of the state, but nothing was done and the conservatives won back control quickly.[120] The ALP returned to power on a more secure basis in 1911, under the leadership of John Scaddon, only to be wracked by the internal crisis produced by the conscription debate. Spending the next two decades out of office, the WA ALP built a strong electoral base in rural areas, the AWU playing a leading role in this. The party avoided making open criticisms of the exploitation of Aboriginal workers by white station owners, in order to gain the owners' support. In the case of the Pilbara seat, which would become a strong Labor district, the ALP forged a dirty alliance with local squatters known for their vicious anti-Aboriginal racism. The fruits of this collaboration would appear during the post-war Aboriginal strike, which came into serious conflict with the AWU officialdom and the Labor Party.

So, in the first decades of the 20th century, racist oppression was becoming more entrenched and the election of Labor governments did nothing to stop increasing attacks on Indigenous rights. While Indigenous and non-indigenous workers had united in some union struggles, this occurred unevenly across the labour movement and depending on the level of participation by Indigenous workers as well as the political outlook of trade union leaders and rank-and-file activists. Even when Indigenous workers were unionised, such as

---

119. Horner 1974, p.10.
120. *Westralian Worker*, 21 October 1904, p.2.

in the AWU, they still often suffered from more exploitative conditions, not to mention the more general effects of anti-Indigenous racism. Among the socialist left, there was some sympathy for the Indigenous population and some understanding that their oppression was because of the capitalist system. But the situation remained relatively undertheorised and practical activity was limited.

While there had been a series of rebellions on Aboriginal reserves during the 19th and early 20th centuries, such as those at Coranderrk and Maloga, these appear to have had little connection with the early workers' movement. However, by the 1920s, high levels of class struggle were shaping the emergence of a new generation of Indigenous activist groups.

Fred Maynard was a member of the Waterside Workers' Federation and encountered radical African American, West Indian and African sailors while working on the Sydney waterfront. He was also involved in the Coloured Progressive Association, an organisation of Black nationalist sailors which held a farewell dinner for heavyweight African American boxing champion Jack Johnson in Sydney in 1907. These experiences influenced the character of the Australian Aboriginal Progressive Association (AAPA), established by Maynard in 1924.[121]

The AAPA's motto – "One God, One Aim, One Destiny" – was a slogan popularised in the United States by Black nationalist leader Marcus Garvey, whose ideas influenced Maynard and other AAPA members. The impact of Maynard's involvement in the waterside unions is evident in his 1927 letter to NSW Labor Premier Jack Lang:

> The members of [the AAPA] have also noted the strenuous efforts of the Trade Union leaders to attain the conditions which existed in our country at the time of invasion by Europeans – the men only worked when necessary – we called no man "Master" and we had no king.[122]

Maynard's familiarity with the ideals of the union movement is here mobilised to enlist support for his campaign for Aboriginal justice. While

---

121. Maynard 2007.
122. Maynard 2007, pp.104–5.

Lang was not sympathetic, the fact that Maynard tried to appeal to him this way shows that he hoped to win over figures from the workers' movement on this basis.

From 1924 to 1928, the AAPA involved hundreds of Aboriginal men and women in campaigns for their rights. Its activities drew the attention of government authorities, who waged a vicious campaign of harassment against the organisation. By 1928, it had been largely driven underground, and it disappeared some time later. The repression was so intense that none of the AAPA leaders appear to have been involved in subsequent periods of Indigenous activism.

In the 1930s, a new generation of Indigenous activist groups emerged, including organisations such as the Aborigines Progressive Association (APA) and the Australian Aborigines' League (AAL). Many of the leaders of these groups also had backgrounds in trade union organising.

AAL founder William Cooper, as the letter quoted at the start of this chapter shows, was involved in the shearers' strikes of the 1890s. Shadrach Livingstone James, Cooper's nephew and an important activist in his own right, was also a member of the AWU for many years and was a union representative at shearing sheds in Cheviot Hills, Penshurst and Brie Brie.[123] Caleb Morgan, also an activist with the AAL, had written a letter to the *Worker* about Aboriginal issues some time before joining the new group, and his wife Anna spoke about Aboriginal issues at a 1935 meeting organised by the International Women's Day Committee. William Ferguson, who founded the APA, had strong links to the workers' movement, in particular the AWU, thanks to his many years working as a shearer. In 1916, Ferguson and his family settled in Gulargambone, a small town in the central west of NSW. In Gulargambone, he led a campaign to reform the local branch of the ALP and helped establish a new Trades and Labour Council, which elected him as its secretary for two years. He was also a leading local campaigner against conscription during the First World War. Ferguson was clearly trusted as an important working-class leader in the region, by non-indigenous and Indigenous workers alike.[124]

---

123. *The Australian Worker*, 10 July 1929, p.2.
124. Stanbrook and Fieldes 2019.

Several white allies attracted to the AAL and the APA also had left-wing or trade union backgrounds. Helen Baillie, while coming from a Christian background, had political connections "as much with the labour movement and left-wing organisations as…with Christian humanitarian ones", having been involved in the Ethiopian Relief Committee, organised by left-wingers to protest Mussolini's invasion of Abyssinia, as well as volunteering as a nurse for Republican forces in the Spanish Civil War. She once described herself as "a Christian communist". Baillie was a close supporter of the AAL and William Cooper. Another white supporter of the AAL, Arthur Burdeu, was more moderate than Baillie, but came from a working-class background and was president of the Victorian division of the Federation of Salaried Officers of Railways Commissioners during the period in which he was helping Cooper and the AAL.[125]

While the rise and fall of the AAPA had gone mostly unnoticed by the workers' movement, the APA and the AAL rapidly gained substantial support from unions and the socialist left. This is largely because, in the period between the 1928 suppression of the AAPA and the formation of the AAL in 1933, and the APA in 1937, a radically different organisation – the Communist Party of Australia – had started to reshape the Australian left.

---

125. Attwood 2021, pp.117–32.

Chapter five

The Communist Party of Australia and Indigenous liberation

> Hitherto, the conditions of the Aborigines have not been considered by workers in the revolutionary movement, and the rank and file organisation set up by the aborigines was allowed to be broken up by the A.P.B., the missionaries, and the police, but henceforth no struggle of the white workers must be permitted without demands for the aborigines being championed; no political campaigns without political programs applicable to our fellow exploited – the aborigines – being formulated.
>
> — Communist Party of Australia's 1931 "Draft Programme of Struggle Against Slavery".[126]

URBAN WORKERS HAD THE POTENTIAL to support Indigenous rights, but in order for this to become a reality the intervention of a party of working-class socialist activists was essential. Throughout the 20th century, the Communist Party of Australia (CPA) made important contributions to the struggle for Indigenous rights. For decades, Communists went against the grain of racism in Australian society, criticised the mainstream of the labour movement for its failure to take Indigenous rights seriously and condemned the Australian Labor Party for its role in enforcing oppression and racism at both the state and federal level. These weren't just words. Communists sought to build solidarity with Indigenous struggles and promoted anti-racist ideas among its predominantly working-class membership and audience. No other predominantly non-indigenous organisation contributed as much to the Indigenous struggle in Australia as the CPA.

Even compared to other Communist parties in countries with minority Indigenous populations, the CPA was ahead of the curve. Communists in

---
126. *Workers' Weekly*, 25 September 1931, p.2.

New Zealand didn't start to do much about Māori rights until 1935.[127] The Canadian CP didn't adopt a program for Indigenous rights until 1937 (six years after the CPA, and its program was much more limited than the CPA's 1931 draft program) and didn't begin to take up the question in a practical sense until after the Second World War. The contribution of the CPA to Indigenous struggles also significantly dwarfed that of the Communist Party USA.[128] In America, there are no examples of Communist-organised working-class support for Indigenous rights on the scale of the support seen in Australia.

It was in the turmoil of the Great Depression that Communist militants first began to integrate the struggle for Indigenous rights with working-class politics. At first, the contribution was primarily in the form of propaganda: articles drawing attention to the exploitation of Indigenous workers and making arguments for why their struggle should be seen as a part of the movement for working-class self-emancipation. As the Communist Party grew in influence throughout the 1930s, they took these arguments into the arenas of left-wing struggle – in the unemployed movement, the trade unions, and in broader political campaigns.

In the process, the CPA trained hundreds, if not thousands, of working-class activists to be sensitive to the oppression of Indigenous people and to be ready to show solidarity when Indigenous people fought back against the racism of Australian society. Throughout the first half of the 1930s, the CPA conceived of the fight for Indigenous liberation as a potentially revolutionary, anti-capitalist struggle, taking place in the broader context of the rise of anti-colonial and anti-racist movements across the globe. They argued that the working class were natural allies of Indigenous people, much more so than naive, vacillating and paternalistic middle-class do-gooders. During the late 1920s and early 1930s, the CPA believed that while Communists should strive to combat racism and promote Indigenous rights in day-to-day struggles, the ultimate liberation of Indigenous people would only be possible with the overthrow of Australian capitalism and the establishment of a workers' state.

---

127. McNeill 2015.
128. Drachewych 2017.

The formation of the Communist Party of Australia is often presented as a radical break with the previous development of the socialist left and the labour movement in Australia. This is particularly the case with regard to the attitude of the left and the labour movement towards racism in general and Indigenous oppression in particular. As Bob Boughton has argued:

> Communists who took up the cause of Indigenous rights in the 1920s were clearly reflecting concerns more widely held in non-Aboriginal society, concerns stimulated by Indigenous peoples' own struggles, but this does not explain why they adopted such "advanced" positions, nor why, alone among working class political organisations, the CPA consciously set out to become a major force in the movement for Indigenous rights. Australian communists were led to this position largely by the international movement of which they were members.[129]

There is an important element of truth in this argument. The CPA would articulate a more politically advanced and practically effective conception of their relationship with Indigenous struggles than the socialist groups and working-class organisations that came before them. However, a one-sided emphasis on the Communist Party's advancements in this regard can obscure previously existing working-class tendencies towards solidarity with Indigenous people, however underdeveloped they may have been. The CPA was only able to have the impact they did because the international Communist politics that influenced them were at least to some degree applicable to the situation of Indigenous people in Australia.

---

129. Boughton 2001.

The Communist Party of Australia, the Communist International and Indigenous rights

The Communist Party took some time to move beyond the politics and practices of the left that preceded it. This is not particularly surprising given it spent much of the 1920s as a small and beleaguered organisation, numbering only in the hundreds, regularly wracked with internal crises, splits and a high turnover of both rank-and-file members and political leadership. Despite these challenges, from 1923 the CPA's newspaper *Workers' Weekly* began publishing articles about Indigenous oppression. One article, about the exploitation of Torres Strait Islanders on Badu Island, ended by stating: "[F]acts show that wherever the capitalist system plants itself the native population is subjected and ruthlessly exploited. Let us speed the day when the workers – black, white or brindle – will be free from the blighting influence of brutal Capitalism".[130] An article in 1924 criticised mainstream labour newspapers the *Worker* and the *Labour Daily* for whipping up a hysterical campaign "denouncing the blacks as treacherous murderers" in the Northern Territory. The author, C Arfeldt, while accepting the idea that Indigenous people were a "dying race", also pointed to the benefits that capitalism had gained out of exploiting the Aboriginal population in the Northern Territory.[131]

From 1925 *Workers' Weekly* regularly reported on the conditions of Aboriginal workers. Articles from 1925–27 criticised Labor party state governments for not stopping the exploitation of Aboriginal domestic servants, and attacked the AWU for refusing to organise Aboriginal workers in Western Australia and the Northern Territory. In January 1928 they published an interesting account of a conversation between a Communist Party member and some Aboriginal workers in Western Australia. According to the account, the Aboriginal workers said that they were "treated very harshly by some white people". When the Communist replied that this would change when workers "woke up and ruled Australia", the Aboriginal workers reportedly said, "we wish they would hurry up and do it". The Aboriginal workers also said they wanted control over their own land, to which the Communist replied

---

130. *Workers' Weekly*, 23 November 1923, p.1.
131. *Workers' Weekly*, 7 November 1924, p.3.

that when the "white worker would control Australia...then they would have land and freedom too". Whether this account is accurate or embellished for propaganda purposes, it reflects that the party was starting to think about the issues.[132] Unfortunately during this period their theoretical journal, *The Communist*, published a series of anthropological articles that approached the Indigenous question from a racist standpoint common in the academy at the time.[133]

From 1928, the CPA was thrown into disarray by a factional struggle out of which a new leadership came to power, backed by the Stalinised Communist International (Comintern).[134] The victory of this new leadership spelled the end of the Communist Party as a revolutionary socialist organisation and saw it transformed into a Stalinist organisation in line with Communist parties across the globe. This would have important consequences for how the party came to understand the question of Indigenous oppression.

The approach of the CPA to Indigenous oppression in the 1920s has often been criticised as being economistic, meaning that they allegedly had a narrow focus on the economic aspects of Indigenous exploitation rather than any consideration of broader political issues.[135] It is then argued that this shifted from 1928 onwards due to the influence of the Comintern, which pressured the Communist Party to take the issue of Indigenous oppression more seriously and to develop a political analysis of that oppression and strategies to combat it.

While there is some truth to this argument, most writers on the subject end up avoiding an examination of the broader context in which debates within the Comintern around colonialism, racism and anti-imperialism took place, in particular the impact that the rise of Stalinism had on the formulation of its policies towards colonially oppressed and Indigenous peoples.

Unlike the old Socialist International, which maintained ambiguous positions on colonialism, the Comintern was established on a clearly anti-imperialist basis. This was important because, in the aftermath of the

---

132. *Workers' Weekly*, 20 February 1925, p.2; 20 July 1926, p.3; 27 January 1928, p.2.
133. See *The Communist*, September–October 1925; November–December 1925; January–February 1926; March 1926.
134. The general analysis of the CPA in this chapter comes from O'Lincoln 1985.
135. Townsend 2009.

First World War, a series of national independence movements had erupted across the globe. The Bolshevik party in Russia and the leadership of the Comintern saw an alliance between the revolutionary workers' movements of the advanced capitalist countries and the anti-colonial movements of oppressed nationalities as a key strategic question. At first, the Comintern essentially conceived of the world as split between the large imperialist powers, like Britain and Germany, and the colonies that they oppressed and controlled. The colonial world was seen as relatively homogeneous, with only limited attempts made to differentiate between different categories of oppressed nation.[136]

At the Fourth Congress of the Comintern in 1922, the Indian Communist MN Roy argued for a more sophisticated analysis of different colonial nations. Roy distinguished between three different "tiers" of colonial societies. First there were the "countries in which capitalism has reached a rather high level of development", such as Australia and Canada. In these countries "industry has developed due to the inflow of capital from the great centres of capitalism" and a "native capitalism has gained strength". Second were those countries where capitalist development has occurred, but "it is still at an elementary level" and "feudalism" was supposedly still economically dominant. Lastly were countries where capitalist development had barely started at all, "primitive conditions still prevail, and the social order is dominated by patriarchal feudalism".[137]

In this schema Australia's position was still ambiguous. While it was seen as having a high level of capitalist development and a native capitalist class, it was still a colony of Britain and therefore the fight for Australian independence was presumably progressive. This was at any rate how leading members of the CPA and Comintern officials in charge of Australian affairs chose to interpret Roy's schema. For the CPA this fitted conveniently with the strong current of Australian nationalism dominant on the socialist left and in the wider labour movement. It wasn't until 1928 that the nature of Australian capitalism and the place of Indigenous people within it was further clarified. That year, the Sixth Congress of the Comintern adopted theses on

---

136. The following is largely drawn from Drachewych 2021.
137. Riddell (ed.) 2012, p.687.

colonies and semi-colonies which argued that it was "necessary to distinguish between those colonies of the capitalist countries which have served them as colonising regions for their surplus population, and which in this way have become a continuation of their capitalist system (Australia, Canada, etc.) and those colonies which are exploited by the imperialists primarily as markets for their commodities…"

> The colonies of the first type, on the basis of their general development, became "Dominions", that is, members of the given imperialist system with equal or nearly equal rights. In them, capitalist development reproduces among the immigrant white population the class structure of the metropolis, at the same time that the native population was, for the most part, exterminated.[138]

Australia was now understood not as a colony, but as an independent capitalist power with "equal or nearly equal rights" with Britain and a social structure that reproduced the main features of a class society that was part of the advanced capitalist world, albeit with an additional element in the form of the Indigenous inhabitants. While this was an important development in the analysis of countries like Australia, the political strategies put forward for combating racism and imperialism were negatively influenced by the growing Stalinisation of the Comintern.

From 1925 politics in the USSR became dominated by the "right-centre" bloc of Stalin and Bukharin, and this flowed through into the Comintern, with Bukharin in charge of the International from 1926. He pursued a policy of seeking alliances with any national liberation movement on whatever basis possible. When criticised for this opportunism, he argued that Communists across the globe should subordinate themselves to anyone willing to ally with the USSR, whatever impact this might have on the development of class struggle within their own countries. This policy was pursued in the interests of the new Soviet bureaucracy, who were concerned about increasing imperialist pressures on the USSR from the Western powers. Even after Bukharin was driven out of the leadership, the Soviet bureaucracy largely maintained the policies on race and colonialism entrenched during Bukharin's time.

---

138. Quoted in Drachewych 2021, p.2419.

What does this have to do with the CPA and the question of Indigenous oppression? At a meeting of the Comintern Information Department in 1926, CPA member Hector Ross was grilled over his attitude towards the Indigenous populations in Australia and New Zealand. The questions reflected little concern for combating racism, but were instead about clarifying whether the Indigenous populations in the two countries could generate national movements that the USSR could support in order to undermine British imperialism from the inside. Ross appears to have been confused by this line of questioning and vaguely replied that while the Māori were antagonistic to the British, "the Australian natives are not to be reckoned with at all".[139]

The shift to seeing Indigenous Australians as a colonised national minority striving for national independence, and therefore a potential ally for the Australian Communist movement, took place sometime between 1928 and 1931. This change was shaped by the broader shift in Comintern thinking with regard to various oppressed peoples across the globe. The origins of this shift appear to be in the intervention of the Comintern officials Nikolai Nasanov and Max Petrovsky, although it has been argued that it was directly influenced by Stalin himself and his writings on the national question. In several countries with a history of colonialism or racism, Petrovsky and Nasanov proposed that the Communist parties adopt new demands to relate to these questions. For South Africa, Petrovsky and Nasanov developed the Native Republic thesis and, for the United States, the Black Belt thesis. A similar proposal was also put forward by Comintern representatives at the first meeting of Latin American Communist parties in 1929; they raised the demand for an "Indian Republic in South America" made up of the Indigenous peoples of the continent.[140]

While the theses of both the Native Republic and the Black Belt would shape the CPA's response to Indigenous oppression, it is the Black Belt thesis that was drawn on most directly. This was a perspective which argued that African Americans concentrated in the southern US states of Louisiana, Mississippi, Alabama, Georgia and the Carolinas constituted an oppressed

---

139. Quoted in Drachewych 2017, pp.226–7.
140. See Zumoff 2014, pp.342–52 for a detailed discussion about the origins of the Black Belt thesis.

nation which had tangible borders within the US, and that they should fight for their national right to self-determination – up to and including the right to secede from America.

For revolutionary anti-Stalinist critics, there were several points of concern with the Black Belt idea.[141] The first was that they believed the motivation behind it had little to do with developing serious concrete strategies for combating racism and strengthening Communist working-class forces. Instead, they said, what lay behind the thesis was a desire to propose demands that would allow the Communists to relate to middle-class layers within oppressed groups. This related to the broader shift in Comintern policy regarding anti-colonial movements which was criticised by Trotsky and others in the 1920s.

Secondly, the demand for a Black Belt was viewed as yet another example of the Comintern coming up with reasons to endlessly defer the socialist revolution. This approach was outlined at the Sixth Congress of the Comintern, which divided the world between countries where proletarian revolution was on the agenda and countries where the immediate goal should be a so-called "democratic dictatorship of the workers and the peasantry", distinct from a revolutionary workers' state. This was the beginning of the Stalinist revival of the Menshevik two-stage theory of socialist revolution. The American Trotskyist Max Shachtman, in his book *Communism and the Negro*, drew out how the Black Belt demand accepted the idea that there "is still room in the United States for a national-democratic revolution distinct from the proletarian revolution". However, for anti-Stalinists like Shachtman,

> no other revolution, intervening between the present rule of finance capital and the final proletarian upheaval, is conceivable in the United States. A theory which does conceive of one is utopian and reactionary. Yet it is precisely such an "intermediate" revolution which is visualized by the new theory.[142]

The third problem with the Black Belt thesis is that it conceptualised African Americans in the United States as an oppressed nation engaged in a movement

---

141. For a more modern critique of the Black Belt see Sustar 2012. For anti-Stalinist critiques from the time see Shachtman 2003, Trotsky 2001 and James 2018.
142. Shachtman 2003, p.86.

for national liberation. As leading Black Communist Harry Haywood put it: "The Negros in the United States reveal amongst themselves all the characteristics of a nation... Therefore, the struggle of the Negro masses for liberation...must take the form of a movement for national liberation".[143]

For anti-Stalinists like Max Shachtman and CLR James, this argument did not stack up. They did not rule out the possibility of African Americans developing a nationalist consciousness. Nonetheless, they saw this as being explicable within a framework which understood African Americans as an oppressed racial minority, rather than a nationally oppressed group striving for national independence from America. The idea that African Americans constituted a "nation" was undermined by numerous factors, including the mass migration of Black people from the south to the north, the diverse social and economic conditions in which they lived, and the lack of any precedent for a campaign to create a Black nation in the proposed region. But aside from its lack of sociological grounding, the theory had big political problems. It pushed against the idea of trying to unite Black and white workers together in militant struggle – something which would in fact take place throughout the 1930s and again later during the civil rights movement. It also went against the grain of early Comintern thinking on African Americans, which was sometimes unclear and imprecise, as Shachtman acknowledges, but which definitively did not raise the demand for national self-determination nor consider them to be a nation. Thus for Shachtman and other Trotskyist critics, the theory was further proof of the Stalinist desire to seek alliances with middle-class layers in the Black community, and to move away from a class-based analysis of Black oppression towards a race-based or nationalist one.

A contemporary Marxist historian, Bryan D Palmer, has written a similar critique:

> [I]n placing undue emphasis on the 1928 self-determination thesis there is a danger of understating other communist initiatives in the 1920s and overplaying what was undoubtedly a highly problematic theoretical and practical direction taken for the first time with the articulation of the Black Belt nation thesis.

---

143. As quoted in Shachtman 2003, pp.68–9.

In actuality, the notion that African Americans in the Deep South could form a distinct nation not only compromised severely Marxist understandings of historical materialism and "the national question," but also flew directly in the face of black aspiration, undermined the very racialized class solidarities that communist organizers repeatedly promoted as the critical component of progressive politics in both the North and the South, and retreated from significant unities that were developing across the United States, especially in northern cities such as Chicago and New York.[144]

The Peruvian Marxist José Carlos Mariátegui developed a similar argument against the demand for an Indian Republic in South America. He argued that the oppression of the Indigenous peoples of South America was clearly rooted in the socio-economic structure of the continent, and that the Communist movement must strive to recruit the most militant sections of the Indigenous working class and "give the movement of the Indigenous and Black proletariat, whether agricultural or industrial, a clear character of class struggle".[145]

He saw the promotion of the Indian Republic demand as a barrier to this goal, because it would lead to the Indigenous peoples being marginalised in the developing workers' movement and, as the Trotskyists argued with regard to the Black Belt thesis, it was based not on a concrete examination of the actual dynamics of Indigenous struggle in South America, but rather was a preconceived model enforced on the Communist parties by an increasingly bureaucratic and conservative Comintern leadership. Instead of raising the illusory demand for a separate Indigenous republic, Mariátegui argued that the Indigenous population had to be won to the idea that a socialist republic would destroy the economic roots of their oppression, while the rest of the working class had to be educated about why they should support the struggles of their Indigenous comrades.[146]

There is no direct evidence of the Comintern developing a comparable strategy for the CPA. Instead it seems that the CPA developed its policy on

---

144. Palmer 2004, p.199.

145. Mariátegui 2021, p.71.

146. Becker 2006; see also Mariátegui's "Race in Latin America", collected in Mariátegui 2021. Trotskyist oppositionists in the Communist Party of South Africa similarly "rejected the slogan of an 'independent native republic' and its corollary, the two-stage revolution in South Africa, in which a bourgeois democratic state would abolish racial discrimination prior to a socialist transformation" (Hirson 1990).

Indigenous issues through internal discussion, although its approach was obviously shaped by the Native Republic and Black Belt theses. This can be seen in the first major CPA publication on the Indigenous question, "Communist Party's Fight for Aborigines: Draft Programme of Struggle Against Slavery", released by CPA leader Bert Moxon in September 1931.[147] This draft program contains a systematic overview and denunciation of the exploitation and oppression of Aboriginal people. It then presents a long list of demands for "full economic, social and political rights", the abolition of the Aborigines Protection Boards, the release of all Aboriginal people from prison and their trial by Aboriginal juries, and other quite advanced and radical slogans.

The 1931 draft program was strongly shaped by local conditions. A number of its demands were very similar to those put forward by the Australian Aboriginal Progressive Association (AAPA), founded by Aboriginal activist Fred Maynard in 1924, and the program itself positively references the existence of the AAPA. Moxon would also have been influenced by his own direct experience and those of other leading Communist Party members. In 1931 he went on a semi-clandestine tour of Indigenous communities in central and northern Australia. The tour was not announced publicly in the Communist press, presumably because of their fear that the authorities would be alterted to his project. However, it came to the attention of the public anyway when Giles Roper, the secretary of the South Australian branch of the CPA and future Trotskyist, was arrested at a public meeting in the Botanical Gardens during which Roper reported on the findings of Moxon's tour, in particular the abuses perpetrated by station owners and the police. Roper was found guilty of offensive behaviour for criticising police attacks on Aboriginal communities, and was fined.[148] After the tour, Moxon wrote an article about his experiences for the Communist press.[149] Norman Jeffery, a leading Communist who showed a particular interest in Indigenous issues, was reportedly influenced by his time working alongside unionised

---

147. *Workers' Weekly*, 25 September 1931, p.2.

148. *The Advertiser*, 18 December 1931, p.26; *Workers' Weekly*, 27 November 1931, p.3; *Workers' Weekly*, 25 December 1931, p.3.

149. *Workers' Weekly*, 11 September 1931, p.1. This was also republished in two parts in *Red Leader*, 11 September 1931, p.4 and 25 September 1931, p.2.

Aboriginal workers in rural NSW. Tom Wright had some experience with Aboriginal working-class activists in the Unemployed Workers' Movement in Glebe, in particular the irrepressible Eatock family.[150] EA Knight, Sydney district secretary of the CPA-led Militant Minority Movement during the 1930s, similarly noted that his views on Aboriginal oppression were shaped by "personal experiences in my youth".[151]

However, the draft program also raised a demand directly influenced by broader Comintern thinking:

> The handing over to the aborigines of large tracts of watered and fertile country, with towns, seaports, railways, roads, etc., to become one or more independent aboriginal states or republics. The handing back to the aborigines of all Central, Northern, and North West Australia to enable the aborigines to develop their native pursuits. These aboriginal republics to be independent of Australian or other foreign powers. To have the right to make treaties with foreign powers, including Australia, establish their own army, governments, industries, and in every way be independent of imperialism.[152]

The Aboriginal republics section of the draft program has often been dismissed as a kooky idea that, while misconceived, had no negative impact upon the CPA's practical approach to Indigenous issues. Some have even celebrated it as evidence that they were starting to take the question seriously.[153] Other writers see the demand as confused, but nonetheless expressing a commitment to a demand for Indigenous self-determination that foreshadowed the struggles of the '60s and '70s.

But to what extent are the criticisms of the Black Belt thesis applicable to the CPA's 1931 draft program? The question of whether the CPA was relating to a middle-class Indigenous leadership was not a concern, as during this period such a layer was basically non-existent in Australia. Nor does the CPA's demand for Aboriginal republics seem to have been conceptualised

---

150. Macintyre 1998, p.266.
151. *Workers' Weekly*, 7 April 1939, p.2.
152. *Workers' Weekly*, 25 September 1931, p.2.
153. Townsend 2009, p.13.

as part of a two-stage theory of revolution. The CPA insisted that the establishment of Aboriginal republics would only come after the socialist revolution and the creation of a workers' state in Australia.[154]

The main issue with the draft program's demand for Aboriginal republics was that it was not based on a serious analysis of Australian conditions, but rather represented the mechanical adoption of a cynical slogan invented by the Comintern bureaucracy. The adoption of this demand created a series of confusions and ambiguities surrounding the Indigenous question which would make it difficult for Communists to understand the changing dynamics of Indigenous struggle over time. Like the Black Belt thesis, it conceptualised Indigenous people as a national minority striving for national independence. But this threw up some difficult problems for the CPA. After all, significant sections of the Aboriginal population did not live in the Northern Territory or Western Australia. Some had become integrated, to varying degrees and not without significant racist discrimination, into Australian society. The 1931 draft program dodged this dilemma by arguing that the "fifty thousand aborigines in the Federal territories, the few hundred in each State, and the tens of thousands of half-caste workers in each State and the territory must be mobilised" around all the demands in the draft program: for civil rights and Aboriginal republics.

Compare this for instance to the actual development of the Australian Aboriginal Progressive Association (AAPA). Unlike some Indigenous activist organisations in the 1930s, the AAPA did not narrowly advocate for the ending of discriminatory laws in order that Aboriginal people could assimilate into white Australian society. Though it did campaign against racist discrimination and called for the abolition of the Aborigines Protection Board, the AAPA also argued for the protection of Aboriginal cultural independence, and the right to plots of land for Aboriginal families owing to their ownership before invasion. It strongly rejected the idea that Aboriginal culture was inferior. As Maynard wrote in his 1927 letter to NSW Premier Jack Lang:

> I wish to make it perfectly clear, on behalf of our people, that we accept no condition of inferiority as compared with the European people. Two distinct

---

154. See for instance *Workers' Weekly*, 6 May 1932, p.3 and *Proletariat*, August 1934, p.14.

civilisations are represented by respective races. On one hand we have the civilisation of necessity and on the other the civilisation co-incident with courteous supply of all the requirements of the human race. That the European people by the arts of war destroyed our more ancient civilisation is freely admitted, and that by their vices and diseases our people have been decimated is also patent, but neither of these facts are evidence of superiority. Quite the contrary is the case...[155]

Maynard's letter goes on to explain that while Aboriginal people have "accepted the modern system of government which has taken the place of our prehistoric methods" this did not mean the AAPA had any intention of abandoning either Aboriginal culture or a distinct Aboriginal identity.

This assertion of Aboriginal identity was not connected to a demand for national separation. In fact, when white sympathisers proposed to campaign for a "Model Aboriginal State" in the Northern Territory, the AAPA explicitly rejected the idea – twice. As the Indigenous historian John Maynard explains, the "AAPA's fight was not for a separate and segregated Aboriginal state but for the provision of enough land for each and every Aboriginal family in Australia".[156] Of particular concern to members of the AAPA was the fear that if such a state was created, the entire Indigenous population would be forcibly resettled there – establishing a segregationist state. So while the AAPA saw itself as connected to the worldwide struggle against racism and colonialism, it was able to do so without mechanically applying demands from other countries and different contexts.

This raises a number of problems with the CPA's draft program and other writings. The leadership of the AAPA, and many of its hundreds of members, had some European heritage. Many engaged in work alongside white workers in the country or the cities. They wanted both an end to discrimination and a positive affirmation of their identity and culture. On the other side of the equation, in the pastoral industry of north-western Australia and the cattle industry in the Northern Territory, hundreds of Indigenous workers were employed by capitalist landowners. Though the

---

155. Maynard 2007, pp.104–5.
156. Maynard 2007, p.83.

conditions Indigenous workers faced were uniquely terrible, they were nevertheless participating in a capitalist labour process. At the same time, they were able to keep alive more of their cultural traditions than Indigenous people in the eastern states, including their connection to Country. The example of the AAPA also didn't fit with the 1931 draft program's conception of Aboriginal people as a national minority striving for the establishment of Aboriginal republics.

Throughout this period, the CPA attitude towards Indigenous struggle went through important changes, with substantial shifts of substance and emphasis. However, despite the various changes, for most of the 1930s, the CPA strongly associated the struggle for Indigenous rights with a revolutionary working-class struggle against capitalism. The draft program was an extremely radical and intransigent document. It connected the struggle for Indigenous rights to a revolutionary fight against capitalism and imperialism, while also raising several politically advanced demands that had not been raised widely, or in some cases at all, in Australia beforehand. In 1932, it was reprinted in the Comintern publication *The Negro Worker* as part of an overview of revolutionary movements against imperialism and colonialism across the globe.[157] The CPA would bring this militant spirit into the class battles of the Great Depression.

The Unemployed Workers' Movement

It was in northern Australia that the Communist Party first systematically organised around Indigenous rights. In doing so, they were forced to challenge the approach of the established labour movement in Darwin. The trade union movement in the Northern Territory, centralised under the leadership of the Northern Australian Workers' Union (NAWU) often had an antagonistic attitude towards the multi-racial working class that it was supposed to represent.[158] Chinese labourers were an early and persistent target of the NAWU, which successfully lobbied to restrict their employment from 1911 onwards. During the 1920s, the leadership of the NAWU was also often

---

157. *The Negro Worker*, 2 (4), April 1932, pp.10–12.
158. The two best accounts of Indigenous workers in the Darwin labour movement are Martínez 1999 and Brian 2001.

dismissive of Indigenous workers. Even when the NAWU argued that they should be covered by union agreements, this was usually in the hope that it would lead to their replacement by white workers.

Seizing the latent possibilities for multi-racial working-class solidarity would thus require a sharp break in the development of the Darwin labour movement. Two things made this possible: the existence of an increasingly frustrated left-wing opposition within the NAWU, and the establishment of a small branch of the CPA, the two of which quickly merged. A key role in bringing the two together was played by Lawerence James Mahoney and his friend and comrade John Waldie. Mahoney and Waldie had been part of a growing left-wing opposition trying to unseat the conservative NAWU leadership of Robert Toupein. The issue of Indigenous workers came to the fore during a union boycott campaign of local pubs over the employment of Aboriginal workers. While some NAWU members argued for the boycott on the basis that the workers were being underpaid, the majority of the union supported the boycott, more or less explicitly, with the goal of driving the Aboriginal workers out of the industry and replacing them with white workers. As the boycott went on, the tensions over this started to come to the fore. Mahoney had played a prominent role during the boycott, demanding heavy penalties for workers who drank at the pubs, against the moderation of the NAWU leadership. The racist support for the boycott, though, sat uneasily with Mahoney, who was friendly with Aboriginal workers through his position as a referee at the local football club. As the boycott came to an end he started to raise the issue of Indigenous exclusion. This came to a head in the aftermath of the boycott's victory, when the NAWU leadership proposed that it be extended to Chinese merchants who employed Aboriginal workers. Mahoney and his friend Waldie raised a stink, pointing out that it was hypocritical of the union to do this when Aboriginal workers were excluded from membership of the NAWU and when some NAWU members personally employed Aboriginal workers. Mahoney and Waldie pushed for a vote on allowing Aboriginal workers and some other "coloured" workers to join the union, although it was unsuccessful. Mahoney also organised union support for a strike of Malay pearlers and protested against racist discrimination in the football league.

Mahoney and Waldie's arguments dovetailed with those being made by the CPA. *Workers' Weekly* had criticised the boycott campaign from the beginning, and the broader hostility of the NAWU towards Aboriginal workers which underpinned it.[159] In theses passed at a meeting of the Central Committee of the CPA in June 1930, it was proclaimed that in "such places as Darwin, where there are masses of coloured workers, our Party must become the leader of these masses and bring them into political struggle against their capitalist exploiters". The theses noted the strikes by Indigenous workers in the pearling industry and went so far as to argue that "[t]he majority of our Party members in such districts should be coloured":

> Let the contemptible scoundrels of social fascism scornfully sneer at us as a "coloured party" in such districts. We will accept it as a tribute to our revolutionary determination to unite the working class for the destruction of capitalism.[160]

The CPA would never achieve this goal in Darwin, but it would fight admirably for an anti-racist working-class culture in the city. It is unclear exactly when Mahoney and Waldie joined the CPA; by November 1929 they had resigned from the Darwin branch of the ALP, though they had already been active in various Communist-led organisations and campaigns. As Mahoney and Waldie started attacking the leadership of the NAWU more stridently around a range of issues, including its racism, the NAWU moved to punish them by pushing them out of delegate and organiser positions.

Having been essentially isolated from the centre of the union movement in Darwin, Mahoney, Waldie and their supporters instead focused their attention on the struggles of the unemployed, where they would find an easier audience both for their militant tactics and their arguments about racism. They established a local branch of the Unemployed Workers' Movement (UWM) and engaged in a number of high-profile, militant actions. The most famous saw Mahoney climb onto the roof of a local government building, occupied by the unemployed at the time, and fly the red flag. Mahoney and

---

159. *Workers' Weekly*, 13 April 1928, p.4.
160. Communist Party of Australia 1930, p.39.

the Darwin Communists also brought the CPA's support for Indigenous rights into the unemployed struggle. In July 1929, the local Communists supported and promoted a mass meeting at Police Paddock, an area where much of the local Aboriginal and non-white community lived. The meeting demanded that the government give ownership of the area over to the local community, end racist discrimination and grant them full citizenship rights. When Police Paddock was raided by the cops, the Communists organised an open air meeting denouncing the repression.

Many Aboriginal workers were involved and arrested at the militant unemployed protests. Photos show several Aboriginal and Asian workers participating in the famous unemployed occupation of government offices in January 1931. One of these Aboriginal workers was Joe McGinness, the future national president of the Federal Council for Aboriginal and Torres Strait Islander Advancement. At a meeting of the Darwin UWM in 1931, a motion was adopted supporting the "complete emancipation" of Aboriginal people from economic and political oppression.[161] When an Aboriginal man was arrested for murder by Darwin police, Mahoney tried to intercede to have the man released in his role as the local representative of the the International Class War Prisoners Aid, a Comintern organisation. Mahoney would regularly write letters to the *Northern Standard* about Aboriginal oppression. While Mahoney and Waldie had some success building anti-racist sentiment among the unemployed workers, the mainstream labour movement remained mostly hostile. They had some success getting the NAWU to protest the banning of "half-caste" workers from drinking at Darwin pubs. However, at the annual conference of the NAWU in 1930, their motion to end all racial discrimination in union membership was ruled out of order by the chair.[162]

Over time opposition from the NAWU leadership and the repression by the police began to take their toll on Mahoney and Waldie. The NAWU whipped up a slanderous campaign accusing Mahoney and Waldie of plotting to replace the white workforce with their "coloured" allies.[163] They both spent considerable time in jail over various offences related to the unemployed

---

161. *Workers' Weekly,* 6 November 1931, p.4.
162. *Northern Standard,* 2 September 1930, p.2.
163. *Workers' Weekly,* 30 May 1930, p.2 has a reply to these accusations.

protests and unpaid fines. The NAWU leaders effectively abandoned them and manoeuvred to limit their support within the Darwin workers' movement, with some success. The repression reached its farcical climax when Mahoney was arrested while waving goodbye to a friend on an outgoing ship. His crime? Standing on the wrong side of the wharf.[164]

In January 1933 Mahoney left Darwin, and Waldie followed suit shortly afterwards. They would both remain active in Communist politics in Sydney, but clearly felt that they had been defeated in Darwin and that their efforts to build an anti-racist working-class movement had been in vain. But within a few years, a new generation of Darwin Communists inspired by Mahoney and Waldie would continue their fight for militant unionism and anti-racism.

It wasn't just in Darwin that Communists took up the issue of Indigenous oppression within the unemployed struggle. At the beginning of the Depression, the membership of the Communist Party was primarily concentrated in the capital cities, particularly Sydney, plus a handful of mining communities. But as the Depression forced hundreds of thousands of people out of work, the unemployed struggle opened up opportunities for the Communists to spread into new areas.

One of these areas was country NSW. Most readers are probably inclined to think about rural NSW – then and now – as an undifferentiated reactionary mass. After all, it was in the country towns that the fascistic Old Guard drilled its militias in preparation for the overthrow of the Lang Labor government. Rural newspapers were filled with dire warnings about the Communist hordes gathering in the industrial cities, and some advocated for rural regions to separate from the NSW state in protest. When the rural elite heard that Communists were attempting to build a base in country towns they hit back with a wave of attacks on Communist activists, culminating in an estimated 3,000-strong protest in Dubbo that surrounded the home of local Communist activists and demanded their immediate expulsion from the town limits.[165]

Throughout the 1920s and 1930s, there was also a wave of racist agitation against Aboriginal communities, with a number of country towns pushing for greater levels of segregation in schools, cinemas and public spaces, as well as

---

164. *Northern Standard*, 13 September 1932, p.4.
165. *Wellington Times*, 23 November 1931, p.3.

the further removal of Aboriginal missions. This was led by the "respectable" middle-class elements in rural NSW, who saw Aboriginal people as unwanted pests. As the Depression set in, the NSW government issued instructions that unemployed Aboriginal workers should receive rations instead of the dole. Aboriginal people didn't accept these attacks without a fight. In 1931 Aboriginal unemployed workers protested in Wellington, NSW, demanding the dole instead of rations. The *Yass Tribune-Courier* reported that the change was "much resented by the colored people", and that strikes were being advocated by Aboriginal communities and petitions organised to be sent to Jack Lang.[166] According to historian Heather Goodall, these actions culminated in a wave of "stop-works, protest and strikes at Wallaga Lake, Menindee, Burnt Bridge, Brewarrina and Purfleet from 1936 to 1938".[167]

In the face of these attacks, Indigenous and non-indigenous working-class activists started to draw together in some places, with a key role often being played by members of the Communist Party. In June 1931 a meeting was organised in Dubbo to launch a local branch of the Unemployed Workers' Movement by a small group of Communist activists. It was immediately controversial with the conservative Dubbo establishment, who condemned it as a Communist front.[168] Criticism also came from the local ALP leadership, who attempted to stop Communist activists from dominating the movement and, when that failed, set up a rival unemployed organisation. The mayor repeatedly refused to give the UWM Dubbo branch permission to hold public rallies.

As the unemployed struggle in Dubbo took off, it intersected with the local Aboriginal community. Aboriginal activists Tom Peckham and Ted Taylor, who lived in the area, both got involved in the unemployed protests. They then spoke to the white unemployed about the discrimination of the Aborigines Protection Board and asked them to take up Aboriginal issues.[169] The Peckham family would be involved in trade union and socialist politics for many decades.

---

166. *Yass Tribune-Courier*, 15 June 1931, p.2.
167. Goodall 2008, p.218.
168. *The Dubbo Liberal and Macquarie Advocate*, 21 November 1931, p.6; *Dubbo Dispatch and Wellington Independent*, 20 November 1931, p.1.
169. Goodall 2008, pp.218–19.

Their appeal had an impact. At a mass meeting in Dubbo in 1932, the unemployed movement moved a motion demanding full rations for Aboriginal workers and urged the labour movement to take up the issue more generally.[170] During the 1932 municipal elections, the platform of the Dubbo branch of the CPA included the demand for the "enfranchisement of aboriginals and foreign workers of all races", and the "right of all aboriginals to own property and participate in municipal affairs".[171] There was also a small Communist group in the nearby town of Wellington, which supported unemployed Aboriginal workers through the local branch of the UWM. At a meeting of western NSW unemployed organisations and trade unions in Orange in 1936, the Wellington and Dubbo branches of the UWM initiated a discussion about the treatment of Aboriginal people, which led to the conference moving that "a definite campaign be launched throughout all areas to demand equal treatment for all classes and colors".[172]

This activity wasn't confined to western NSW. The Waratah-Mayfield UWM branch in Newcastle repeatedly discussed the issue of Aboriginal rights. In February 1932 it sent a letter to the local branch of the Australasian Society of Patriots drawing their attention to abuses against Aboriginal people in the Northern Territory. In March of the same year, it sent a protest to the Queensland government over reports of attacks on Aboriginal communities and in July it protested against the lower dole rates for unemployed Aboriginal workers. At a 1932 meeting of the Kempsey Unemployed League a Mr. Stevens, who was at the very least a close supporter, if not a member, of the CPA, argued in favour of equal rights for Aboriginal unemployed workers – and won the debate.[173] In 1932 Communists tried to organise a joint protest of Aboriginal fisherman and wharf labourers at Port Kembla after they were all kicked off the dole.[174]

This support for unemployed Aboriginal workers spread further still, with the Innisfail, Queensland branches of the UWM, the Australian Railway Union, and the Waterside Workers' Federation, as well the Mourilyan mill

---

170. *Workers' Weekly*, 1 July 1932, p.4.
171. *Dubbo Dispatch and Wellington Independent*, 8 January 1932, p.2.
172. *Wellington Times*, 27 February 1936, p.3.
173. *The Macleay Chronicle*, 14 September 1932, p.6.
174. *Workers' Weekly*, 3 February 1932, p.3.

workers demanding that "aboriginals and other colored workers be placed on the same footing as other unemployed as regards rations and relief work", at a meeting in May 1933. The meeting also protested "against the police intimidatory methods which are used with these workers".[175] That motion was moved by CPA member Pat Clancy. By 1938 even the Tasmanian unemployed movement was passing motions about Aboriginal rights.

What Darwin, Dubbo, Innisfail and the working-class suburbs of Newcastle had in common is that the Communist Party had built up a base of support among working-class activists through the unemployed struggle, and in some cases trade union activity, which then opened up the space for them to pursue anti-racist arguments and activity.

Evolving Communist theory on Indigenous oppression

The Communist contribution to the struggle for Indigenous rights in the first half of the 1930s wasn't confined to practical activity. There was also a wide-ranging discussion in the Communist press about the origins and nature of Indigenous oppression. As has already been noted, in the 1920s this discussion had been mainly of an anthropological nature, often with strong paternalistic or racist undertones due to the influence of the academic framework commonly used to understand these issues. However, during the 1930s Communist writers pushed past this to develop a more serious examination of the relationship between Indigenous oppression and Australian capitalism.

Communists were well placed to reject the founding myths of Australian capitalism. While the shearer unionists, socialists and some liberals had in the past acknowledged that the establishment of the colonial government had rested on a morally unjustifiable invasion which resulted in death and misery for Indigenous people, Communists took this further.

The 1931 draft program had laid out the general arguments, but they were now expanded upon in numerous articles. One of the most advanced statements on Indigenous issues came from a 1934 article in *Proletariat*,[176] a

---
175. *Cairns Post*, 26 May 1933, p.12.
176. *Proletariat*, August 1934, pp.12–14. All quotes in this section are from this article.

publication of the Melbourne University Labor Club run by CPA members. The article begins by noting that "there has been a great awakening of interest in Australian Aborigines over the last two or three years". However, while noting the growing interest in the conditions of Aboriginal people shown by humanitarian, religious and scientific organisations – and more cynically by the "smug bourgeois" – the article argues for a specifically communist approach to the question of Indigenous oppression. The *Proletariat* article argues forthrightly that Indigenous oppression is embedded in the capitalist system. Due to the integration of Indigenous workers into certain sectors of the economy such as the pastoral industry, Indigenous exploitation is "now part of the economic life of the country". The exploitation of Indigenous peoples, much like those in Australia-controlled New Guinea, is the ground from which "the colonial super-profits of the Australian bourgeoise" arises. The article also argued that Indigenous oppression is not just economic but political in nature, explaining that "the aborigines, like the million masses of Asia and Africa, suffering from European and Japanese imperialism, are robbed of all political rights", as they have no political representation, constitutional recognition or legal control over their own land.

At the time this oppression was often justified with the idea that the invasion of the continent was beneficial for the Indigenous population, and that at any rate, they were a "dying race". The *Proletariat* article took issue with both of these arguments, further revealing the distance between Communists and middle-class humanitarians. On the question of the supposed benefits that British imperialism gave to Indigenous people, the article is very clear. According to the article, British capitalism came to Australia already, in the words of Marx, "dripping from head to foot in blood and dirt". The Indigenous experience of British colonisation was one of massacres and exploitation in which "the aborigines have been brought very close to total annihilation at the hands of the imperialists". However, this annihilation was not total, and the article argues that it won't be if working-class forces throw themselves into the anti-racist struggle. "We must decisively reject the bourgeois theory that aborigines are doomed to extinction. Even without Socialism, they may be saved from extinction" by concerted political action.

The involvement of the working class, and the Communist Party in particular, was seen as vital for the advancement of Indigenous rights. The capitalists are "not concerned with the emancipation of the aborigines". Bourgeois academics, while feigning concern about Indigenous people, are content "to see they depart in peace". The work of religious missionaries has been a total failure with regard to protecting the Indigenous population, and while sympathetic anthropologists might help to gather scientific evidence of the exploitation of Indigenous people, the reality is that "we already possess sufficient information... What is wanted...[is] political action to prevent further oppression".

Despite this quite brilliant polemic, when it came to solutions the *Proletariat* was still trapped in the framework provided by the 1931 draft program. It envisioned the establishment of an "autonomous aboriginal republic under the leadership of the working class" as the only fundamental means of achieving emancipation. This "aboriginal republic" however was not seen as an achievable goal under capitalism, but rather its success is "contingent on the formation of a Soviet Australia". As evidence for the viability of this strategy, the article pointed to the experience of the national minorities during the 1917 Russian Revolution which showed that "where the working class succeeds in emancipating itself from capitalism it simultaneously emancipates all oppressed peoples within its territories".[177]

Solidarity and struggle

As the Communist Party drew young militants towards it through its work in the Unemployed Workers' Movement, it also began to rebuild a left-wing current within the trade unions. A key role in this was played by the Militant Minority Movement, modelled on overseas examples of rank-and-file initiatives. As they rebuilt a class struggle wing of the labour movement, the CPA also sought to integrate their support for Indigenous rights into trade union battles.

---

177. It should be noted though that the CPA regularly contrasted how the USSR treated the oppressed nationalities in Eastern Europe with Australia's treatment of Indigenous people. In reality, the USSR, from the time Stalin took power in the late '20s, pursued a policy of ruthlessly exploiting the oppressed nationalities of the former tsarist empire and terrorising tendencies towards national self-determination. For a classic look at this question see the Ukrainian dissident Ivan Dzyuba's *Internationalism or Russification?: A Study in the Soviets Nationalities Problem*, published in English in 1968 by Weidenfeld and Nicolson.

Red Leader, the publication of the Minority Movement, published extensively on Indigenous oppression.[178] While other Communist publications mainly focused on developing a platform for Indigenous rights, *Red Leader* articles were more agitational, highlighting particular examples of exploitation and oppression. These articles were important in popularising support for Indigenous rights among a layer of left-wing working-class militants, alongside the more local publications of the CPA. As Communist influence increased within the union movement, they were then able to take practical steps on a number of fronts in solidarity with Indigenous struggles. In 1932 the Communist Party's "Agit-Prop" committee proposed pro-Aboriginal slogans for that year's May Day. The CPA also organised for Aboriginal activist Anna Morgan to speak at a meeting of the International Women's Day Committee and at the Women's Anti-War Conference in 1935. It also published one of her articles in the CPA publication *Working Women*. When Aboriginal shearers were refused award wages by an employer in Mukinbudin, Western Australia, the CPA's Perth branch took up the issue with the state government. Norman Jeffery, the Communist organiser of the Pastoral Workers' Industrial Union, used his time visiting rural workers' committees to urge workers to support Indigenous rights and investigate conditions at local Aboriginal missions.[179]

The greatest impacts made by the CPA came through its intervention into two of the most significant and sustained union-backed Indigenous campaigns of the time: the 1932–34 Caledon Bay campaign and the 1938 Day of Mourning and Protest.

---

178. For example *Red Leader*, 11 September 1931, p.4; 25 September 1931, p.2; 9 October 1931, p.2.
179. *Workers' Weekly*, 15 March 1935, p.3.

The Caledon Bay campaign

In September 1932 five Japanese fishermen were killed near Caledon Bay in the Northern Territory. Suspicion fell on the local Yolngu Indigenous community. One of the police officers dispatched to investigate also turned up dead. In Darwin's establishment, opinion demanded that a significant police expedition be sent to arrest those accused. The Melbourne *Herald* captured the mood:

> The Administrator…[a]nd the Superintendent of Police…consider that unless prompt action is taken to punish the natives, it will be unsafe for any white man or trepangers [fishermen] to call at any part of the north-eastern portion of Arnhem Land.[180]

In August 1933 a committee was set up in Darwin to campaign against the organisation of the police expedition due to fears it could lead to a massacre.[181] The Australian branch of International Labor Defence (ILD), a legal advocacy group under the umbrella of the Comintern, was a part of the committee along with local union, humanitarian and religious groups.[182] The CPA campaigned across the country to build opposition to the proposed police expedition. In September a large meeting of waterside workers in Sydney voted to condemn the expedition.[183] While the committee's action managed to stop a police attack, Dhakiyarr Wirrpanda and three other Aboriginal men were brought back to Darwin by a group of missionaries, and a trial began.

The campaign continued right through the trial and into 1934. In June, 2,000 attended a rally at the Sydney Domain, organised by the ILD to demand a retrial after Dhakiyarr Wirrpanda was sentenced to death and the three other men to 20 years' hard labour. Throughout the year the campaign received support from unemployed organisations in Brisbane, Punchbowl, Redfern and Bankstown, from branches of the

---

180. Quoted in Gray 2007, p.115.
181. *Workers' Weekly*, 19 August 1933, p.3.
182. *Workers' Weekly*, 8 September 1933, p.1.
183. *Workers' Weekly*, 15 September 1933, p.2.

Australian Railway Union and other unions, and a further two rallies of thousands were organised in Sydney during August. The Aboriginal men were eventually released thanks to the pressure of the campaign. But Dhakiyarr Wirrpanda disappeared soon after he was released from Fannie Bay gaol, possibly murdered by the police.

The work that the CPA did around this campaign brought it into greater contact with Indigenous people. A report on the work of the party in Western Australia in June 1934 noted that, due to the campaign, "aborigines are in contact with the D.C. (District Committee) – they write to the party and party members go down to where they are preparing facts to present to the Royal Commission when it meets".[184] The Caledon Bay incident and the consequent widespread opposition to the police in Darwin was a turning point. For a long time after 1932, governments no longer felt confident that they would have the level of public support, or indifference, necessary to launch large-scale police expeditions into Indigenous communities.[185]

The anti-sesquicentenary and the 1938 Day of Mourning and Protest

The sesquicentenary of the arrival of the First Fleet in Australia was intended by the Australian bourgeoisie to be a celebration of Australian nationalism, conservatism and loyalty to the British empire. It immediately came under criticism from the workers' movement, the socialist left and sections of the progressive middle class. After all, what version of Australian history was going to be celebrated in 1938? The struggles of the Eureka Stockade, the 1890s strikers and the anti-conscription campaign? Or the ties to British imperialism, the values of colonialism and the dominance of the Australian ruling class?

The CPA initially supported the day's festivities, arguing that the history of working-class and democratic struggle should be the focus.[186] In this vein they argued that Aboriginal people should be included in the official

---

184. Docker 1934, p.17.
185. For a more detailed look at this campaign see Gibson 2022, particularly pp.177–267.
186. *Workers' Weekly*, 24 December 1937, p.2.

celebration as an acknowledgement of their continued existence.[187] This backward outlook was shaped by the CPA's turn to what became known as the Popular Front, a shift that pushed the CPA to abandon its former hostility to all forms of Australian and British nationalism, and instead to frame the Communist movement as the continuation of a progressive Australian national tradition.

The CPA was forced to change its position as it became clear that Indigenous activists were organising to demonstrate against the celebrations. On 30 November 1937, *Workers' Weekly* reported that Aboriginal activists were planning to hold a day of protest and argued: "The Australian people should make it a day for heaping coals of fire on their own heads and at the same time a day of determining that white chauvinist beastliness be relegated to the past".[188]

One of the Aboriginal activists who played a key role in organising the Day of Mourning and Protest was William Ferguson. In 1937 Ferguson founded the Aborigines Progressive Association (APA) at a meeting in Dubbo. Ferguson, as mentioned previously, had a long history of union and Labor Party activism. The CPA had welcomed the creation of the APA and promoted its activities in *Workers' Weekly*.[189] In October 1937 Ferguson spoke at a public meeting in Sydney organised by the CPA.[190] Afterwards, Ferguson was invited by Tom Wright, the Communist leader of the Sheet-Metal Workers' Union, to a meeting of the Sydney Trades and Labour Council to talk about Indigenous oppression. The Trades and Labour Council then voted to endorse a list of progressive demands around Indigenous issues proposed by Wright. Alongside Wright, a number of Communist union leaders played an important role in getting the Trades and Labour Council to endorse this position, including Lloyd Ross, state secretary of the NSW Australian Railways Union, and Bill Orr, the CPA leader of the Miners Federation.[191]

In the lead-up to the sesquicentenary, a meeting of the Trades and Labour Council passed a resolution moved by Ross that condemned the celebration

---

187. *Workers' Weekly*, 10 December 1937, p.3.
188. *Workers' Weekly*, 30 November 1937, p.3.
189. *Workers' Weekly*, 23 July 1937, p.3
190. *Workers' Weekly*, 8 October 1937, p.4; 15 October 1937, p.4.
191. Holt 1988, p.299.

and urged the labour movement to organise its own pro-working class, anti-sesquicentenary events. The resolution noted the slap in the face to Indigenous people embedded within the official celebrations:

> We seize the opportunity to draw the attention of the Government and the people to the tragic position of the aboriginals, and declare that immediate attention must be given to their needs. We demand that the perversion of history in the celebrations should cease and a correct view be given of the treatment of the aboriginals, the place of the convict, and the role of the masses. We appeal to the Trade Unions to feature working-class history and analysis in their journals and meetings.[192]

Coverage of the Day of Mourning and Protest itself was front page news for *Workers' Weekly*, and the various meetings and events held over the week by Indigenous activists were reported on as historic events. However, several articles pointed to tensions that had arisen between the CPA and the APA.

On 25 January, *Workers' Weekly* published a reply to reports in the media that Ferguson was accusing the CPA of refusing to hand over money raised at one of the meetings he spoke at. The CPA argued that this had arisen over a misunderstanding, however it was a foreshadowing of future debates.[193] The Day of Mourning was organised by the APA with the support of the Australian Aborigines' League, based in Victoria. Its organising meetings were open to Aboriginal people only, and while white supporters were encouraged to attend a meeting afterwards, the Day of Mourning and Protest itself was also to be an Aboriginal-only event.

The CPA was very critical of this approach. While they positively covered the Day of Mourning and Protest in detail, they also published articles criticising the "separatist" politics of the organisers. One article laid out the general argument:

> It is most admirable that a movement should take place among the aborigines on their own behalf, but that movement must not be limited or confined in

---
192. Holt 1988, p.301.
193. *Workers' Weekly*, 25 January 1938, p.4.

any way. All progressive and democratic people must be rallied to their cause. Their struggle is ours as well as theirs. While praising the aborigines for taking up the fight, we, the whites, must help them, fight for them, use all means in our power to see that they get justice. Representatives of the trade unions, of all progressive bodies, should be present on their platforms, present in the Australia Hall with them on their Day of Mourning. Whoever tries to limit their movement is foe, not friend, of this fine and terribly maltreated people.[194]

These debates have been seen by some as a precursor to arguments over autonomous organising and Black nationalism in the second half of the 20th century. While concern about white influence over the movement by Indigenous activists probably played some role, there were other factors at work as well.

In the lead-up to the Day of Mourning, considerable conservative pressure was building on Indigenous activists involved. So David Unaipon, a prominent Aboriginal figure, pulled out of the protest a few days before it began, on the basis that the Lyons government had contacted him to assure him that changes were to be made to Aboriginal policy.[195] The Lyons government also accepted a proposal that it would meet with a delegation from the protest, provided that it only included Aboriginal people. This was motivated by a desire to exclude representatives from the socialist left and the unions. At any rate some white people did attend the meeting, but they were handpicked by the government.[196]

There were other conservatising pressures on the Indigenous activists who organised the Day of Mourning. While establishing the APA, Ferguson and another Aboriginal activist, Jack Patten, had come into contact with the publisher William Miles and the writer PR Stephensen. Stephenson had once been a member of the CPA but had drifted away. Both were now part of a tradition of far-right nationalist politics that had some sympathy for Indigenous people. It included such figures as John J Moloney, editor of the nationalist newspaper *The Voice of the North*, who had supported the

---

194. *Workers' Weekly*, 25 January 1938, p.1. Also discussed in *Workers' Weekly*, 1 February 1938, p.2.
195. *Workers' Weekly*, 25 January 1938, p.4.
196. *Workers' Weekly*, 4 February 1938, p.2.

Australian Aboriginal Progressive Association.[197] Later, Miles and Stephensen would establish the proto-fascist Australia First Movement. While Ferguson had initially been friendly to Miles and Stephensen, he became increasingly suspicious of their motives.[198] The tensions were heightened when they arranged the funds to have a newspaper called *Abo Call* published with Jack Patten as the editor. Divisions started to open up within the APA, between Ferguson, who was closer to the union movement and the socialist left, and Patten, who looked to nationalist allies. Patten used *Abo Call* to publish articles attacking Ferguson,[199] and sent a letter to *Workers' Weekly* explaining that the APA would no longer be accepting "unsolicited" donations.[200] ALP members like Albert Thomspon also pressured Ferguson to put limits on his relationship with the Communists.[201]

Despite arguments between the CPA and the APA, they continued to work with each other after the Day of Mourning. On May Day, four months after the protest, the APA accepted an invitation from Communist union leaders to march in the parade, and at the end of the march Tom Wright spoke alongside William Ferguson at a massive meeting on the Domain. The CPA also worked with the APA in establishing a new campaign group, the Campaign for Aboriginal Citizen Rights, which included CPA member Jean Devanny, Ferguson for the APA, plus Mark Davidson and Albert Thompson representing the ALP state executive.[202]

The political divisions within the APA would also shape, and unfortunately ultimately undermine, the important struggle at Cumeroogunga. The Cumeroogunga station and reserve was on the New South Wales side of the Murray River and had long been a site of Aboriginal resistance and unrest. Tensions came to a head in February 1939 when Jack Patten was arrested while agitating among the Aboriginal people at the station. Several hundred Aboriginal people living there then staged a walk-off in protest at the arrest, crossing over the Murray River to northern Victoria.

---

197. Maynard 2007, pp.39–40.
198. See Horner 1974, pp.68–80 for an overview of the dispute between Ferguson and Patten.
199. For instance *The Australian Abo Call*, 1 June 1938, p.2 and 1 May 1938, p.1.
200. *Workers' Weekly*, 11 March 1938, p.1.
201. Horner 1974, p.71.
202. *Workers' Weekly*, 22 April 1938, p.4.

The walk-off was highly controversial in both Indigenous and non-indigenous activist circles. The issues involved were muddled due to the tensions between Patten and other Indigenous leaders, plus Patten's relationship with the right-wing nationalists in Sydney. William Ferguson opposed the walk-off and made it known to those involved in Aboriginal campaigning that he believed Patten had stirred up trouble at Cumeroogunga for his own purposes. The Campaign for Aboriginal Citizen Rights "claimed that Patten represented no known Aboriginal organisation and disassociated itself from his methods".[203] In Victoria, however, the situation was somewhat different. PR Stephensen's Australia First organisation seems to have collapsed shortly before the walk-off began, and despite the Sydney left's hostility, the walk-off found support among the socialist left and the workers' movement in Victoria. William Cooper and the Australian Aborigines' League in Melbourne were more supportive of the walk-off than Ferguson and the Campaign for Aboriginal Citizen Rights. In March, the League brought the issue to the attention of the ACTU, which passed a motion calling on the NSW government to hold an inquiry into the conditions which led to the walk-off. The Victorian branch of the CPA started to run a series of articles about the walk-off and protest meetings were held at Melbourne's Yarra Bank, with socialist, CPA and Aboriginal speakers. A new organisation, the Aborigines' Assistance Committee, was formed with a number of Aboriginal representatives, as well as socialists like JF Chapple, general secretary of the Australian Railways Union. Young Aboriginal members of the Committee such as Margaret Tucker "were keen to accept the support of socialists and communists".[204]

After nine months, the walk-off ended in defeat. The NSW government rejected any demands for a public inquiry and successfully convinced the Victorian government to refuse aid to protesters who had crossed the state border.

---

203. Attwood 2021, p.187.
204. On left-wing support for the walk-off see Attwood 2021, pp.187–94.

Torres Strait Islanders and the North Queensland Communists

So far this chapter has primarily focused on the struggles of Aboriginal people. The oppression of the other Indigenous group in Australia, the Torres Strait Islanders, was also an issue that Communists in North Queensland took up. In the process, they began to grapple with some of the distinctive features of the Torres Strait Islander population and the particular dynamics of their struggles.

More than anywhere else in Australia, it was in North Queensland that the Communist Party took on the character of a mass working-class movement, with a considerable degree of hegemony over left-wing politics in the region, particularly during the two decades between 1930 and 1950. It was in the North Queensland state electorate of Bowen that the Communist Party's first and only parliamentarian, Fred Paterson, was elected in 1944. In the northern towns, ports and mining communities of Townsville, Collinsville-Scottsville, Ingham, Innisfail and Cairns, Communists built an industrially militant and politically radical working-class movement, led by Communist activists who also had substantial influence over rank-and-file members of the ALP.[205] By 1936, *Workers' Weekly* had a circulation of 3,000 in northern Queensland, its second highest after Sydney and its highest per capita in Australia. In 1937, Communists launched the *North Queensland Guardian*, which achieved a circulation of 5,000.[206]

While the Communist Party had drawn attention to the issue as far back as 1923, once it had built a stronghold in North Queensland it was much better placed to take up the oppression of Indigenous people on the Torres Strait Islands, which at the time were under the direct political control of the Queensland state government.[207]

In 1936, a strike erupted among Islanders who worked as pearling luggers for the Queensland Native Affairs Department. It appears that at least some of the strikers were influenced by Communist activists in northern Queensland. A strike participant told historian Nonie Sharp they believed that one of the Islander strike leaders "was with the communists before.

---

205. See Menghetti 2018.
206. Menghetti 2018, p.10.
207. See *Workers' Weekly*, 23 November 1923.

He had a lot of contact with old-time buddies like one South Sea man in Cairns. He'd been feeding him that stuff from the watersiders in Cairns".

Based on her research into the strike, Sharp concluded that the striking Islanders had "longstanding experience in the principles of trade unionism and direct action", and that for those Islanders who had "associated with unionists, with the white left, with communists", there seemed to be a "continuity between the Islanders' conceptions of 'sharing' and the ideals of communism". During the strike itself a newspaper noted that some of "the more advanced boys...are reading the papers and trying to emulate the seamen's strike now being carried on in Australia".[208]

As soon as the 1936 strike started, *Workers' Weekly* began to promote it, writing on 17 January that "though officials decline to give information, Thursday Island natives report that, with two exceptions, all the Torres Strait islanders controlled by the Protector of Aborigines are on strike and refuse to work their boats".[209]

When the Queensland government sent in police to break up the strike and arrest the strike leaders, the CPA campaigned against the repression and exposed the abuses of the cops and the government. A *Workers' Weekly* article entitled "Terrorism against Aborigines" stated:

> A police party has been sent by the Queensland Labor Government to suppress the discontent among the Torres Strait Islanders. The discontent arises from the shameful and cynical way in which the aborigines are exploited by the Government... This state of affairs must be wiped out. Unionists throughout Australia should send in protests to the Queensland Government. Queensland workers should use all their efforts to prevent the terrorising of the Torres Strait islanders by the police party.[210]

This engagement with the struggles of the Torres Strait Islanders continued into the post-war period. Gerald Peel, a full-time writer and organiser for the CPA, took a particular interest in the Islanders. Peel came from an upper-class

---

208. Sharp's quotes from Boughton 2001.
209. *Workers' Weekly*, 17 January 1936, p.1.
210. *Workers' Weekly*, 21 January 1936, p.3; 28 January 1936, p.2; 21 February 1936, p.3.

British family – his great grandfather was Prime Minister Robert Peel – and he had been headmaster at Christ Church Boys' High School, one of the top European schools in India. During the war he had moved to Australia and joined the CPA, becoming a prominent Communist writer on colonial questions such as Indian and Indonesian independence.

By Peel's own account, he became interested in the issue when a Torres Strait Islander visited the CPA's offices in Sydney after the war. The Islander had read some books on political economy he had borrowed from a Communist sailor and discussed with Peel the history of oppression on the islands. Inspired by the conversation, Peel wrote a short book called *Isles of the Torres Strait: an Australian responsibility* that exposed the conditions of the Islanders and advocated for a radical break with government policy. In the book, Peel advocated for the transfer of the islands from the control of the Queensland state government to administration by the Commonwealth, declaration of the area as "an autonomous region within the Commonwealth, with sovereign internal rights for its people, including the right to secede", an islands' constitution to be drawn up by a sovereign constituent assembly elected by the people, and the preservation of "all pearling and fishing rights…and all other natural wealth in the region…exclusively for the islanders". While not seeking to pre-empt the Islanders' right to decide their new constitution for themselves, Peel suggested

> that such a constitution be based on an economy of public and/or cooperative ownership of the means of production, barring entry of private enterprise from outside, and that it would be the duty of the Commonwealth to effectively cooperate in policing this.

While it is unknown what influence Peel's book had on the Islanders themselves, it seems to have formed the basis for a CPA program on the Torres Strait called *Let the sun shine! Derum gair kaurge, goiga buia nagi mura lagia: a plan for the Torres Islands people*, published in 1954. The program was printed in Kala Lagaw Ya, Merriam Mir, as well as in English.[211]

---

211. Peel 1947.

The Popular Front and *New Deal for the Aborigines*

From 1934 onwards, a significant shift in the politics of the international Communist movement, and therefore the CPA, was underway. This was the turn to what became known as the "Popular Front".

For the first half of the 1930s, the Comintern had argued for a "class versus class" policy based on the idea of the "Third Period", which claimed that proletarian revolution was on the immediate agenda and denounced the reformist left as "social fascists". This was a time of extreme sectarianism, which in some cases led to important defeats for the workers' movement – the rise of Hitler in Germany, for example. It limited the growth of Communist parties around the world at times when they could likely have found a mass audience. This was demonstrated in Australia during the period of radicalisation under the Lang government in New South Wales. Nonetheless, this period saw the CPA lead hundreds and then thousands of working-class fighters in battles on the streets and in the workplace.

The turn towards the Popular Front involved a shift away from this perspective, but it was a shift that led even further from revolutionary Marxist politics. In contrast to the Third Period's insistence on a sharp distinction between middle-class and working-class approaches, the emphasis was now on winning over sections of the progressive middle class, and even the capitalist class, to a common struggle against fascism. This led Communists around the world to pursue cross-class alliances, downplaying the importance of working-class struggle. Within the workers' movement in Australia, it involved toning down criticisms of the ALP and "left" trade union leaders, which ultimately led to the adoption of a reformist and left nationalist approach.

In taking up the Popular Front, the CPA began attempting to relate more to anthropologists, scientists, religious leaders and middle-class humanitarians. This is not to suggest that socialists should always oppose working with such people, but by relating to them at the expense of a clear working-class orientation, the CPA opened itself up to the political and ideological influence of the liberal middle classes. It began to adapt itself to the assimilationist currents growing among these layers of society. This was particularly notable in Tom Wright's 1939 pamphlet *New Deal for the Aborigines*.

This pamphlet marked a shift in how the CPA understood Indigenous oppression. It now conceived of a much stricter separation between Indigenous people still living on the fringes of Australian society, and "half-castes" who had become more integrated. As a result, it essentially adopted two different strategies for these separate categories of Indigenous people:

> It would be an important step towards a better understanding of the aborigines question if it were clearly recognised that there are two separate problems.
>
> The most urgent problem is that of the Aborigines proper, the full-blooded natives, thousands of whom still live under tribal or semi-tribal conditions, and who could be saved from extinction if appropriate measures were adopted immediately by the Australian people. It is this problem, the real aborigines problem, that is the subject of this pamphlet.
>
> A second problem, often wrongly referred to as the aborigines problem, is that of the half-castes and others of mixed blood. Most half-castes and their descendants are denied social equality with other Australian citizens, and are subjected to social indignities that are a disgrace to our community. This second question has only passing reference in this pamphlet. It is a separate problem, not the aborigine problem, and requires a different and separate treatment.[212]

Wright doubled down on this distinction in a 1947 report to the Central Committee of the CPA:

> One of the demands of the party is that the terms "Aborigine," "Aboriginal" and "native," used in the various acts and ordinances, should not apply to persons of mixed blood. However, we find people of mixed blood, particularly in NSW and Victoria, who think it is necessary and correct to represent themselves as Aborigines in conducting a campaign for full civic rights. These persons of mixed blood confuse the right of the Aborigines with their own problems, which is not the Aborigine fight.[213]

---
212. Wright 1944 [1939].
213. Wright 1947.

Wright's distinction was an attempt to respond to the divergent experiences of Indigenous people in Australian capitalism at the time, but this rigid division of the Indigenous population created new problems. It will be obvious to contemporary readers that it is mistaken to deny the Aboriginality of those with mixed ancestry or those who live in urban settings. This is not simply because doing so means uncritically accepting a reified, capitalist understanding of race and racial identity. Politically speaking, it also results in a schematic understanding of Indigenous oppression and excludes the possibility of urban and regional communities being inspired by each other's struggles and grievances.

It also dovetailed with assimilationist ideas promoted at the time by certain sections of the middle class which sympathised with Indigenous suffering. While assimilation wouldn't become official government policy until 1951, from the late '30s there was a growing assimilationist wing within academic and government circles, represented in particular by the Australian National Research Council, which funded most anthropological research into Indigenous communities.

As discussed in chapter two, a 1937 conference of Commonwealth and state government authorities made a recommendation that so-called "half-caste" Indigenous people should assimilate into Australian society by abandoning any connection to their Indigenous heritage. The rest of the Indigenous community were divided into the categories of "detribalised", "semi-civilised" and "uncivilised". It was recommended that so-called "detribalised" Indigenous people also be assimilated, while the "semi-civilised" and "uncivilised" would be segregated from the rest of Australian society, with strict limits on contact with both whites and assimilated Indigenous people.[214] These recommendations were endorsed by figures such as anthropology professor AP Elkin, who had spoken on platforms alongside Communists during the campaigns of the mid- to late 1930s.[215]

Wright pointed the Communist strategy for Indigenous people in the Northern Territory and Western Australia in a much more conservative direction which had been deeply influenced by such liberal academics.

---

214. Commonwealth of Australia 1937.
215. *Workers' Weekly*, 10 August 1934, p.1.

He was particularly influenced by the outlook of dissident anthropologist Donald Thomson.[216] Thomson, who had become friends with Wright in the '30s, was more on the fringes of the academic establishment than Elkin, but their proposals for government policy on the Indigenous question were both marked by paternalism. Thomson's main difference with mainstream assimilationist thought was that he placed a much greater emphasis on the need to rigorously segregate the still "tribalised" Indigenous communities. In his view, echoed by Wright, this was in order to prevent the total destruction of the last remains of true pre-invasion Indigenous culture and society.[217]

The acceptance of such middle-class attitudes towards Indigenous people was not the only problem with Wright's writings. The 1931 draft program, despite its own issues, had been a *radical* document which emphasised the revolutionary nature of anti-racist solidarity, the role of the working class and the need for a socialist revolution in order to destroy the roots of Indigenous oppression found in the capitalist imperialist system.

New Deal for the Aborigines and its various reprints made not a *single* reference to class struggle, socialism, capitalism or imperialism. It also made not a single reference to the role that unions or the working class can play in the struggle for Indigenous rights. As Hannah Middleton has argued:

> CPA policy was weakened by the introduction of bourgeois, reformist ideas. The anti-imperialist essence of the struggle for Aboriginal rights, the recognition of Aborigines as members of the working class and the key importance of land rights were replaced by New Deal for the Aborigines... The pamphlet offered not radical changes but measures to alleviate the conditions of the Aborigines. It viewed their position as static rather than a process of change and development and did not consider the active role that the Aborigines themselves were playing and would have to play in their own struggle.[218]

---

216. Macintyre 1998, p.266.
217. For the views of Thomson, Pink and Elkin see Gray 2007, pp.115–71.
218. Middleton 2008, p.50.

For the so-called "half-caste" Indigenous population, Wright proposed a civil rights campaign with no class content whatsoever. Wright's main criticism was that the Australian government had failed to follow through on its promise of assimilating Indigenous people into white society:

> The Conference of Commonwealth and State Aboriginal Authorities held in April 1937, resolved that, in regard to people of mixed aboriginal and white blood, they must aim at their "ultimate absorption by the people of the commonwealth". No explanation is given for delay in acting on the resolution, and conceding full social equality.[219]

At the same time, Wright also downplayed the working-class character of Indigenous people in the Northern Territory and Western Australia. In a 1947 report to the CPA Central Committee, Wright positively notes the Aboriginal strikes in the Pilbara and Darwin but goes on to argue that they have no particular working-class content, stating:

> If we spoke of the natives as a "reserve of the proletariat" we would also be making a wrong approach. It is true that in the north and north-west of Australia they constitute a majority of the population, and that their welfare is of great importance to the working class in those areas, but if we speak about our movement as a whole we cannot say that the Aborigines represent a reserve of the proletariat. We take up the fight of the Aborigines because they are oppressed, as oppressed as any people in the world, and our task is to fight for all the oppressed.[220]

Wright had reframed the struggle for Indigenous rights as an essentially liberal one – as simply a part of the general advance of the broad front of democratic progressive forces against fascism and the power of monopolies. While this could serve as a day-to-day guide for CPA members campaigning for equal rights for some Indigenous people, it could not lead to the development of a revolutionary Marxist perspective on Indigenous struggle.

---

219. Wright 1944 [1939].
220. Wright 1947.

New Deal for the Aborigines quickly replaced the half-forgotten 1931 draft program as the authoritative text on the Aboriginal question for Communist Party members. Many of the positions in Wright's pamphlet would be challenged by important developments in Indigenous struggle which came about in the post-war era, leading to further changes in CPA policy.

Chapter six

Post-war struggles: from civil rights to land rights

> In America they call color prejudice Jim Crow. In Germany Hitler called it the "superiority of the Aryan race." In Australia we pretend it doesn't exist. But it does exist, and at times takes as filthy and poisonous forms as it ever did under Hitler or in the lynch law Southern US States.
>
> — *Tribune*, 1950.[221]

> Marx once pointed out that in creating the working class, the capitalists were at the same time creating their own grave diggers. The Australian Aborigine is no exception. As long as the white man limited himself to poisoning and shooting them, they had little means of reprisal. But, having decided to exploit them as slave labor, the pastoral monopolies have unwillingly helped them organise and learn the ways of the world Labor Movement. Therein lies the key to the final emancipation of the Aborigines.
>
> — *Tribune*, 1957.[222]

As the Second World War came to a close, there was an explosive upsurge of class conflict in Australia. The number of strikes reached historical highs, shop committees which brought together workers from different unions spread throughout large industrial workplaces, and among a broad section of workers there was a general desire for revenge against the ruling class after the bitter years of depression and war. This upturn in working-class struggle also imbued those fighting for Indigenous rights with greater levels of confidence.

---

221. *Tribune*, 14 January 1950, p.5.
222. *Tribune*, 27 February 1957, p.8.

The Pilbara strike: 1946–49[223]

The origins of the Pilbara strike lie in the clash between an intensification of discrimination against Aboriginal workers during the Second World War and a growing anti-racist sentiment in a section of the workers' movement and in left-leaning society.

In Western Australia, the exodus of white workers from the pastoral industry into the army, combined with the importance of continued wool production for the war effort, led to the hardening of the exploitation of Aboriginal workers on the stations. Despite many Aboriginal workers volunteering to help the war effort, authorities were suspicious about their loyalty, and so military personnel carried out surveillance of Aboriginal communities in order to detect subversion. Stricter segregation was also put in place across the state in order to keep Aboriginal people away from soldiers, with the authorities citing concerns about "sexual misconduct".

At the same time, the 1940s were a period of growing sympathy for the plight of Aboriginal people among an important minority of the Western Australian population. Edward Beeby, a Communist and founder of the Anti-Fascist League (AFL), hosted a weekly radio broadcast on human rights issues which regularly discussed the oppression of Aboriginal people. The broadcast was the basis for discussion groups of the AFL, which by 1943 had 2,700 members and 72 branches holding weekly meetings across Western Australia. Anti-racist working-class communities had started to emerge in some areas of the state. In a Port Hedland community of mixed European and Aboriginal descent, residents established a "Euralian Association", which campaigned for the rights of Indigenous people to decent housing, education, employment and equal status with the non-Aboriginal community. Some of the Association's members were employed on the wharves or the railway line, and were members of the AWU. The Association won a considerable degree of support in the town, leading to a significant undoing of segregation in Port Hedland. This changed in November 1942 when the authorities clamped down – the area in which the Euralian community lived was declared a prohibited area and then forcibly segregated, with a pass system established.

---
223. This section draws heavily upon Scrimgeour 2020.

A campaign against this segregation started to take off. One link between the Euralian Association and the Anti-Fascist League was white activist and future Communist Don McLeod, who would go on to play an important role in the Pilbara strike. McLeod attended a "big half-caste meeting" in Port Hedland which discussed how to organise against the pass system. He helped to promote the struggle through the AFL's radio program and articles written for the *Fremantle Districts Sentinel*. Through this work, he came into contact with a vibrant community of Communists and left-wing anti-racist activists in Perth, including the writers Katharine Susannah Prichard and Mary Durack, the anthropologist Fred Rose, and Edward Beeby. They connected McLeod with a broader network of Communist activists who were involved in the struggle for Aboriginal rights across the country. During this time, McLeod read Communist literature on Aboriginal rights.

The plan for a strike of Aboriginal workers started to become more concrete through discussions between McLeod, Aboriginal men who worked with him sinking wells and local Aboriginal Lawmen. Also playing a central role was Clancy McKenna (Warntupungkarna), the son of a white pastoralist and a Nyamal woman, who had recently resigned from his job in protest over discriminatory wages.

While there had been rising anger in the Aboriginal community about their conditions before McLeod got in contact with them, there was also underconfidence about how to fight. The key ideas McLeod promoted were that Aboriginal labour was essential to the pastoral industry, that because of this strike action was key, that if they fought, working-class allies across the state could be mobilised to support them, and that it was unlikely the police and pastoralists would just murder them all – a widespread and understandable fear among Aboriginal station workers at the time. As Scrimgeour, who generally takes a rather critical view of McLeod's influence at this time, argues:

> [A]lthough he played down his role in instigating the strike, McLeod clearly took an active role in sowing the seeds of the strike idea. Among a disempowered Aboriginal population seeking a way "to help ourself", his ideas found fertile soil.[224]

---
224. Scrimgeour 2020, p.78.

The idea of a strike was discussed in large meetings of Aboriginal workers at Nullagine, Moolyella and Marble Bar. McKenna and the Lawman Dooley Bin Bin travelled across the state visiting far-flung stations to promote and organise the strike. At the same time, McLeod started to popularise the idea in Communist Party circles, writing to leading party members about the development of plans for the strike and seeking advice about the way forward. By 1945, the idea of a strike had spread widely, and while McLeod might have been its inspiration, it quickly became driven by the Marrngu people themselves. As McKenna put it: "McLeod gave us a hint about the strike, and we took it up".[225]

After years of preparation, the strike began on 1 May 1946. Hundreds of Aboriginal workers took part, and strike camps were organised across the Pilbara. Strike action was also taken by hotel workers, domestic servants and miners in Marble Bar on 1 May. One large coastal station on the De Grey River had already gone on strike before 1 May in order to take action just as the mustering began, revealing that workers were thinking about how best to use their power. The strike immediately came up against all the racist institutions of Western Australian capitalism, which had previously been sceptical about the organising capacities of Aboriginal workers. Many employers simply sacked the Aboriginal workers who went on strike and expelled them from their properties. The police went from station to station threatening the workers with exile if they joined the strike. Then McKenna and Dooley were imprisoned and McLeod was arrested.

The leaders of the Pilbara strike knew that for their campaign to be successful, they needed what McLeod called "power behind us", i.e. solidarity action from workers in industrial cities. Following the arrests of McKenna, Dooley and McLeod, a vigorous campaign broke out in the south of the state. Trade unions, civil liberties groups and women's groups campaigned against the imprisonment of the strike leaders and in support of the strike movement. Open meetings were held, and protests organised in Perth. Encouraged by the growing show of support from the south, the strike movement spread. In Port Hedland, strikers marched on the jail in which McLeod was imprisoned and he was freed. As it became clear the strike was going to continue, support

---

225. Scrimgeour 2020, p.94.

flowed in from around the country. Nineteen unions in Western Australia, seven national unions and four Trades and Labour Councils supported the strike and sent money.

The decisive moment came in August 1949, when the Seamen's Union banned the shipment of wool from the Pilbara. Three days after this, the government caved in. Substantial gains were made in wages and conditions.

While the strikers garnered significant union support, this was not universal. The leadership of the Australian Workers' Union (AWU) worked with the Department of Native Affairs to oppose the strike. This approach had its roots in a combination of the AWU leadership's poor record on the Aboriginal issue and its vicious anti-communist stance. While the AWU didn't deny Aboriginal membership, it left the final decision to local union representatives. So the AWU in Port Hedland welcomed members of the Euralian community into the union, while in Broome they were barred from well-paid employment. When Pilbara strikers tried to find temporary employment on the wharves during the long strike, the AWU refused to give them union tickets.[226] The state secretary of the AWU, Charlie Golding, is reported to have believed that the Pilbara strike "had been inspired by the Communist, Donald McLeod",

> and because he did not favour the tactics of this individual he proposed to telegram the Union representative at Port Hedland stating that Union tickets were not to be issued to persons deemed to be natives according to the Native Administration Act.[227]

The AWU also campaigned against the employment of strikers on the Port Hedland railway and joined an anti-communist crusade against the white stationmaster who allowed them to be employed. These attitudes didn't go totally unchallenged within the AWU; at a members' meeting on 19 February, the decision to refuse membership to the Pilbara strikers was overturned and the meeting declared that members would refuse to work on the wharves if Aboriginal men were not given equal opportunity for jobs. The attitudes of

---

226. Scrimgeour 2020, pp.255–70.
227. Scrimgeour 2020, p.258.

the AWU leadership also stand in contrast to railway workers who helped Aboriginal strikers board trains after police had attempted to ban them.[228]

The CPA played a very positive role in building support for the strike in WA, where they were a very minor political and industrial force, and even more so around the country. However, the impact of the turn to the Popular Front on the CPA's intervention was also evident.

The Labor Party governed Western Australia in the years 1933–47. After the adoption of the Popular Front, the CPA came to believe that it was in an alliance with the ALP from the late '30s until Labor lost power. This impacted how they understood the relationship between the ALP and Indigenous rights. For instance, in 1935 the CPA's Western Australian newspaper *The Red Star* had ruthlessly criticised the failures of the Labor WA state government on Indigenous issues.[229] Yet by 1939 *Workers' Weekly* welcomed the inclusion of Bob Coverly and Emil Nulsen into the state Labor cabinet, as they were apparently strong supporters of Aboriginal rights.[230] In fact, Coverly was a consistent mouthpiece for the white station owners who exploited Aboriginal people in the Pilbara. At the 1934 Moseley Commission, Coverly had voiced his opposition to any government regulations limiting the exploitation of Indigenous workers, criticising what he called the "stupid system of protecting the aborigines to the detriment of the settlers as a whole".[231] He would be one of the most hostile politicians opposing the Pilbara strike. Contrary to the CPA's claims, Coverly had only criticised the Commissioner of Native Affairs in so far as he believed the commissioner was organisationally and financially ineffective – and not doing enough to protect the rights of the station owners against Aboriginal people.

Don McLeod played a key role in preparing Aboriginal workers for the 1946 strike. However, in 1945, despite Aboriginal workers seeming ready and willing to go on strike, McLeod convinced them to delay by a year in order not to undermine the supposedly "progressive" war effort. The war was in reality an inter-imperialist conflict which was being used to justify restraints

---

228. Scrimgeour 2020, pp.261–6.
229. *The Red Star,* 8 March 1935, p.2.
230. *Workers' Weekly*, 11 April 1939, p.3.
231. Scrimgeour 2020, p.20.

on wage increases and strikes across the country.[232] In the initial aftermath of the war, McLeod found new reasons to oppose an immediate strike. He argued that the Aboriginal workers would be defeated without access to resources, and instead must focus on winning control over some areas of land from the government. Mines and farms could be built on these lands, which would give the strikers the economic independence necessary to mobilise support for the strike across the Pilbara. This attitude was informed by the extremely optimistic perspective of post-war Australia promoted by the CPA, heavily shaped by its Popular Front politics. They saw huge opportunities for social and economic advancement under a post-war federal Labor government and emphasised that this would be possible through an alliance of middle-class, working-class and even "progressive" capitalist forces. As historian Ken Mansell has argued, the CPA "entered the post-war period with a positive attitude towards reconstruction and its own version of the peoples' anti-monopoly democratic revolution based on a gradualist perspective".[233]

Influenced by this framework, McLeod believed that in the Pilbara the large station owners were detested by the majority of the population. He envisaged uniting small business owners, small farmers, rural workers and urban business interests around a program for economic development in the Pilbara. Such a program would benefit all, except the large station owners, and would include provisions for greater autonomy for the local Indigenous population.[234] McLeod thus focused his efforts on winning over the North-West and Kimberley Advancement Association.[235] Unsurprisingly, this organisation – which was the representative of small and large business interests in the region – was not receptive to McLeod's ideas. Harry Greene, owner of Talga Talga Station and a strong opponent of McLeod, was elected chairman at the first convention of the Association, and the meeting then endorsed the interests of the pastoralists. McLeod then tried to set up a more sympathetic branch of the Association in Marble Bar. However, at the first meeting of this branch a motion was moved to effectively

---

232. Scrimgeour 2020, p.86.
233. Mansell 1980, p.23.
234. Scrimgeour 2020, pp.86–9.
235. The following account is based on Scrimgeour 2020, pp.87–9.

censor McLeod. The motion passed overwhelmingly. In the aftermath of the meeting, Department of Native Affairs Inspector Lawerence O'Neill wrote that McLeod had "no standing in the community but...a small following among poor class whites".[236] The North-West and Kimberley Advancement Association would go on to vigorously oppose the 1946 strike and to advocate for the segregation of Indigenous children in schools. The WA branch of the CPA endorsed McLeod's orientation towards the North-West and Kimberley Advancement Association, publishing his program in the *Workers' Star* newspaper.[237]

McLeod's program, inspired by the Popular Front, crashed up against the realities of capitalism in the Pilbara region. While small business owners and farmers might not particularly like the large station owners, they were ultimately subservient to them. Nor did they have any particular interest in campaigning against the racist controls on Indigenous people. Having been rejected by polite society, McLeod soon refocused his efforts once again on planning for the strike. This was helped by the revival of class struggle at the end of the Second World War and the rift this produced between the CPA and the ALP federal government.

The Darwin Aboriginal workers' strikes: 1947–51[238]

In February 1947, a strike broke out among Aboriginal workers in Berrimah Native Compound, outside Darwin, as a result of poor pay and living conditions. Then, in December 1950–January 1951, Aboriginal workers employed as cooks, gardeners, painters and general labourers on the Bagot reserve went on strike.

These strikes were organised by the workers themselves, who held mass meetings to decide their course of action. Serious repression was unleashed on the strikers. One strike leader, Fred Waters, was banished to Haasts Bluff, a desert area about 1,000 miles from Darwin, for "organising the natives to strike". Another leader who "neglected to obey a lawful instruction" was imprisoned for four months.

---

236. Scrimgeour 2020, p.89.
237. *Workers' Star*, 1 June 1945, p.5; 8 February 1946, p.6; 5 April 1946, p.4.
238. The following account comes from Middleton 1977, pp.99–101 and Day 2019.

Two important factors shaped these strikes. The first was the contradictory impact of the Second World War on the situation of Indigenous and non-indigenous workers in the Northern Territory, and the resulting effects on their consciousness. The war broke down the isolation of northern and central Australia, as railways and airports were built in order to facilitate travel and communications to the military base in Darwin. At least 1,000 Aboriginal workers were recruited to work in food production, in the Civil Construction Corps and as labour aids to the military. Middleton writes that "these measures made a considerable contribution to the breakdown of the Aboriginal traditional hunting and gathering economy" which were "destroyed and replaced by new, wider affiliations".[239]

The experiences of these Aboriginal workers stirred a greater desire for equality, while also frustrating those desires. The workers were paid in cash wages and, despite not being paid the same as white soldiers, they were paid many times more than the nominal amount that station owners "paid" Aboriginal workers in rations. Some Aboriginal workers received training in semi-skilled industrial trades, drove trucks, and were housed in the military barracks. At the same time, however, the war destroyed much of what remained of traditional Aboriginal communities in the areas surrounding Darwin, resulting in the further integration of Aboriginal workers into the exploitative capitalist economy, in greater numbers than ever before.

They interacted with white soldiers and workers in a far less segregated environment than they could experience during peacetime. Middleton describes the effects of this on both Indigenous and non-indigenous workers and soldiers:

> They were the first white Australians in contact with the Aborigines who were not involved or interested in exploiting them. The experience of living and working with such people, the contrast between army conditions and the ways in which they were exploited and treated by the pastoralists, and the observation of the Black soldiers all had important ideological consequences for the Aborigines. Their world view was expanded, particularly their consciousness of support and sympathy among a section of the white population and their

---
239. Middleton 1977, pp.78–9.

shared experiences and aims with other groups of Aborigines. The basis was laid for the unity which was developed and for organisations and campaigns which were begun after the war.[240]

One expression of the growing consciousness of at least some white workers regarding the plight of Aboriginal people was the novel *No Sunlight Singing* by Joe Walker. The novel details the exploitation of Aboriginal workers in Darwin during the 1930s and '40s. Although the book was only published in 1960, it was based upon what Walker learned from Aboriginal people he worked with in the Civil Construction Corps during the war and then, after the war, in his role as a left-wing union organiser and editor of the union newspaper *The Northern Standard*, which openly supported the Aboriginal strikes in Darwin.[241]

Middleton makes the important point that a "reciprocal process" took place during the war, in which consciousness of the exploitation and oppression of Aboriginal workers "was raised in both the Aborigines themselves and in the white population".[242] She also argues that "Communist Party of Australia members particularly used these experiences as the basis for the development of their theoretical policy and practical support for Aboriginal people".

The role played by the Communist Party was the other important factor in the Darwin strikes. The North Australian Workers' Union (NAWU) organised financial and legal support for the striking workers and their families. This was only possible because, in 1946, the NAWU had been taken over by a group of Communist activists led by George Gibbs, defeating the right-wing, AWU-aligned leadership of the union. The Communist-led NAWU went to the High Court of Australia in an attempt to challenge the Aboriginals Ordinance, which was used to deny Aboriginal workers the right to strike or to join a union in the Northern Territory. This was a constant source of complaint by the NAWU; at a 1947 conference, a request that Aboriginal workers be allowed to join the NAWU was denied by the Labor government.[243]

---

240. Middleton 1977, p.80.
241. Thanks to the excellent website run by Joe Walker's son Alan Walker, which is dedicated to keeping alive *No Sunlight Singing*. https://www.nosunlightsinging.com
242. Middleton 1977, p.81.
243. See Townsend 2009, p.27.

There is also some evidence that Communists in the NAWU helped the Aboriginal strikers in more direct ways. In his memoirs, Murray Norris, a Communist Party activist in the NAWU, recalls:

> Early in '46 the first of the Aboriginal strikes took place. I can't remember the date now, but it was after the first strike that took place on the wharf. I had come up from the Centre to report, which I generally did about every four months, and was sitting in the union office when I heard a stone drop on the roof. I had a look around and couldn't see any kids about. A little later I heard another one on the roof so I figured that I had better take a better look. As I walked all around the buildings and at the back I heard the familiar sound "Eh", the sound that an Aborigine makes when he wants to get your attention. I walked over to some long grass and hidden there were seven Aborigines. They told me that they wanted to talk to the union about striking. They wanted assistance and advice what to do. As I am tone deaf I have great difficulty in translating broken English and they had to keep repeating what they were saying. I told them to hold on and went back to the union office. Frank Whiteoak, the Darwin Organiser, was there so I told him about it and took him back down. Some of them knew him and he was the bloke they had really come to see. They were too polite to tell me that they didn't know me. Frank took over and formed a strike committee with himself as adviser in the background. I still have a photo of this first strike committee with Frank.[244]

This support shown by the NAWU was then reciprocated by the Aboriginal workers themselves. During a six-week-long hospital strike in 1948, wealthy women attempted to act as scabs. In response Aboriginal domestic workers who were employed by these women went on strike, refusing to do the laundry or clean the house. As Norris puts it in his memoirs, "as soon as the 'silver tails' found that there was nobody at home to do all the dirty work, they quickly turned tail and went home".[245]

---

244. Norris 1982.
245. Norris 1982.

Indigenous rights, Communists and trade unions in the 1950s

The Pilbara and Darwin strikes took place when Communist influence within the trade unions was at historical heights, having emerged from the industrial upsurge of the immediate post-war years. The 1950s and early '60s were a much more difficult period for Indigenous and left-wing trade union activism. The onset of the Cold War, the 1949 defeat of the coal miners' strike at the hands of the Chifley Labor government and the subsequent election of Liberal Party Prime Minister Robert Menzies had thrown the workers' movement onto the defensive. Militants found themselves isolated and the Communist Party felt besieged by conservative forces both inside and outside the workers' movement. CPA members, trade unionists and Indigenous activists organised a number of small-scale campaigns against racist discrimination during the '50s, but the initial sense of hope which had been prevalent in the immediate post-war years evaporated and was replaced with the realisation that it was going to take a long battle to rebuild the earlier momentum for Indigenous rights.

As the conservative Cold War atmosphere set in, society shifted to the right. Indigenous rights campaigners and left-wing activists more generally were put on the back foot. Any activism around Aboriginal issues was denounced as a Communist plot and the red-baiting of activists was out of control. As a result, campaigns around Indigenous issues in the '50s and early '60s were politically quite conservative, as activists sought to maintain a respectable image. Petitions were the usual form of activity and a key focus for supporters of Indigenous rights was appealing for the United Nations to put pressure on the Australian government. When protests did occur, they usually took the form of a silent vigil, in contrast to the more militant style of direct action which would emerge in the late 1960s. This moderate approach, reflecting the conservatism of the period, was also reinforced by post-war developments within the CPA. In 1955 the Labor Party expelled the right-wing, Catholic anti-communist forces known as the "Groupers". Following this, the Communists further softened their stance on the ALP, believing that by embedding themselves within its left wing they would be protected from the isolation of the Cold War years. This perspective was also spurred on by the

Soviet Union, which was increasingly moderating its own political rhetoric, embracing the line of "peaceful coexistence" with the Western powers.[246]

Despite these problems, left-wing trade unionists, Indigenous activists and Communists continued campaigning across the country to expose racist injustices and uproot segregation. During the 1950s, CPA members either initiated or participated in campaigns against racist segregation in every major city, as well as dozens of country towns and remote communities. Victories were few and each was hard won. It was not until the 1960s that the tide began to turn in favour of Indigenous rights.

Continuing to strengthen the links between the left wing of the workers' movement and Indigenous struggles was key to keeping activism alive in this period. And while the going was tough, it was during the Cold War that support for Indigenous rights was cemented as a common sense for left-wing workers to even greater extent than before. An important role was played by four of the main left unions of the time: the Waterside Workers' Federation, the Building Workers' Industrial Union, the Sheet-Metal Workers' Union and the Seamen's Union. During the 1950s, Aboriginal rights became one of the stock standard demands of the left-wing unions, alongside equal pay for women, voting Menzies out, an end to the anti-union penal powers and world peace. It was very rare for a state or federal conference of the left unions to go by without mention of support for Aboriginal workers. Indigenous activists, for their part, also recognised the importance of sustaining a relationship with the trade unions and the socialist left. Ray Peckham remembers that when he first got involved in Aboriginal activism in Sydney, his guide, the veteran activist Pearl Gibbs, told him that "the first thing we got to do…is to take you down and introduce you to the Trades and Labour Council in Sussex Street".

> So she took me down there…and took me right around to all the trade unions…from top to bottom. From the basement right to top. And then up to the Seamen's Union, the Teachers' Federation, the national secretary to the BWIU (Building Workers' Industrial Union).[247]

---

246. See for example the article "Activists for peace" in *Tribune*, 18 July 1962, p.2.
247. Peckham and Willis 2012.

The Communist Party also began to recruit a number of leading Indigenous activists in the '40s and '50s. Kath Walker (later known as Oodgeroo Noonuccal), who would go on to become a famous Aboriginal poet, joined the CPA towards the end of the war while working as a switchboard operator for the Australian Women's Army Service. In 1945, she was a delegate to the Brisbane and South Eastern District Conference of the Communist Party and was involved in a protest against segregation at a dance hall in Scarness, Queensland.[248] Similarly, the Aboriginal activist Charlie Leon joined during the war while working as a painter and docker on Garden Island, and Louise West, who became secretary of the Surry Hills branch of the party, joined in 1942. Leon would later become a pentecostal Christian and Walker ended up rejecting communism once the Cold War became entrenched, but other Indigenous activists would remain members of the party for decades.[249]

Ray Peckham, whose father Tom had been involved in the Dubbo branch of the Unemployed Workers' Movement, joined the party in the 1950s. Peckham had met members of the CPA through Pearl Gibbs and her trade union contacts. In 1951, Peckham was elected as a delegate to the Berlin World Youth Festival along with fellow activist Faith Bandler. Complications arose when Peckham tried to get his passport for the trip. He described what happened when he was waiting to see if the government would approve his passport:

> We're all waiting anxiously for this passport to come down. There was one of the girls, she was a young woman, she was secretary to one of the main unions. And she was doing all the paperwork and that see. And she was back and forth to the office. They kept knocking her back. And then word got that the might of the trade union movement was moving in… And they said, "No, Peckham doesn't go on this ship, and this ship doesn't leave this harbour. And we'll tie up every ship that's important around the shores of Australia." Down comes the passport hey, four hours later.[250]

---
248. *Tribune*, 19 July 1945, p.4; 18 January 1946, p.7.
249. Horner 2012 and Boughton 2001.
250. Peckham and Willis 2012.

The powerful maritime and seamen's unions had used the threat of a strike to get Peckham his passport – yet another reminder of how the industrial power of the working class could be brought to bear around the issue of Indigenous rights. In 1959, the Aboriginal activist Gladys O'Shane and her husband Patrick, a militant wharf labourer, joined the CPA following O'Shane's involvement in the women's auxiliary of the Waterside Workers' Federation. At the 19th National Congress of the CPA in 1961, *Tribune* could report that a small group of Aboriginal members had been elected as delegates, including an Aboriginal woman.[251]

The Federal Council for the Advancement of Aborigines and Torres Strait Islanders

Throughout the late '50s and early '60s, various civil rights organisations sprang up around the country, with Communists and left-wing trade unionists often playing a role in their formation and activities. In 1951, the Council for Aboriginal Rights (CAR) was founded in Melbourne, originally in order to support the Darwin strikers. Henry Wardlaw, a CPA member, was elected honorary secretary of CAR alongside two clergymen, while CPA member Shirley Andrews and CPA supporter and academic Mollie Bayne were members of its inaugural executive. In 1956, the Aboriginal-Australian Fellowship was founded in Sydney by Indigenous activists Pearl Gibbs and Faith Bandler, Aboriginal Communist Ray Peckham and Communist writer Len Fox. Eighteen trade unions and the Communist-led Union of Australian Women quickly became affiliates of the Fellowship.

In 1958, many local civil rights organisations joined together to form the Federal Council for the Advancement of Aborigines (FCAA) on the initiative of Shirley Andrews. FCAA encouraged the formation of Aboriginal Advancement Leagues around the country; the Cairns League (CATISAL) was formed in 1960, while the Northern Territory Council for Aboriginal Rights (NTCAR), the Queensland Council for the Advancement of Aborigines and Torres Strait Islanders (QCAATSI) and the South Coast Aboriginal Advancement League

---

251. Best 2022; *Tribune*, 14 June 1961, p.1. Gladys O'Shane gave a report to the 1964 CPA conference on the work of the party in the Cairns Aboriginal movement; see *Tribune*, 24 June 1964, p.3. See also her obituary in *Tribune*, 19 January 1966, p.8.

were all established in 1961. Throughout the 1960s many country towns also set up local Aboriginal Rights Committees or Advancement Leagues, particularly in Western NSW. In 1964, FCAA changed its name to the Federal Council for the Advancement of Aborigines and Torres Strait Islanders (FCAATSI).[252] While these organisations shared the common goal of advancing civil rights for Aboriginal and Torres Strait Islander peoples, there were also important political and social differences between and within them.

The Newcastle and South Coast Advancement Leagues were set up by CPA activists as essentially campaign committees of the local Trades and Labour Councils. While they involved a number of local Aboriginal people, most of the members of these leagues were white Communist-affiliated trade unionists. CATISAL and NTCAR, based in Cairns and Darwin respectively, had a much greater number of Indigenous activists involved from the very beginning. While the NTCAR had been created on the initiative of white CPA members Brian Manning and Terry Robison, its constitution included a clause requiring that 75 percent of its executive members be of Aboriginal descent. Similarly, Aboriginal and Torres Strait Islanders formed the majority of the members of CATISAL and held all of the main executive positions, while most of the white members of the group were CPA trade unionists.

CAR in Melbourne and the Fellowship in Sydney were composed of a mixture of white Communist activists and a broader layer of Christian, peace movement and left ALP personalities, although they also included some prominent Indigenous members like Pearl Gibbs, Ray Peckham and others. The Aborigines Advancement League of South Australia was led by the Presbyterian social reformer Charles Duguid and dominated by Indigenous and non-indigenous Christian activists. Most of the affiliates to FCAATSI, as well as the Federal Council itself, were dominated by white activists, who controlled most of the important executive positions. As the next chapter will explore, debates over Indigenous control of FCAATSI would come to the fore in the late 1960s, eventually leading to the organisation's demise. During the '50s and early '60s, however, the main political battles were those which pitted FCAATSI's more left-wing supporters against religious and often anti-communist forces led by Christian activists. In Queensland,

---

252. Taffe 2005 and Taffe 2009.

white Christian reformers Joyce Wilding and Muriel Langford organised a hostile split from QCAATSI in 1961, forming the One People of Australia League, which was openly pro-assimilationist and hostile to the socialist left.

Ray Peckham and the struggle to desegregate New South Wales

> The strength of the working people can help us aborigines crack through the curse of the color bar in Australia.
>
> — Ray Peckham, 1961.[253]

The activity of Ray Peckham gives a sense of what campaigning for Indigenous rights during the early '60s could look like. Following Peckham's return to Sydney from a visit to the Eastern Bloc in 1951, he was involved in the Builders Labourers Federation and the Communist Party, joining the Newtown CPA branch and attending the party school in Minto. Peckham would visit Aboriginal communities across the state and began to connect different campaigns together, publicising their efforts in trade union and left-wing circles. The Builders Labourers Federation helped by raising money for Peckham to do this work full-time.

At the start of 1961, the NSW Labor government launched court action to have Horace Saunders, an Aboriginal man, evicted from Purfleet Mission Station in Taree. Purfleet had been taken over by the Aborigines Welfare Board and the Aboriginal families who lived on the reserve were supposed to pay rent, but the Board had let the unpaid rent accumulate for several years without doing anything about it. In 1960, the Board pushed for Aboriginal families to start paying and took legal action against Saunders, who represented four families, when they refused. Left-wing unions rallied to support Saunders and the Newcastle Aboriginal Advancement League brought him to Sydney to speak to hundreds of workers at workplace meetings. The well-known Communist lawyer Fred Paterson acted as Saunders' legal representative and trade union leaders lobbied the Labor government to abandon the case.[254]

---
253. *Tribune*, 28 March 1961, p.12.
254. *Tribune*, 15 February 1961, p.11.

The Saunders campaign was seen as a part of the broader fight against racism in NSW. As *Tribune* noted: "[T]rade union and public support in the Purfleet eviction case has lifted it from a housing struggle to a struggle for equal rights for the whole Aboriginal people".[255]

Peckham played a key role in building support for the campaign and in raising these broader issues. He toured the South Coast speaking at workplace meetings and winning union backing for Saunders. At the time, 130 coal miners at Nebo Colliery were on strike and after a meeting with Peckham, they decided to donate a levy in support of Saunders. At another meeting of miners in Coalcliff, Peckham reported:

> [T]he miners were actually meeting to hear a report on the strike at Nebo pit, but they deliberately delayed the vote on whether they would strike in sympathy in order to hear me. They wanted to be sure I had an undivided hearing.

Peckham went on to hold similar meetings at B & W Steel in Fairymeadow, at a caravan park at Windang (where a residents' committee was set up in order to support Saunders), at the Tallawarra Power House and for wharfies at Port Kembla.[256] Reflecting on this South Coast tour, Peckham told *Tribune*:

> At every meeting, I was given a very enthusiastic reception. The white workers' moral and financial support for the struggles of Aboriginal people are becoming a source of strength and courage which my people are coming to appreciate more and more.[257]

The local Taree press whipped up a hysterical campaign against the Communist support behind Saunders, even attempting to organise an anti-communist meeting on the reserve. The meeting was a flop, however, when it was boycotted by the entire Aboriginal community, who were also annoyed that the meeting replaced a weekly film night in the same hall.[258]

---

255. *Tribune*, 15 March 1961, p.3.
256. *Tribune*, 22 March 1961, p.5.
257. *Tribune*, 22 March 1961, p.5.
258. *Tribune*, 28 March 1961, p.12.

In May 1961, the courts ruled in favour of Saunders, humiliating the Aborigines Welfare Board and greatly undermining its authority. Peckham said that it "was probably the first time in NSW that the Aboriginal people had taken on the Aboriginal Protection Board and won".[259]

A lengthy article Peckham wrote for *Tribune* in 1961 surveyed other recent examples of fights against racism and segregation, noting how Aboriginal people, backed up by thousands of workers across the state, had ensured that Aboriginal housing was built in Coonamble and Nambucca Heads despite racist opposition.[260]

Peckham campaigned against discrimination and racism across rural NSW. He spent a weekend in Moree with the Aboriginal community at Top Camp, who were protesting against their exclusion from the local hospital despite significant health problems resulting from poverty and poor housing. Pressure exerted by the community and their supporters led the NSW health minister to declare the end of formal segregation in state hospitals.[261]

Peckham then visited Armidale, where 14 new homes had been built for the Aboriginal community by the Aborigines Welfare Board – but on the outskirts of town, next to the rubbish dump. While some Aboriginal people welcomed any new housing, Peckham found that "many had voiced their disgust and further disappointment in the deceitful and domineering manner in which the board has acted".[262]

The houses had also been built with the support of the local branch of the Assimilation of Aborigines Association, who while trying to "do something constructive" had only "isolated themselves, and…won mistrust and ridicule from the Aborigine population". This situation led Peckham to reflect more widely on the relationship between the struggles of Aboriginal people and middle-class liberal organisations, as compared to the workers' movement:

> It seems that many influential and progressive organisations will never learn the fundamentals and ways of the Aboriginal peoples. Many have tagged

---

259. Donaldson 2020, p.363.
260. *Tribune*, 10 May 1961, p.8.
261. *Tribune*, 31 May 1961, p.7.
262. *Tribune*, 12 July 1961, p.8.

themselves as being authorities on Aboriginal problems and Aboriginal study and policy.

These people can never know the misery – the struggle and humiliation, but can only guess, for it lies within the Aborigine himself. When he gets the true spirit of organisation, he will be able to cope with the problem of his people. And a very bitter fight and struggle it will be.

It won't be intellectuals or high ranking politicians who will solve his problem for him but it will be solved through class struggle alone, for isn't the Aborigine a section of the working class, though the most backward and disorganised section?

Now, he is very quickly being drawn into the tide of unemployment and mass movement, and is being recognised by trade unions as an equal and a fellow worker. Here alone lies the future of the Aborigines in that mounting tide of progressive struggle, the working class movement.[263]

It was this perspective that guided Peckham's work. He sought to build up local, statewide and national organisations involving Aboriginal people themselves in fighting for their rights. At the same time, he saw the need to form links between these campaigns, the wider workers' movement and the socialist left, in order to ensure they could bring as much pressure as possible to bear on racist governments and bosses.

Peckham saw how racism was deeply intertwined with the economic inequality that Aboriginal people in NSW faced, noting with regard to housing:

[T]he State Government uses the discriminatory provisions of the Aborigines Protection Act to keep the people under those conditions, and then uses these very conditions as an argument why they "should not be given something better."

"Why do the aborigines live in such pitiful shacks instead of building better dwellings?" Simply because the land on which they must live is allocated by

---
263. *Tribune*, 12 July 1961, p.8.

the Government and, as outlined above, in most cases is land that could not be used for any other purpose and is entirely unsuitable for the erection of decent buildings.[264]

In November 1961, Peckham investigated the conditions of Aboriginal people on the NSW South Coast as part of a team which included trade unionists and local activists. He visited Murray's Flat, Wallaga Lake, Eurabodalla, Wreck Bay, Roseby Park, Warriee and Brown's Flat. The team produced a report which slammed the conditions of Aboriginal people, comparing them to those in the "Deep South of the United States". This laid the basis for the formation of the South Coast branch of the Aborigines Advancement League, which would go on to desegregate many areas in the region.[265]

In 1963, the NSW government banned discrimination against Aboriginal people in pubs and hotels, the result of a long campaign in which Peckham again played a key role. When the police commented that they were pleased with the "behaviour of Aborigines" who mixed freely in northern NSW bars on the weekend after discrimination was banned, Peckham told the press, tongue in cheek, that "Aborigines were generally pleased about the behaviour of publicans in carrying out the New South Wales law".[266]

Peckham also saw the struggles of Aboriginal people as linked to other struggles against oppression. He spoke at a 1963 protest against US and Australian intervention in Vietnam, and at an international solidarity rally protesting against attacks on democratic rights in Spain and Greece, the apartheid regime in South Africa and segregation in the United States. He would continue to be involved in activism in the mid- to late '60s, speaking at a meeting of Aboriginal people in Walgett following the arrival of the Freedom Ride in 1965. A 1968 Sydney rally to support the Gurindji land rights struggle involved Peckham and Communist novelist Frank Hardy giving their speeches into a megaphone on the run while the protesters were followed by the police.[267]

---

264. *Tribune*, 30 August 1961, p.5.
265. *Tribune*, 10 January 1962, p.7.
266. *Tribune*, 3 April 1963, p.3.
267. *Tribune*, 5 June 1963, p.10; 18 September 1963, p.1; 1 September 1965, p.1; 26 June 1968, p.3.

The South Coast Aboriginal Advacement League

The efforts of the South Coast Aboriginal Advancement League provide another example of the positive changes these campaigning bodies could achieve.[268] The formation of the League was inspired by a conversation between white Communist Joe Howe and Aboriginal activist Joe McGinness, who met while working on the Cairns waterfront. Upon returning to Wollongong, Howe got in touch with local Communist trade unionists. The Illawarra region had a strong left-wing trade union tradition, spearheaded by Communists in the 1930s and then consolidated during and after the Second World War in the coal mines, docks and briefly at the steelworks. The South Coast Labour Council (SCLC) was notable for its radical positions and its interventions into local unions backing up left-wing challenges to right-wing union bureaucrats.

Prior to establishing the League, the SCLC organised a survey into the conditions of Indigenous seasonal pickers working for white farmers on the South Coast, as mentioned in the previous section. Despite resistance by reserve managers, the survey team travelled south and documented not only widespread exploitation and poor housing conditions, but also the political aspirations of Aboriginal people. When Howe introduced the survey to a meeting of the SCLC, he noted that Aboriginal people had been "deliberately kept in a humiliating condition" by both Liberal and Labor governments:

> Through bitter experience they see governments and employers as their enemies. They are unionists, some of them, they are part of the Australian Labour movement. We in our Unions, do not practice discrimination. Our Aboriginal people are fighting for freedom in common with the African people, American negroes and others. Greet our Aborigines as friends. Your co-operation will end discrimination.[269]

The report noted the desire of Illawarra Aboriginal communities for land rights, plus an end to the abuses of the Welfare Board and the desecration of

---

268. The following section draws heavily from Donaldson, Bursill and Jacobs 2017.
269. Donaldson et al. 2017, p.59.

sacred sites. Once the League was formed, it set about campaigning against discrimination across the Illawarra. The focus of the League was the everyday racism and segregation that Aboriginal people faced. The League worked with the Waterside Workers' Federation to win the right of Aboriginal people to drink at Port Kembla and Wollongong pubs. Throughout the rest of the South Coast discrimination was even more entrenched, particularly in the rural towns; Aboriginal people were not only excluded from pubs but also faced segregation in schools, pools, shops and cinemas.

In March 1962, a branch of the League was set up in Nowra. Fred Moore, a longstanding trade union activist from Wollongong, spoke at its inaugural meeting and was particularly impressed by the involvement of young women. As the new branch's first action, an Aboriginal woman by the name of Norma Sherman entered a café that refused to serve Aboriginal people, along with some of her friends and Moore. Moore explains what happened next:

> Well, we sat there and sat there and they wouldn't serve us. So I got up and said "What's your problem mate?" The man said he did not want the custom of the women because if he served them he'd get no more business from other people. He said he would serve us if we moved to the back of the café, out of sight. We refused. Racism was pretty rampant in Nowra then. Well, we left and put out the word that if anyone refused to serve an Aboriginal person again we would ban all deliveries of food to their business.[270]

A week later the women returned and were served, and by 1964 segregation had been defeated in Nowra. This was a year before the far more famous Freedom Ride organised by Charles Perkins and the student activists at Sydney University. The activism of the League also laid the basis for future struggles in the Illawarra, such as the campaign during the 1967 Referendum and the fight for land rights at Wreck Bay. A layer of Indigenous working-class activists was formed out of these struggles and would go on to play important roles across the rest of the country.

---

270. Donaldson et al. 2017, pp.62–3.

The tide begins to turn: the mid-'60s

From the mid-'60s onwards there was a rising level of concern over the rights and conditions of Indigenous people in Australian society. Several factors underpinned the shift, including the influence of the civil rights movement in America and growing international attention on racism and decolonisation. Anti-racist ideas gained a wider hearing as the high point of Cold War hysteria started to ebb and a slow shift back to the left began. Jennifer Clark explains the effect this had on activism around Aboriginal issues:

> The issue of racial empowerment was not lost on either Aboriginal leaders or their white supporters. Encouraged by events overseas and buoyed by national organisation, they slowly embarked on a political awakening, demanded freedom from the trappings of colonialism and responded to the effects of oppression at worst and neglect at best. They forced wider Australia to recognise that a "wind of change" was blowing their way… By the late 1950s and early 1960s…a new intensity and a new direction were present in Aboriginal politics that turned sporadic activism, local dissent and personal resistance into a discernible movement.[271]

This flowed through into the established Indigenous rights organisations, in particular FCAATSI. In 1964, *Tribune* noted that "the movement for Aboriginal rights [has] began to assume a new quality".

> It is becoming an organised, growing mass movement, in which capable Aboriginal representatives are beginning to take leading parts, with the working class, through a number of trade unions, playing an increasingly important role, together with other organisations of the people.[272]

It was at this point that support for Aboriginal rights also gained a foothold outside of the Communist-aligned unions, with the 1963 ACTU congress adopting a substantial program on Indigenous issues.

---

271. Clark 2008, pp.4–5.
272. *Tribune*, 12 February 1964, p.5.

The emergence of a more stable and ongoing Indigenous rights movement in the form of FCAATSI raised the need for the CPA to modify its approach to issues of Indigenous identity and culture. In 1964, the party adopted a new program, *Australia's way forward*, which included an expanded and rewritten section on the fight for Aboriginal rights. This section was an advancement on the ideas bequeathed to the party by Tom Wright's writings of the late '30s and '40s. In practice, the party had already moved beyond the most rigid ideas of the Wright years, but the drafting of a new program opened up the opportunity to clarify some of the issues involved.

The new program argued that the problems Indigenous people faced may "differ from place to place" – since "some are free, others strictly controlled, some of pure Aboriginal descent, others of mixed origin" – but it is still the case that "all Aborigines are oppressed, to a greater or lesser extent, by Acts of the Federal and State Governments, and by discriminatory practices". In order to attempt to deal with the complexity of Indigenous experiences and different struggles, the CPA acknowledged that the Aboriginal and Torres Strait Islander population had two aspects: many had "been converted into a particularly oppressed section of the working class"; however, they also constituted an oppressed national minority within Australia. Unlike Wright's 1939 pamphlet (as discussed in chapter five), the 1964 program didn't attempt to divide up Indigenous people into these two separate sections. Instead, it argued that both aspects shaped all Indigenous people, and so the working-class movement and the left must take up both the economic and the national-political aspects of Indigenous oppression.[273]

There were also developments in how the question of land rights was understood, particularly in the wake of the 1963 Yirrakala bark petition protest. The issue of the land had long been important for Indigenous campaigners and the left, but previously it had often been understood in a relatively narrow way. Now the issue of land rights was becoming increasingly associated with the growing appreciation of Indigenous people as a national minority, with particular rights rooted in the nature of their oppression.

The adoption of this stance ignited some debate in the Communist Party and in circles of Aboriginal rights campaigners. Dr Barry Christophers, a

---

273. All quotes from *Tribune*, 12 Feburary 1964, p.5.

member of the CPA and president of the Council for Aboriginal Rights (Victoria), wrote a series of articles criticising the new program. Christophers' main objection to the program was that by conceptualising Indigenous people as a national minority it gave "undue emphasis to a discussion on such things as assimilation, integration, identity as a people, right to control their own affairs, etc". Instead, he argued, they should be seen as an ethnic minority and the emphasis should be on equal civil rights and on economic exploitation.[274]

The response from other CPA members revealed there was a growing concern over the need to understand issues of Indigenous identity and to stridently reject the assimilationist policies of state bureaucrats. Ted Zeffertt argued in reply to Christophers:

> [It] is true that Aboriginal culture "should not be artificially retained or exploited". But let us be wary of playing down the pride in their identity and determination of Aboriginal people to preserve it. Let us be wary of opening even the tiniest crack to the danger of spreading the capitalist class policy of assimilation, merely a more "civilised" adaptation of the old policy of extermination. I prefer "national minority" precisely because it does emphasise a sharp line of demarcation from assimilation.[275]

Christopher's criticisms reflected some of the conservative pressures on Indigenous rights campaigners during this period. As another reply by a CPA member to Christophers pointed out, it was the government and public servants who wanted to emphasise that Indigenous issues were purely socio-economic in nature, and not racial, in order to pretend that Australia had no problem with racism:

> If this is what the GOVERNMENT is anxious to have us believe, then we must beware of such statements as "it is more important to have Aborigines as plumbers, electricians, doctors, scientists, etc. than to have them making boomerangs." (Dr. Christophers, *Tribune*, 18/3/64). This last sentence, surely, is an over-simplification.

---

274. *Tribune*, 24 March 1964, p.7; see also 18 March, p.11 and 1 April, p.11.
275. *Tribune*, 10 June 1964, p.13.

Acceptance of Aborigines as a People would entitle them to considerations over and above ordinary citizenship. If we keep on insisting on the importance of the socio economic aspects of their struggle, without recognising that their needs as a People are of PRIME importance to them, we will continue to commit the mistakes of the past. Aborigines want equal status and amenities along with the majority group, but AS Aborigines. This is their emphasis. Separate identity, land rights…from these basic demands they desire social and economic justice. To put the latter first, in the face of evidence when we no longer have the excuse of negligible contact, is presumptuous indeed. Many sincere, capable Aborigines have approached the progressive movement in the past; the tendency then was to direct them into the general wage demands and struggles – these people have drifted. Realizing that the Aborigines' basic demands are consistent with their desire to be recognised as a People, the draft policy envisages the Aborigines in specific organisations and forms of action which correspond to THEIR demands, and this becomes their basic foundation for the general struggle which at the moment appears to them to be of secondary importance. Let us assist the Aborigines to win their demands.[276]

The irony is that by the end of the decade, the CPA was facing criticism for not being sensitive enough to the issues it had started to grapple with during the early '60s.

Another expression of the shifting mood in the 1960s was a new culture of increasingly radical activism among university students. From the early '60s, Australian university students had been involved in demonstrations against South African apartheid and in support of the US civil rights movement. There was a large contingent of students for the first time at the 1964 National Aborigines Day – as well as a bearded folk singer. The week before, 800 Sydney University students had protested for Aboriginal rights outside Parliament House in Sydney.[277]

Then in February 1965, a busload of students from Sydney University toured through the towns of Walgett, Moree, Kempsey and Bowraville in order to campaign against segregation in rural NSW. They were pelted with

---
276. *Tribune*, 10 June 1964, p.13.
277. *Tribune*, 15 July 1964, p.1.

tomatoes, punched, verbally abused, burned with cigarette butts and run off the road as they challenged segregated swimming pools, pubs and hotels. At a follow-up demonstration protesting arrests in Bowraville a Sydney University student, Sue Johnson, burned a copy of the Aborigines Protection Act, to the horror of onlookers.[278] The origin of this "Freedom Ride" can be traced to a 1964 demonstration outside the US Consulate in support of the American civil rights movement, organised by Sydney University students during Orientation Week. Afterwards, a number of the organisers inspired by the American example formed Student Action for Aborigines (SAFA). While building on some of the activity undertaken in previous decades, the Freedom Ride engaged in a different form of activism, revealing a political shift:

> The method the students chose was bold, brazen, direct action... While targeting entrenched discrimination in country towns, the initiative drew on recent interest in the patterns of international race reform, a developing awareness of new racial dynamics, the rise of the New Left, the revival of politics in the universities and the emergence of effective Indigenous leadership. In other words, the Freedom Ride was a dramatic announcement that both Australia's racial awakening and the development of the 1960s had reached a new stage.[279]

When the bus returned to Sydney University, 400 students came to hear the Freedom Riders at a public meeting. One of the Riders explained the impact on the student body to *Outlook*, an independent socialist newspaper:

> "Freedom Rider" has an air of glamour. But if SAFA maintains its momentum, it will become the mainstream of social protest at the University because it has had a success. So often you get into a cause and nothing comes of it; you get battered, you come up against the Establishment and you never get anywhere.[280]

---

278. *Tribune*, 20 July 1966, p.4.
279. Clark 2008, pp.150–1.
280. *Outlook*, April 1965, p.8.

Then, in August 1966, a group of Aboriginal stockmen and their families in the Northern Territory walked off the remote cattle station where they had been working. The "Wave Hill Walk-off", or Gurindji strike, had a huge impact on the growing progressive consciousness around Indigenous issues in Australia, and it cemented the question of land rights as a central issue for decades to come.[281]

The Gurindji strike was a bridge between the Aboriginal strikes in the Pilbara and Darwin and the growing radicalisation of the 1960s. At first, it seemed like a repeat of the post-war strikes, with an important role being played by left-wing trade unionists such as Dexter Daniels, an Aboriginal organiser for the North Australian Workers' Union. It also built on years of campaigning and occasional work stoppages by NT trade unions.

As the struggle developed, however, new elements came to the fore. Once they had walked off the station and occupied the area around Wattie Creek, the Gurindji reformulated their fight as one for land rights.

This wasn't an entirely new idea. A section of the Pilbara strikers had established a co-operatively-owned mining company after the end of their strike – although this was achieved through the normal mechanisms of private proprietary ownership. In 1963, the Yolngu people of Arnhem Land had made the Yirrkala bark petitions, which asserted the Yolngu people's ownership of land over which mining rights had been granted by the federal government to a private company, Nabalco.

The Gurindji strike, however, placed land rights at the centre of the national discussion on Indigenous issues, as historian Charlie Ward explained:

[A] series of slow, seismic changes were in motion, triggered by their Walk-off, their activism in the south, and the equal wages decision. Fuelling talk of Aboriginal work and land issues, the public could see that the Gurindji's homeless status on their own country meant that the whole status quo of race relations in the north was no longer tenable. The fate of all Aborigines on pastoral land, the direction of the nation's Aboriginal policy and the northern cattle industry would all turn on this axis.[282]

---

281. The following account is primarily drawn from chapter two of Ward 2016.
282. Ward 2016, p.38.

The demand for land rights put the Liberal government on the defensive. In response to a petition from the Gurindji for 500 square miles of land to be handed over to them, the Governor-General advised them to apply for a lease on vacant Crown land and in the meantime to be careful not to break any laws that would undermine such an application. This move backfired, increasing levels of sympathy for the land rights struggle across the country and adding to the growing pressure for a referendum on Indigenous rights. Following the successful 1967 referendum, the Liberal government continued to resist the demand for land rights. In July 1968, they announced that the government's "solution" would be to move the Gurindji to the "desolate, infertile, flood-prone Wave Hill Welfare settlement", where they would live in 20 new houses built and paid for by the government. It was a slap in the face for the strikers, reinforced by Minister for the Territories Peter Dixon's comments in parliament that he saw his role as relegating land rights "to its proper position of relative insignificance".[283]

University students also played a role in the Gurindji strike. These students, already alienated by the government's role in the growing Vietnam conflict, were quick to sympathise with the strikers. Angry protests broke out in the capital cities in response to the government's refusal of land rights, and some student activists engaged in tactics more akin to direct action – protesting inside supermarkets, occupying the foyers of office buildings – leading to arrests and clashes with the police. A hostile article in the UNSW student newspaper *Tharunka*, while opposing the tactics of student activists, captures something of the mood:

> Consider the recent protest outside a Cabinet meeting in Sydney. It was meeting to consider, among other things, the question of Aboriginal Land Rights in the Northern Territory and, as a consequence of the precedent to be set, in future cases. Many students, and presumably some at least in this demonstration, were most concerned that [Aboriginal affairs minister] Mr. Wentworth's case be enhanced. Yet in fact gross hostility was directed at the members of Cabinet before and during the meeting.[284]

---

283. As quoted in Ward 2016, p.51.
284. *Tharunka*, 16 July 1968, p.12.

The Gurindji strike also received significant support from the left-wing trade unions and some of the strikers' spokespeople toured around worksites and union meetings. The involvement of the students in solidarity actions was a foreshadowing of the shift taking place on the campuses, however. The Freedom Ride and the Gurindji strike were two more streams flowing into the student population's growing radicalisation which within a few years would explode on campuses across the country, around the issue of the Vietnam War in particular. They would raise new challenges to the established strategies and politics of the post-war Indigenous rights movement.

While in the Northern Territory the Gurindji engaged in an innovative action, a more traditional campaign was taking off in the eastern cities. During the 1930s and the immediate post-war years, the CPA and Indigenous activists had been campaigning for changes to the constitution in favour of Indigenous people, but the conservative 1950s had temporarily halted any serious progress on this issue. The reasons that the issues of citizenship rights for Indigenous people and constitutional change became intertwined are quite obscure and confusing. Essentially it was believed that giving the federal government greater constitutional powers with regard to Indigenous people would override reluctant state governments and somehow give Indigenous people greater social rights, although this was a somewhat erroneous assumption. Part of the explanation for why this became a significant theme for progressive campaigning in the early 1960s lies in the conservative and moderate nature of Indigenous activism during the 1950s. The focus on constitutional changes and empowering the federal government fitted with the focus on appealing to the United Nations and to supposedly progressive Liberal politicians like Paul Hasluck and William Charles Wentworth.[285]

In 1962, FCAATSI launched a renewed push for constitutional change. Its representatives met with both Liberal Prime Minister Robert Menzies and ALP leader Arthur Calwell. The ALP was sympathetic, but Menzies resisted. Shifts in public opinion, strengthened by the 1965 Freedom Ride and then the Gurindji strike, combined with international debates about racism and decolonisation, brought pressure to bear on the Liberal government. Harold Holt became prime minister in January 1966, elected unopposed as Liberal

---

285. A detailed discussion of this issue is found in Attwood and Markus 2007.

leader following Menzies' retirement, and by this point the Liberals had decided to support a referendum on the matter.

An enormous amount of work was put into the 1967 referendum campaign by progressive activists. Dozens, if not hundreds, of stop-work meetings were organised by trade unionists across the country, petitions were gathered, meetings held, materials distributed.[286]

The focus placed on the constitutional changes proposed by the referendum was not uncontested among Indigenous activists:

> [S]everal Aboriginal leaders expressed serious criticisms of it in the lead-up to the poll. Groves expressed the desire of Aboriginal people "to be part and parcel of the community" at the same time as he made it clear they wanted "to do this without losing [their] identity as Australian Aborigines". The policy of assimilation, he stated bluntly, reflected "a failure to accept a minority race on the basis of equality", indeed, he went so far as to call it "a modified method of extermination." Other Council leaders like Kath Walker were no longer so committed to the campaign for civil rights.

> ...In the opinion of the Federal Council's Aboriginal rank and file, the priority the organisation had given to the fight for constitutional change was misplaced. Aboriginal-Australian Fellowship member Ken Brindle later told Bandler: "I couldn't see how it would benefit us…I was more informed than the average Aboriginal, but I couldn't understand it"; Leon later recalled that the thoughts of Aborigines "were always on housing and jobs" and other bread-and-butter issues. At a symbolic level, too, it seems that many Aboriginal people regarded the referendum as relatively unimportant. The right to drink was a more significant marker of equality than the right to be counted in the national census. Sydney Aboriginal figure Mum Shirl later remarked: "As far as being a citizen, it wasn't even a word I even thought about".[287]

These opinions foreshadowed criticisms that would come to the fore several years after the referendum. Despite the limited nature of the demands raised

---
286. See Bloodworth 2006 for an overview of this activity.
287. Attwood and Markus 2007, p.53.

by the referendum, the fact that 90.77% of the population voted in favour of them was a sign of mass sentiment beginning to shift. The radicalisation of the late '60s was beginning to gain momentum. However, the constitutional change delivered nothing concrete to improve the lot of Indigenous people. Along with the Liberals' refusal to support even token land rights, this demonstrated the limits of the government's commitment to reforms. As even Barrie Dexter, a member of the Council for Aboriginal Affairs that advised the government on Indigenous matters, conceded, "the mountain [of the referendum] gave birth to a mouse".[288]

The referendum campaign was in many ways the last roll of the dice for the older, more conservative forms of Aboriginal activism that had become hegemonic in the 1950s. Soon a new generation would take the lead.

---

288. Ward 2016, p.44.

Chapter seven
Black Power

THE LATE 1960S AND EARLY 1970S were a period of mass struggles and radical politics around the globe. University students took to the streets and occupied their campuses in protest against the Vietnam War. In the United States, a powerful struggle for civil rights mobilised huge numbers and inspired struggles against racism internationally. United movements of students and workers erupted in France, Italy, Portugal and Spain.

Australia was not immune to the upheaval. Here too, hundreds of thousands of people marched against the war, and the confidence of the working class to take industrial action surged forwards after the general strike of 1969 which freed the imprisoned trade union leader Clarrie O'Shea. A new radical left began to emerge, critical of the conservatism and moderation of both the Australian Labor Party and the old Communist Party.

It was in this context that a significant radicalisation in the movement for Indigenous rights took place. In the late 1960s, a new generation of younger, more militant Aboriginal activists, many of whom had been inspired by the 1965 Freedom Ride, was increasingly interested in the politics of Black Power. This was a political movement which began among African Americans in the United States who had become frustrated with the slow progress of the mainstream civil rights movement and its strategy of winning over moderate white liberals. In Australia, the failure to win any significant changes in the conditions of Indigenous people following the passing of the 1967 referendum helped point activists in a more radical direction, as Kevin Gilbert has explained:

> The 1967 Referendum gave a huge "yes" vote for full citizenship rights for Aborigines. Many blacks thought that at last a new deal for black people was imminent. The disillusionment after 1967 hit hard. It is little wonder that

younger, more literate blacks began to search for their values in the literature of the Black Panther movement of the United States. They read somewhere about how some white fat cat reckoned that Australia was a "lucky country" and said "Yeah, for the gubbahs (whites)".[289]

The Australian Black Power movement traces its origins to a 1969 meeting of the Victorian Aborigines Advancement League, which had come under the leadership of radicals Bob Maza and Bruce McGuinness. This meeting featured Caribbean Black Power activist and writer Roosevelt Brown, whose speech was widely covered in the press at the time, in often hysterical tones. Black Power activist Gary Foley notes that the event and the media reaction were "closely observed by younger activists in Brisbane and Sydney".[290]

Following Brown's visit, a Black Power group cohered in Redfern, playing an important role in the protests against the 1971 Springbok tour, as well as establishing the Aboriginal Legal Service of New South Wales in 1970 and then the Aboriginal Medical Service. In 1971, an Australian Black Panther Party was formed in Brisbane, composed of a small number of leading Black Power advocates from across the country. In the same year, Lin Onus organised a protest camp in the Dandenong Ranges concerning a land rights claim and told *Tribune* that "Black power has connotations of violence for some people, but we see it as black autonomy. It is the right to be self-determining. And black power is a reality – it's here to stay". In November, there occurred what the *Canberra Times* called "the first violent Aboriginal demonstration in Australia" when Dennis Walker and other activists organised a protest in Brisbane against a new repressive law, leading to clashes with the police. By the beginning of 1972, a "Black Power Group" had formed in Western Australia.[291]

An important development helping to lay the social basis for the emergence of Black Power was demographic changes which had occurred in the Indigenous population, particularly in the eastern states. Hundreds and then thousands of Aboriginal people living in rural areas moved

---

289. Gilbert 2013 [1977], p.106.
290. Foley 2001, p.2.
291. *Tribune*, 17 February 1971, p.4; *Canberra Times*, 29 November 1971, p.2; *Tribune*, 4 April 1972, p.8.

to the cities in the post-war period, reinforcing pre-existing Aboriginal communities in inner city areas like Redfern in Sydney, Fitzroy in Melbourne and South Brisbane.

Some of these demographic changes were rooted in the contradictions of government policy. Assimilationist programs had tried to compel the integration of Indigenous people into white working-class life; while those who were deemed not yet "assimilated" lived on the missions. By the early 1960s, however, this had led to a significant crisis for the Aboriginal Welfare Board in NSW, as it struggled to deal with the significant numbers of Indigenous people who lived in appalling conditions on the outskirts of rural towns, gathered together in unofficial Aboriginal camps. This growing section of the Aboriginal population was unable to be dispersed into the rest of Australian society, but it also no longer lived on the government-controlled reserves and by the 1960s was the fastest growing section of the Indigenous population in the state. In 1969, the NSW government attempted to resolve the issue by making a greater push for Aboriginal people to move into large towns and cities. To achieve this, the Welfare Board was abolished and responsibility for the Indigenous population was transferred to the mainstream government departments of welfare, housing, education, health and so forth.[292]

This reinforced post-war trends towards urbanisation that impacted Australian society as a whole, including Indigenous people. In Sydney, while there had been small numbers of Aboriginal people living in the poor suburbs of the inner city throughout the 19th and early 20th centuries, it was in the 1940s that the first major waves of Indigenous migration occurred. Many moved into the working-class suburbs of Redfern, Waterloo, Surry Hills and Newtown, attracted by greater job prospects. While precise statistics are hard to come by, the process of urbanisation was very rapid. An informal census by the Welfare Board in 1945 had reported around 2,500 Aboriginal people living in Sydney, by the mid-1960s there were reports of around 12,000 in the Sydney area, and by 1971 studies were recording over 10,000 Aboriginal people living in the suburb of Redfern alone.[293]

---

292. See chapter two of Morgan 2006.
293. Morgan 2006, p.47.

This process wasn't confined to NSW, as George Morgan explains in his study of Indigenous urbanisation:

> The movement of Indigenous population to metropolitan centres occurred across Australia. Aboriginal communities were established in places like Fitzroy and Footscray in Melbourne, Fortitude Valley in Brisbane, Adelaide's West End and in Allawah Grove and to the east of Perth, a city where a night-time curfew operated to exclude Aboriginal people from the CBD after 6pm.[294]

The urbanisation of the Indigenous population at a time of growing political ferment in the inner cities had a significant impact, as Foley has explained:

> It should be remembered that this was a time of exciting social and political upheaval in Australia and the rest of the world. The late 1960s saw student rebellion in Paris, riots at the Democratic Convention in Chicago and the emergence of the American Black Power movement. In both America and Australia demonstrations against the War in Vietnam bought together elements of black and white political activists. In Sydney people like Paul Coe, Gary Williams and Gary Foley were starting to encounter new people and new ideas.[295]

Nightly clashes with the police in inner city areas like Redfern increased this openness to new ideas, as young Aboriginal activists saw striking parallels between their own struggles and those of Black Power militants in the US, as well as the potential for solidarity with movements on the campuses and in the workplaces. These experiences also shaped how Aboriginal people understood their own identity:

> As with the formation of working-class solidarity in the new industrial towns, the congregation of Indigenous peoples from different regions in high-density population centres, produced new solidarities. Those who came from small country towns or remote areas were able to relate their particular localised

---

294. Morgan 2006, pp.46–7.
295. Foley 2001, p.8.

experiences to those of other Aboriginal people who came from elsewhere. Solidarity was built on a realisation that what had happened on the reserve was not peculiar but was part of a more generalised set of experiences.[296]

This created a greater social basis for the kind of pan-Aboriginal identity that FCAATSI had been struggling to construct in the post-war years, while also laying the basis for a more radical version of that identity which would challenge older conceptions, as we shall see later in this chapter.

Out of this context a core layer of urban Aboriginal activists emerged who were taking up the politics of Black Power. While it was among these urban activists that Black Power struck its deepest roots, its influence was felt across the country. Bishop Witt, speaking in 1972, explained how in one remote town in the Northern Territory, where newspapers were double the price of those in the city, there was no television and it was almost impossible to receive radio service, he had been stunned one day to come across a group of young Aboriginal men painting the slogan "Black Power Will Rule the World" on the side of an abandoned building.[297]

The fight over FCAATSI

An early expression of tensions between Black Power and older forms of campaigning about Aboriginal issues was a fight within FCAATSI. From the late 1960s, there had been growing agitation for greater Aboriginal control over the organisation, which was still dominated by church figures, progressive parliamentarians and white activists. In 1969, at a meeting of the FCAATSI executive, Kath Walker circulated a document which prefigured later criticisms. In the same year the Victorian Aborigines Advancement League, which had organised the meeting with Roosevelt Brown, publicly embraced Black Power and moved towards being an Indigenous-only organisation.

The leadership of FCAATSI was not ignorant of the discontent that was building. In November 1969, they organised a one-day conference on "Autonomy and Self-Government for Aborigines and Islanders" at which

---
296. Morgan 2006, p.63.
297. *Canberra Times*, 14 September 1972, p.3.

criticisms of white influence over the movement were raised, although any serious debate seems to have been avoided. At least some FCAATSI executive members seem to have publicly acknowledged that the ideas of Black Power might have some validity and interest for Indigenous activists, but behind the scenes they worked to undermine the influence of those ideas within the organisation. The trade union convenor of the council, John Baker, who came up with the idea of the November conference, spoke positively about it to *Tribune*, stating "we shouldn't be timid about bringing forward ideas of autonomy or black power or whatever we call it". Yet the minutes from a March 1970 meeting of the executive reveal that Baker had also claimed the government was secretly funding busloads of Black Power activists to swamp the next conference of the organisation and destroy it.[298]

For those younger Indigenous activists attracted to Black Power, FCAATSI epitomised an older form of conservative, moderate Aboriginal activism which they were moving away from. Barrie Pittock, a white member of the council who became sympathetic to the arguments of the Black Power advocates, summarised the two sides of the debate:

> [O]ne side sees an immediate and obvious community of interest between racial-minority groups and a liberal-humanitarian or socialist-working class movement in the dominant society… [R]acial and cultural group differences are of minor significance and the interests of both groups are best served by an immediate and continuing coalition aiming at the fusion of the two groups, or their assimilation, in some more humanitarian or socialist state which the coalition will bring into being.

> The other side places greater emphasis on the different racial and cultural group experiences and identities. It emphasises the need for the minority group to build up its own pride, leadership, traditions, and strength based on its own experience and condition. It claims that, with rare exceptions, only minority group members have experienced and felt what it means to be born into and raised as members of such a minority. Consequently, it maintains, no matter what theoretical commitment and understanding white people may

---

298. *Tribune*, 19 November 1969, p.7; Pittock 1970, p.5.

have, they cannot in general be relied on to speak for black people. Coalitions must therefore be based, not on some philosophical common ground such as liberal-humanitarianism or socialism, which not all blacks share anyway, but on a pragmatic judgement as to common interests, based on the ability of black people to come or go as equal partners in the coalition.[299]

As the fight heated up, Black Power activists increasingly pushed for FCAATSI to be brought under 100 percent Indigenous control, and for non-indigenous people to be excluded from the organisation. The battle reached its high point at the Easter 1970 conference of the council. A motion to alter the constitution so that only people of Aboriginal or Islander descent could comprise the executive or vote at general meetings split the conference, 48 votes for and 48 against. The Black Power activists then withdrew to establish the breakaway National Tribal Council, and FCAATSI fell into a period of gradual but inevitable decline.

There were certainly both organisational and political problems with FCAATSI, stemming from the conservative context in which it had initially emerged and from the difficulties it had in adapting to the growing radicalisation around the Indigenous issue. However, the split in the organisation was far from a clear left-vs-right break. More conservative Indigenous figures – such as Charlie Perkins, who tried to have the council disassociate itself from Communists at the 1968 conference, and the Aboriginal clergyman Doug Nicholls – also supported the demand for Aboriginal control over the council. Nor was it a straightforward split between Indigenous and non-indigenous activists. Many Indigenous activists, particularly those with working-class backgrounds like Ray Peckham, rejected the arguments of the Black Power militants and instead strongly argued for a multi-racial movement. On the other hand, various non-indigenous academics and students championed Aboriginal control. It was the white academic Pittock, for instance, who wrote and moved the constitutional amendment for Aboriginal control.

Despite these complications, the fight in FCAATSI was an expression of discontent with the moderate liberal-Stalinist coalition politics that had dominated the left for a whole period.

---
299. Pittock 1970, p.1.

Black Power, the student left and the new workers' militancy

> The concept of participatory democracy is easily related to every excluded or repressed section of the population: from workers who are given no say in their conditions, living standards and work value, to aborigines who are subjected to white control and supervision.
>
> — Michael Hamel-Green, "Theory and practice of the student New Left", 1969.[300]

In the anti-Vietnam War movement there had been a clear polarisation against the old peace movement politics of the Communists and their "respectable" middle-class allies:

> The Old Left, dominated by the CPA and its union and ALP left allies, was wedded to the parliamentary road to socialism and a cringing concern for respectability. This meant tailing ALP moderates and church leaders and avoiding radical action that might harm Labor's electoral fortunes.[301]

The Communist Party opposed the call for the immediate withdrawal of Australian troops from Vietnam, even when that was the official policy of the ALP.

The radicalisation among university students, produced above all by the fight against the war, gave birth to a new layer of radical left activists and a militant atmosphere on the campuses. As this left grew and the level of struggle increased, the moderate politics of the old left were challenged across a variety of movements and struggles. In 1965, the Trotskyist Bob Gould initiated the Vietnam Action Campaign, which challenged the CPA's influence on the anti-war movement in Sydney, and since then there had been a wave of militant revolts on campuses across the country. In Melbourne, the CPA was challenged by a variety of new left-wing forces, including the Maoists. The new radical mood also spread to the trade union movement, in which the old strategies were challenged from the late 1960s

---

300. *Tribune*, 12 March 1969, p.5.
301. Armstrong 2007, p.64.

onwards, particularly in the aftermath of the 1969 general strike to free jailed trade union leader Clarrie O'Shea:

> The defeat of the...penal powers signalled a reinvigoration of union mobilisation. Arbitration was discredited among hundreds of thousands of blue-collar workers and not a few white-collar ones too. Workers had not only won back the right to strike; they had gained the confidence to use it... Workers flexed their muscles on a wide range of issues.[302]

One of these issues was, of course, Indigenous rights. The radicalisation on the campuses and more generally around the Vietnam War fed into this working-class militancy by breaking down the conservative political culture of the Cold War years. The emergence of this new militancy was significant; it revealed that the failures of the old left liberal-Stalinist alliance didn't have to mean junking the whole idea that the working class was the agent of social change – although it did mean that the socialist left would have to clarify what this meant. Did it mean the hegemony of supposed "representatives" of working-class opinion such as trade union bureaucrats, Labor MPs and liberal-Stalinist activists? What the Black Power *National Koorier* newspaper had dubbed the "Federal Council for the Advancement of Parliamentarians and Trade Union Officials"? Or did it mean forging a revolutionary movement of the oppressed and exploited built on struggle from below?

One example of the new configuration of political forces produced by this radicalisation was the 1971 strike at the University of Queensland. The strike was responding to a state of emergency which had been declared by Premier Joh Bjelke-Petersen in an attempt to protect the all-white South African rugby team from planned anti-apartheid protests. On 23 July, 3,000 students and staff attended a mass meeting which initiated the 15-day strike and called upon trade unions across the state to join in. The mass meeting was a turning point, as one account recalls:

> Something big had happened, an "impossible" step taken – the feeling that somehow this campus would never be the same again. It was a breakthrough

---
302. Bramble 2008, p.46.

from the original only nominal response to a strike-call earlier. Dan [O'Neill – a radical staff member from the New Left] had originally spoken to the meeting with the intention of suggesting strike action, with a later call for a strike, probably on Monday. However, after this suggestion there were calls for "strike now", with an obvious mass approval. The strike motion was put, and overwhelmingly passed. Then came the question, what does it mean, what do we do now? How many realised the implications? It was suggested then that Strike Committees be set up, including a committee to look after the Refec. These were then elected, and began operating immediately.[303]

The strike transformed the university into a centre of political debate and activism. It was not just the racism of the South African apartheid regime that was under discussion, as Dan O'Neill explained in an interview at the time:

> Denis Walker of the National Tribal Council (NTC) was speaking and participating in the strike from the first days, as was Len Watson on the NTC. Pastor Don Brady also played an important role. It was from Monday on, however, that large numbers of black members of the NTC came on campus and helped in the strike. We were preparing for student participation in a Tribal Feast due for 31 July. On Thursday we raised $3,000 to help the NTC. After Monday's meeting, the stress began to swing from the tour and racism in general, to the situation of the Australian black population in particular. The black NTC leaders spoke daily on campus, putting their case. There was a great exchange of ideas.[304]

The strike demanded that Aboriginal studies courses be adopted at the university, run by Aboriginal people themselves. A national conference on racism and education was also organised and a campaign against the racist Queensland laws which controlled Indigenous people began to emerge.

One of the most dramatic intersections between the radical left, the workers' movement and the campaign for Indigenous rights was in the NSW Builders Labourers Federation (BLF). The radical leadership of

---

303. *Semper Floreat*, 41 (11), 1 September 1971, p.4.
304. *Tribune*, 8 September 1971, p.7.

the NSW BLF, which dominated the union in the '60s, began as a tiny rank-and-file reform group formed in 1951. At that time, the union was controlled by a corrupt right-wing clique, and the Communists in the rank-and-file group were isolated. The building boom of the '50s and '60s, however, created greater space for industrial action, and in 1961 the old right-wing leadership of the union was defeated after years of organising by the opposition. At first, the new leadership, while a definite break from the old, was not radically different from the officials typically found in other left unions of the time. By the late 1960s, however, they were swept up by the sharp leftwards shift taking place in the working class, on the campuses and in society more broadly. Eventually the NSW BLF became one of the most radical expressions of this shift.[305] The 1970s saw the union engage in a series of militant, democratically controlled strikes which won significant wage rises and improvements in conditions. The demonstration of these workers' industrial strength, combined with the leftist politics of union members, gave them the confidence to take industrial action around broader social issues as well.

The NSW BLF welcomed the emergence of the Black Power movement in Redfern during this period, building an important alliance with it. This was a continuation of earlier work of the union to build solidarity with Indigenous struggles. As a union of unskilled manual labourers, the NSW BLF had a significant Aboriginal membership. In April 1962, it sent Aboriginal builders' labourer Monty Maloney, who had previously represented the union at an international conference, to the 5th National Conference on Aboriginal Affairs in Adelaide. During the 1966 Gurindji strike at Wave Hill, BLF fundraising efforts were strong, with two job sites alone contributing over $600; the Aboriginal strike leaders received rousing welcomes on the many New South Wales job sites they visited at the invitation of the union. In 1967, Dexter Daniels, an Indigenous organiser for the North Australian Workers' Union and leading figure in the Gurindji strike, spoke at a BLF meeting in Sydney.

The construction workforce at the time was very ethnically mixed, so the lines of racial segregation were less rigid than in society as a whole. The BLF took a strong stand against anti-migrant racism from the bosses and argued

---

305. See Armstrong 2020 for an overview of the NSW BLF.

against anti-migrant attitudes among workers. This put the leadership in a strong position to discuss the issue of Indigenous rights with the union's rank and file. Kevin Cook, Aboriginal activist and BLF organiser, explained how the racism of the bosses helped them build an opposing culture of solidarity:

> I think the bosses played right into our hands, because, on a building site, most of the bosses, whether they be foremen, leading hands, thought they were a cut above everybody else and they'd go along and say, "Get out of here you wog bastards" and all of that, and the Builders Labourers' union got onto that, and started pulling the bosses up and in fact sacking the bosses for being racist.
>
> So that built the migrant people up too, no longer could the boss come up and call an Italian a wog, in a detrimental way. He might say, "Hey you wog bastard" if he was a mate of his, but on no account could he do that if he was angry or had the shits, he just couldn't do it, because he'd get the sack. That made it a lot easier when you were talking about black issues, it was a social issue the same as not calling migrants "wogs" on the site. And the bosses done that a hell of a lot and the migrants got very, very angry.[306]

From the late 1960s, the NSW BLF also formed strong links with the Black Power activists in Redfern, who had connections with the radical left organisations and movements flowering in Sydney at the time – in particular the Indigenous activists had close ties to BLF leaders Jack Mundey, Bob Pringle and Joe Owens. The BLF saw itself as a democratic workers' organisation that could use its industrial power to take stands on broader social issues. Both the BLF and the Black Power activists in Redfern played a key role in the anti-apartheid protests against the 1971 Springbok rugby tour, with Bob Pringle arrested for trying to saw down a goalpost at the Sydney Cricket Ground.

Perhaps the most important collaboration between the BLF and the Black Power activists took place in Redfern itself, in a fight over housing. In the early 1970s, building developers targeted "the Block", two streets of semi-derelict houses near Redfern railway station which had become an important social and political centre for the Indigenous community in Sydney. With

---

306. Cook and Goodall 2013, p.41.

the building boom at its height, the developers wanted the houses torn down and replaced with new high-rise housing and offices. The BLF immediately banned any demolition or construction work on the Block, essentially ending the developers' plans to purchase the land. The pressure brought to bear on the Whitlam Labor government by the Redfern Black Power activists and the BLF led the government to fund the land's purchase by an Aboriginal-controlled organisation, the Aboriginal Housing Company, in the first urban land rights claim of the 20th century.[307]

The radicalisation of Black Power

In 1972, there was a sharp shift to the left in the Aboriginal movement, which reflected the deepening of the radicalisation in Australian society more generally. In January, the Aboriginal Tent Embassy was established outside the federal parliament in Canberra by four Black Power activists from Sydney: Michael Anderson, Billy Craigie, Tony Coorey and Bertie Williams. It quickly became a lightning rod for the Indigenous struggle and an embarrassment to the conservative federal government. Arson attacks by racists and eventually a police operation to remove the Embassy brought hundreds of Indigenous and non-indigenous supporters to Canberra in protest. Bob Pringle from the BLF was involved in one of these protests in July and recalled that "362 Robots of the law marched out in military fashion and turned about in unison and then mechanically smashed us. Many people were seriously injured".[308]

On 14 July, a Black Moratorium march was organised in Sydney to demand land rights. This protest was initiated by the Black Power activists in Redfern, who looked to mobilise support from their allies in the student socialist left and the workers' movement. It became an important unifying moment for the Black Power movement, student radicals and left-wing trade unionists. When Aboriginal protesters wanted help with advertising the Moratorium, the NSW BLF arranged for banners to be hung from the jibs of cranes around the city. One dogman, Roy Bishop, was dismissed for refusing to take a sign down and the union fought for his reinstatement. The march itself attracted

---
307. Cook and Goodall 2013, p.50.
308. Burgmann and Burgmann 2017, p.136.

thousands of left-wing workers, students and Indigenous people, although it also had to struggle with the police who fought to keep the protest on the footpath. Pringle was arrested, receiving a black eye, bruising, abrasions and a four-hour stint in a police cell.[309]

At the end of 1972, discontent was brewing among over 1,000 mostly Aboriginal cotton chippers in the rural NSW town of Wee Waa.[310] The cotton industry in Wee Waa was run by racist American cotton growers and the conditions were horrendous. The work was seasonal, so from December to February hundreds of mostly Aboriginal workers and their families would travel to Wee Waa from across NSW to work the cotton. Cotton chipping involves a gang of workers walking up and down the rows, "chipping" out weeds with a hoe.

The Wee Waa Aboriginal Cotton Chippers Caucus was set up by a mix of younger Aboriginal workers who had spent some time involved in Sydney Black Power circles and prominent local Aboriginal activists, such as Arthur Murray. Establishing the caucus was necessary because the Australian Workers' Union (AWU) had failed to organise the workers, as had ACTU leader Bob Hawke, who while claiming to support the workers refused to do anything about it unless the AWU asked the ACTU to intervene. The caucus began meeting at the back of the Royal Hotel and organised a series of protest meetings in the first days of January 1973. These meetings rapidly grew to include hundreds of workers and attracted harassment from the police. Preparations started to be made for a strike, and the caucus was renamed the Cotton Chippers' Union.

Tensions in the town grew. On 6 January 1973, 47 Aboriginal cotton chippers were arrested after one protest meeting. Then on 9 January, 300 cotton workers protested outside the Imperial Hotel, which denied service to most Aboriginal people in the town – the publican locked the doors to the hotel and refused to speak to the protesters. This was followed two days later by a march of 500, and then a 24-hour strike at the Glencoe farm owned by Paul Kahl, who had been one of the first Americans to grow cotton in Wee Waa. An indefinite strike began on 22 January; the *Northern Daily Leader*

---

309. *Tribune*, 14 March 1972, p.10; *Tharunka*, 13 June 1972, p.5; *Tribune*, 11 July 1972, p.3.
310. The following account of the Wee Waa strike and all quotes are from Humphreys 2022b.

reported the next day that the strike had widespread support, with only 60 refusing to participate out of a workforce of around 1,500.

Crucially, this was right in the middle of the chipping season. The bosses and their supporters went berserk. The 25 January editorial in the *Wee Waa Echo* – titled "The Communist Strategy" – argued that "what is happening in Wee Waa at present is indicative of the kind of strife which radicals and professional trouble-makers can make", adding "it is not fanciful to see the Aboriginal problem as the powder keg for Communist aggression in Australia". *Tribune* reported that white vigilantes, rumoured to be employees of the cotton bosses, attacked the cotton chippers' camps in the dead of the night and burnt down their tents. Michael Anderson recalled that one night during the strike he was told his life was in danger, and he went to stay with family in town. After he had fled, "two shot gun blasts [*sic*] were fired into the tent and the people said a white 4WD had sped off into the darkness".

Anderson and another activist, Billy Craigie, had arrived in Wee Waa before the strike as representatives from the Aboriginal Tent Embassy in Canberra. Anderson, whose family were from the Wee Waa region, stayed in the area throughout cotton chippers' campaign and became the spokesperson for the workers. As the campaign took off, the Aboriginal Legal Service in Redfern – which had been set up by Black Power activists in 1970 – sent Paul Coe and Sol Bellear to provide legal support for the arrested strikers.

The Black Power activists also brought their connections with non-Aboriginal workers in the left wing of the Sydney trade union movement. Michael Anderson organised for cotton workers to be toured around construction sites in Sydney by builders' labourers in order to raise money for the strike fund, and Communist trade unionists arranged for some of the strikers to speak at a meeting of the Labour Council of NSW, which then endorsed their struggle. This example of non-Aboriginal trade unionists and Black Power activists in the cities coming together with rural working-class Aboriginal people was an important step in breaking down the racism in country NSW. It also showed that those who portrayed the Black Power activists in Redfern as an urbanised elite, who supposedly alienated the majority of poor Aboriginal people with their militant tactics and ideas, couldn't have been more wrong. The struggle of the cotton chippers was an opportunity to show that the

Aboriginal radicals in the cities could connect the struggle against racism with the interests of rural Aboriginal workers, as well as win support for that fight from working-class whites. Six days into the indefinite strike, the cotton bosses met with the leaders of the Cotton Chippers' Union; they agreed to raise the hourly pay rate to $1.45 and introduce double-time for Saturday and Sunday work. While issues such as housing and sanitation remained unresolved, this was still a big victory. The cotton bosses had been forced not only to negotiate with an unofficial breakaway from the AWU but also to concede some of their demands.

In many ways, the Wee Waa strike was the last expression of a high point for the mid-'70s radicalisation in the Aboriginal movement. The movement went into retreat following the election of the Whitlam government in December 1972. The 1971 ALP national conference had committed Labor to an extensive list of reforms on Indigenous issues; once in government, Labor continued to make grand promises, but delivered far less. What it did achieve, however, was a strategic victory against the radical left, by co-opting activists from the women's, anti-war, student and Aboriginal movements into various government roles. Prominent Indigenous activists were given jobs and a concerted effort was made to build up an Aboriginal middle class, which had been largely non-existent up until that point.

In Redfern, both the limitations of the Whitlam government's reforms and its efforts at co-option were clear. After Whitlam came to power in 1972, Aboriginal organisations in Redfern received a significant increase in government funding through the Department of Aboriginal Affairs (DAA). Yet tensions emerged over the limits the DAA wanted to set on "self-determination". The Aboriginal Legal Service, for instance, was free to allocate the funds given to it, but the DAA required that it be consulted about any major new projects and that financial statements be submitted. The Black Power activists involved in the Legal Service, however, wanted the role of the government to be "limited to providing funds", and they believed "attempts to limit expansion undermined its promise of self-determination". When the Legal Service resisted government constraints, the DAA began to introduce tighter financial control. It was a similar story with the Medical Service, the Aboriginal Housing Company and other organisations that were meant to be Aboriginal-controlled. This pressure increased with the outbreak of an economic recession in 1974. The Whitlam government was far more interested in creating a compliant bureaucracy than genuine self-determination, particularly when the capitalist economy started to falter.[311]

The limitations of Black Power

The Black Power movement had many strengths, including its defiance, militancy, and links to the wider radicalisation of Australian society at the time. However, there were also important weaknesses. Often Black Power activists engaged in flamboyant gestures and radical rhetoric which was fairly superficial. While they had connections with the radical left, they had little orientation towards a broader strategy of building working-class support for their movement outside of those workers already directly involved.

This was reinforced by a significant degree of political eclecticism. They were inspired by an uneven mix of American Black nationalism, Maoism, anarchism, radical liberalism, the counterculture and other ideologies in the air at the time. On the one hand, they saw themselves as affiliated to the avowedly "Marxism-Leninist" Black Panther Party in the US and the anti-colonial writer Franz Fanon, while on the other hand they denied the relevance of Marxist politics for the Black struggle in Australia. So in 1972, Paul Coe argued that:

> The concept of white capitalism and white communism is not applicable to the black man because the black man is trapped first and foremost by the colour of his skin… He must develop his own conceptions with his own theories in order to solve his own problems, problems which face the black race, which have not before existed in the concepts of capitalism and communism.[312]

Similarly, Black Power activists could form strong links with organisations such as the NSW BLF without fundamentally changing what they thought about the Australian working class more generally.

---

311. See Perheentupa 2020, pp.56–8.
312. d'Avigdor 2019, p.182.

The eclecticism of Black Power was also expressed in the smorgasbord of political strategies put forward by many of its leading activists. So Paul Coe and Bobbi Sykes argued for the formation of a "Black Mecca" state in the Northern Territory, while others emphasised the importance of a cultural and spiritual revival not tied to the unlikely creation of an Indigenous nation. On the other hand, Gary Foley argued that Black Power was rooted in political and economic demands, not spiritual ones.[313] Pat O'Shane expressed the frustration felt by many of the Black Power activists:

> In any event, groups in the community have to develop their own analysis of their own oppression. That was an object lesson for Aboriginal groups. The sad thing was that movement did not develop. It was curtailed because there was in fact no ideological base there and there never has been an ideological base. There are many factors missing.[314]

In many ways, these weaknesses were not primarily the fault of the Black Power activists themselves, but an expression of the political confusions and limitations of the far left that emerged from the radicalisation of the '60s. This far left was influenced by a variety of often contradictory ideas and struggled to build stable, significant organisations which could begin to seriously challenge the established left organisations of the ALP and the CPA.

The Black Power leaders' attempt to create a kind of revolutionary Black nationalist movement, similar to the Panthers in the US, was limited by the reality that the Indigenous population in Australia was so small it could only provide such a movement with a very narrow base. The question of who the Black Power activists would form an alliance with was a vital one, then, even on a pragmatic level. In the context of a historically large and well-organised workers' movement which was shifting sharply to the left by the late 1960s, as well as a flowering of radicalism on the campuses, an orientation towards the new left-wing forces emerging at the time was the logical choice. This choice was often presented as merely pragmatic, however, rather than being based on the common interest of Black and white workers in fighting oppression, or on

---

313. d'Avigdor 2019, p.183.
314. *Tribune*, 3 April 1991, p.8.

a clear ideological convergence between the socialist left and the Aboriginal movement. In a 1973 interview with the Trotskyist newspaper *Direct Action*, Bruce McGuinness argued:

> I don't think that the black movement can associate itself with any ideology that isn't intrinsically their own. Although obviously, some aspects of Marxist ideology are similar to black ideology. I can see coalitions of black militants and the left movement in Australia, on certain issues, just as I can see its importance for small "l" liberal blacks to form coalitions with their white counterparts.[315]

In 1972, McGuinness had expressed even greater scepticism towards the possibility of joint action between the socialist left and the Aboriginal movement, and towards the relationship between anti-capitalist politics and the fight against racism. In an editorial for *Identity* magazine, he wrote:

> Many white (and some disillusioned blacks) believe that blacks can attain freedom, through a black and white revolutionary coalition. That is just plain B.S. Oppression is just as bitter a pill to swallow under a socialist regime, as it is under a capitalist regime. In other words, we blacks must smash racism, before we consider letting whites piggyback on our backs to aid their cause. I agree that capitalism is a pig system, but capitalism is kindergarten stuff compared to racism.
>
> I know many Marxists, Leninist Maoists, as racist as any capitalist I know. If we can smash racist doctrines, under a capitalist system, then let's do it. I am sure that freedom from racism would be just as sweet, no matter what political set-up we exist in.[316]

For many Black Power activists, the role of the white left was confined to campaigning against racism among non-indigenous people. This sidestepped the whole question of political strategy, however. Because Indigenous people

---
315. *Direct Action*, 39, 20 April 1973, p.21.
316. *Identity*, November 1972, p.1.

made up a small minority of the Australian population, with limited economic or political power, the key question that had to be grappled with was: which class forces in Australian capitalist society should the Black Power movement ally itself with?

In order to move beyond a pragmatic and limited relationship between the Black Power activists and the workers' movement, towards the creation of a sizeable radical movement with deep roots in the working class, the radical left which emerged out of the '60s and '70s would have needed to cohere itself into even the beginnings of a real mass socialist organisation. It unfortunately failed to do so.[317]

The CPA and Black Power

The socialist organisation that should have been in the strongest position to relate to the radicalisation of the Indigenous struggle was the Communist Party. However, as we have seen, in the post-war period the CPA's approach to the Indigenous issue was marked by the moderation that had come to dominate Communist politics more generally.

This perspective was challenged by the arrival of Black Power in Australia. At first, the CPA was suspicious of the rise of Black Power, seeing it as a threat to the creation of a unified movement of white and Black activists. But the CPA's conception of a "unified movement" was the standard Popular Front that it had been promoting throughout the post-war period on a range of social issues – an alliance of moderate Stalinists, liberal progressives, church leaders, trade union officials and MPs.

In the aftermath of the battle over Aboriginal control of FCAATSI in 1970, the CPA softened its criticisms of Black Power and announced in *Tribune* that the Indigenous struggle had now entered into "a phase of national liberation", liberally quoting the anti-colonial writer Franz Fanon. The section of the CPA most hostile to the rise of Black Power was the hardline Stalinist wing of the party, which would leave to form the Socialist Party of Australia (SPA) in 1971.[318]

---

317. For an explanation of why this was the case see Armstrong 2023.
318. *Tribune*, 6 May 1970, p.4. They also published statements on the issue of Aboriginal autonomy by FCAATSI and other organisations in *Australian Left Review*, 23, 1970, pp.29–31.

The founding of the SPA was a right-wing reaction to the Communist Party's move away from high Stalinism. In their eyes, the CPA was engaged in an unprincipled alliance with the "trendy" ultra-left movements of student revolutionaries. The SPA's hostility towards Black Power fitted with this broader hostility towards the more left-wing elements of the '60s and '70s radicalisation: the new left on the campuses, the rank-and-file revolt in the unions, the NSW BLF, as well as the women's and gay liberation movements. Hannah Middleton, the key SPA writer on Indigenous issues, argued that the Aboriginal Tent Embassy "was contradictory and finally harmful in its results" and that Black Power activists "expressed various racist and anti-white ideas… in the interests of the capitalist establishment".[319]

The exit of the future SPA members reinforced the Communist Party's adoption of a more supportive attitude towards the Black Power activists. In 1974, this was codified in the CPA's new program, which embraced the slogans of the Black Power movement. However, it also deleted any references to the economic aspects of Indigenous oppression and the role of trade unions or the working class. This was in line with the rest of the 1974 program, which embraced ideas popular with the new left-wing sentiments of the time, but in a shallow and eclectic manner. This trend was also present in Eric Aarons' 1972 book *Philosophy for an Exploding World*. Aarons was a leading intellectual in the CPA and, as Tom O'Lincoln notes, in Aarons' book the "struggles of third world peoples and Aborigines are given their due, but the working class doesn't appear to have anything to do with them".[320]

This shift to the left was a pretty shallow one, then. Rather than trying to build on the strong points of the Black Power activists (their militancy, self-confidence and defiance), while criticising their weak points (their political eclecticism, understanding of socialism and conceptions of the working class) and fighting to win them to Marxism, the CPA simply tailed behind Black Power. As Gary Nicholls, a left-wing dissident within the CPA, argued in 1975, the Communist Party had "effectively mirrored…changing demands

---

319. Middleton 1977, pp.134–49. See also "The Australian National Minority" in the SPA's theoretical journal *Australian Marxist Review*, 5 (1), January 1976 and 5 (2), June 1976, also by Middleton.
320. O'Lincoln 1985, p.151.

in its changing policy on 'Aborigines' but too often this is where it has left the matter. The Party has not attempted a true **class analysis** of the Black movement".[321]

This put the CPA in a weak position when the movement went into retreat. Following the 1974 recession and the constitutional coup against the Whitlam government, politics started to shift significantly to the right as the balance of class forces moved in favour of the bosses. While strikes continued to be an important feature of Australian society from the late '70s into the '80s, they were no longer underpinned by the same political radicalisation. Weaknesses in all the social movements, already noticeable before 1974, became more pronounced, and what would be identified today as identity politics became more and more dominant as the connection between struggles against oppression, the working class and socialism appeared to fragment.

In this context, the CPA abandoned even the shallow left shift it had undertaken in the early '70s and moved sharply to the right, a turn epitomised by its key role in the stifling Prices and Incomes Accord of 1983, which saw unions enter into a conservatising class-collaborationist pact with the ALP government and the capitalist class. Communist-led unions played an essential part in this. Whatever lingering commitment party members had to the idea that the working class was the agent of social change, that revolution was possible, even that socialism was a realistic goal and that a revolutionary party was essential, these ideas were all massively downplayed, if not totally junked. A 1991 letter to *Tribune* by Joyce Stevens, who had been a CPA member since the 1940s, expressed this growing scepticism:

> Marxism has already demonstrated that it was unable to predict or elaborate the relationships between economic development and the finite nature of the world and its resources, between men and women (even in economic terms) and the depth and resilience of nationalism, racism and the exploitation of indigenous peoples... I do not believe that it is probable or desirable that there will be a return to the years when communist or Left parties appeared to, or in many instances did, provide the central focus for social dissent. New

---

321. Emphasis in the original, *Australian Left Review*, 47, July 1975, p.51. It is also notable that this was the first article on Aboriginal politics to appear in the CPA's theoretical journal since March 1970, a gap of five years.

movements and political concerns have broken up our comfortable "solidarity" and certainty about theories.³²²

Similarly, Sue McCreadie, then economic research officer for the Textile, Clothing and Footwear union and a member of the *Australian Left Review (ALR)* editorial board, argued in an article entitled "Is the Left braindead?":

> Recently I noticed a poster advertising a May Day march which also invited us to "celebrate socialism." The first thing that came to my mind was the slogan from the bicentennial year: "what is there to celebrate?" Because it's not really clear to me what's left of socialism, nor what the Left project is.³²³

This pessimism flowed into the broader left-wing circles influenced by the CPA. The early forms of contemporary privilege theory and settler colonial theory were to a large extent transmitted to the left through Communist Party circles. The theory of internal colonialism, a kind of precursor to settler colonial theory, was adopted by academics around the left, and a series of decolonial study groups were set up throughout the CPA in its last years which emphasised the racism of the Australian working class, its lack of concern for Indigenous issues and the inadequacy of Marxist theory. So Jo Stafford in a 1987 *Tribune* article chastised the left for its "racism" and argued that the "left must realise that all non-Aboriginal people benefit from the theft of Aboriginal land". A lengthy article in the *ALR* on theories of racism argued that "colonialism and post-colonialism are extremely important and poorly understood in Australia, despite the continued existence of colonial attitudes and institutions". Another in *Tribune* explained that the left should adopt a program of racism awareness workshops developed by Christians.³²⁴

The inability of the Communist Party to reconcile Marxism (which it had long since abandoned at any rate) and Indigenous liberation was just one more thing pushing the organisation towards its dissolution in 1991.

---

322. *Tribune*, 3 April 1991, p.23.
323. *Australian Left Review*, 140, June 1992, p.24.
324. *Tribune*, 17 June 1987, p.12; *Australian Left Review*, 89, Spring 1984; *Tribune*, 7 December 1988, p.9. See also CPA member and former Australian Union of Students organiser Marilyn McCormack's speech to the Sydney Socialist Feminist Conference and its call to decolonise the left, reprinted in *Tribune*, 14 October 1987, p.9.

PART THREE

Marxism and the fight for liberation

Chapter eight
Racial, national or colonial oppression?

> The revolutionary left has never been very strong in Australia. While particular historical circumstances have imposed practical limitations, a continual and profound source of weakness has been the absence of revolutionary theory... With this history it is not surprising that the Australian revolutionary left has still not developed a knowledge of the workings of Australian capitalism and its distinctive characteristics.
>
> — Editorial in *Intervention: revolutionary Marxist journal*, 1, April 1972.

WE ARE NOW IN A BETTER POSITION to evaluate the strengths and weaknesses of various approaches that the Australian socialist left and the workers' movement have taken to Indigenous oppression. For the most part, the genuine Marxist tradition has been weak in those "Western" countries with minority Indigenous populations: Canada, the United States, Australia and New Zealand. So it is not particularly surprising that the classical revolutionary Marxist tradition – running from Marx and Engels through the revolutionary left wing of the Second International (especially in Russia and Germany), to the Bolshevik party in Russia and the early years of the Communist International and preserved, in the most difficult circumstances possible, by the Left Opposition and the Trotskyist movement in the 1930s – did not directly produce much writing about the question of Indigenous oppression in general, let alone Indigenous oppression in Australia in particular.

While there has been plenty written about the dynamics of national liberation movements, the oppression of African Americans and migrant populations, there is relatively little in the Marxist canon substantially exploring how Indigenous oppression fits in with revolutionary Marxist politics. To the extent that socialist writers have taken up the question, the vast majority have been strongly influenced by reformist, Stalinist or liberal ideas, severely limiting their ability to navigate the issue.[325]

As we have seen, the Australian socialist left historically viewed Indigenous people in one of two ways. The first emphasised that they are a part of the working class; the second framed them as a separate people, trapped in a colonial relationship with the rest of society. Within these two tendencies, there have been various shades of opinion and nuances, and there have also been some attempts to combine them.

The sections of the early Australian labour movement and socialist left which sympathised with the plight of Indigenous people focused on what made them similar to the rest of the working class. Drawing attention to their indigeneity was viewed by left-wing workers with the suspicion that it was most likely motivated by racial bigotry. Instead, they emphasised how, if given the chance, Indigenous people could be like good white workers, and how they were different from other non-European people perceived as more of a threat, such as the Chinese. So the Aboriginal worker Andy Stepney, leader of the Cobar shearers' camp in the 1894 shearers' strike, could be described as a "real white man at heart" by a newspaper of the shearers' union.[326]

This was a defensive reaction, by both non-indigenous and Indigenous workers themselves, to the extreme racism of Australian society at the time. Its positive side was that, at a time when almost every institution in Australia sought to exclude Indigenous people, this attitude attempted to include them in the broader working-class struggle for self-emancipation. The negative, of course, was that by downplaying the particular way that Indigenous people were oppressed by capitalism, it failed to appreciate how, in order to create a genuinely united working-class movement, the specific aspects of oppression suffered by Indigenous people would have to be challenged.

The Communist Party was able to move beyond some of the limitations of the early labour movement by conceiving of Indigenous people as a specially oppressed section of the working class. This combined the earlier

---

325. A partial exception to this is writings on the Latin American left, but both the general context of Indigenous struggle and the history of the socialist movement in these countries is substantially different from that in "Western" countries with minority Indigenous populations.

326. *The Worker* (Wagga), 8 September 1894, p.2.

emphasis on brining Indigenous people into the wider labour movement with a much greater sensitivity to the political aspects of the oppression Indigenous people faced. It therefore pointed to the need to develop concrete proposals for fighting that oppression within the broader framework of socialist politics.

The CPA, however, was also the originator of the second perspective: that Indigenous people remained colonised. This idea was also taken up by various offshoots from the Communist Party and broader left-wing circles in the trade union movement, as well as academics and the sections of the middle classes influenced by the Communist Party's politics.

The idea that Indigenous people were a colonially oppressed people can only be understood with broader reference to the Stalinist politics of the CPA. From the mid-1930s the Communist Party argued that Australia was not an independent capitalist country and that all Australian people (including the Indigenous population) were exploited by imperialism. From this standpoint, Indigenous people were considered the most oppressed and exploited section of a whole population oppressed and exploited by the multinationals and US imperialism. So, in 1967, the CPA program for Indigenous rights argued:

> Those who benefit chiefly from the wage-robbery of Aboriginal and Island workers and from the theft of Aboriginal lands are the big (mostly foreign) pastoral and mining concerns.
>
> It is the power of these and other monopolies over State and Federal Governments that stands in the way of the liberation of the Aborigines and Islanders, prevents abolition of the backward state of life forced on them and denies them land ownership and control of their own affairs.
>
> The struggle for Aboriginal and Islanders' rights therefore, is an important part of the struggle of the Australian people against monopoly and its governments, for radical social change and for socialism.
>
> For this reason, the fight for Aboriginal and Islanders' rights should be regarded as an important aspect of the whole political struggle in Australia,

not a matter for a few well wishers, but one to be taken up by all progressive people, all true patriots.[327]

This section of the program is entitled "the concern of all" and begins by arguing that the key divide in white attitudes towards Indigenous people is between "the democratic, humanist viewpoint of the great majority" and the "viewpoint of the few who profit from exploitation of Aborigines and Islanders". The end goal of Indigenous liberation was particularly ambiguous, as the CPA's understanding of "socialism" at this point was reformist, focusing on the election of a left-wing Labor government committed to nationalisation.

Maoists who split from the CPA embraced an even cruder version of this argument. In *The Black Resistance*, Fergus Robinson and Barry York argued that Aboriginal people were the first great Australian patriots. They fought a heroic battle for Australian independence against British colonialism. And they are part of a pantheon of supposedly patriotic rebellions, including the early convict revolts, the Eureka stockade, the WWI campaign against conscription, the struggle against the Kerr coup and so on. Robinson and York concluded:

> In the light of the quarrying of Australia by foreign monopolies the demand for Aboriginal land rights effectively calls for the expulsion of the multinational mining conglomerates from our shores. Dramatically it poses the question who should rule our Continent, the Australian people or foreign imperialism?... Those militant Aborigines today who heroically defend their land from imperialist encroachment are performing the highest patriotic duty to the whole Australian people.[328]

The Maoists were but the crudest edge of a broad-left consensus on the issue. The idea that Australia was dominated by US imperialism or multinational companies – or that, at the very least, it needed to break with subservience to the US and pursue an independent foreign policy – was accepted by virtually everyone on the left except for some, but not all, Trotskyist groups. The

---
327. CPA 1967.
328. Robinson and York 1977, pp.124–5.

analysis was not only wrong in theory but was used to justify a Popular Front approach that was totally incapable of challenging Indigenous oppression in practice. It deflected attention away from the key enemy of both Indigenous people and the working class – the Australian bourgeoisie – onto foreigners. It promoted a class-collaborationist Australian nationalism. As we have seen in the previous chapter, these issues were not clarified within the CPA during its "left turn" of the early 1970s.

The legacy of these Stalinist conceptions of nationalism, anti-imperialism and Indigenous struggle can be found among sections of the Australian left within the broader framework of identity politics and a kind of third worldist romanticism. For example, the recently established Black People's Union (BPU), a "First Nations-led revolutionary organisation", while acknowledging that the "Australian state is not exploited in the US-led imperial system but is itself a sub-imperial power", claims that the "continued colonisation of this continent is played out in the destruction of land and extraction of resources for foreign profit, namely the United States and Britain". It argues that anti-imperialism is relevant for Indigenous struggles because they are the struggles of "300+ sovereign Indigenous nations" against the Australian state, which oppresses them to help multinational corporations exploit Indigenous land.[329]

Here, a Stalinist-influenced analysis of Indigenous struggle is used not to promote a class-collaborationist approach, but to provide an equally inaccurate portrayal of the place of Indigenous people in modern Australian society. While the BPU states that it supports the struggles of workers and even recognises that "workers are the backbone of society", this is undermined by its conception of an Indigenous struggle centred on sovereign Indigenous nations fighting an anti-imperialist struggle against the colonial state. This neither describes nor explains the situation of the vast majority of working-class Indigenous people living in large industrial cities, whose experiences with racism result from the actions of capitalist institutions (the police, government departments, bosses and politicians) rather than foreign multinationals.

Even the struggles of Indigenous people living in remote communities rarely have the dynamics presented by the BPU. Many of the problems in these communities stem more from the direct material interests of Australian

---

329. Black Peoples Union 2023.

capitalism than its enabling of foreign companies to exploit land and labour. As discussed in chapter two, while some communities face off against exploitative fossil fuel companies, a significant problem for many remote communities is the total lack of interest from government or private capital in their development on any basis whatsoever. They are seen as ghetto camps to be "administered" until such a time as they can be rationalised out of existence to save government departments a bit of money and trouble.

There are certainly Indigenous campaigns that do pit themselves against multinational corporations. But this is not always the case, and many of the immediate challenges such struggles face have little direct relationship to imperialism.

Even in the classic land rights struggle of the Gurindji, things were more complicated. The struggle started as a fight against the British-owned Vestey Group. But as the years went on, Vestey became more and more irrelevant – the main struggle took place between the Gurindji people and the federal Whitlam government. This in turn was shaped not just by the interests of multinationals, but by the concerns of domestic pastoralists in northern and central Australia about what the nature of the Gurindjis' claim to the land would be, and thus the nature of Aboriginal land rights more generally.

The BPU is a small organisation drawing on a more worked-out Stalinist worldview, but the idea that Indigenous peoples are nations fighting some kind of anti-colonial or anti-imperialist struggle is common among left-wing people. Independent Aboriginal senator Lidia Thorpe, for instance, views herself as being part of a "Blak sovereign movement". While many Indigenous people have important links to, and identity relations stemming from, their connection to Country and community, Indigenous people in Australia are *not* organised into sovereign Indigenous nations and are not likely to be anytime soon.

It is true that there are separate Indigenous communities across this continent, many of which have established organisations that are supposed to represent general community interests, from land councils to smaller bodies. But it is worth noting that many Indigenous people have only weak links with such communities, and most of the difficulties these community bodies face result from modern capitalist society, which places business profits above human life. Indigenous communities and their organisations cannot escape this – precisely because they *don't* have any real sovereignty or autonomy within Australian capitalism. What these Indigenous bodies have ended up looking like is not much different from organisations set up historically by migrant, LGBTI+ or women's groups – that is, campaigning, lobbying or administrative organisations established to advance the claims of particular sections of the Australian population.

More radically minded Indigenous and non-indigenous activists can agree with much of this criticism, but still argue that existing Indigenous community organisations need to be reformed or replaced by new bodies that can lay the basis for sovereign Indigenous nations. This is not realistic either. While Indigenous identities and cultures might be strengthened into the future, there is little possibility of there being even one sovereign nation co-existing on the Australian continent, let alone "300+". For this to be achieved, there would need to be a social force capable of causing a political crisis of such enormity that it would fracture the Australian state. Indigenous people are less than 4 percent of the population; they do not have the socio-economic or political weight to carry out such a project, and there is no reason why any of the social classes in Australian society (the working class, the middle classes, the capitalist class) would engage in such a struggle. Indigenous "nations" are likely to remain Indigenous communities and associated organisations. Some may be more or less democratic or grassroots or activist, but they are not capable of challenging the Australian state.

At any rate, to narrow the nature of contemporary Indigenous struggles to only those land rights struggles taking place against or involving foreign multinationals is to render much of modern Indigenous political life inexplicable. Addressing the various challenges faced by Indigenous people today will primarily mean a confrontation with Australian capitalism, not a struggle of Indigenous nations against foreign imperialism. This is not to say that there is no connection between anti-imperialist struggles and the fight for Indigenous rights; it is healthy that many left-wing Indigenous people see parallels between their issues and global campaigns against racism and injustice. However, the links presented by groups like the BPU are misleading.

To further untangle some of the issues in the socialist left's historical understanding of Indigenous oppression, we must clarify some of the terminology being used. In the Marxist tradition, a *racially oppressed minority* is a group of people who are structurally discriminated against due to their "race", however it has been particularly socially constructed. Socialists should fight against every manifestation of such oppression, but if this is the only characteristic of a group, then it is not struggling either for national liberation nor against colonial oppression.

A *colonially oppressed group* is a population, often a majority, colonised by another nation-state which occupies the region in which this group lives. Such a situation is defined by a central antagonism between the colonially oppressed people and their oppressors, even when both these categories contain within themselves various classes and other divisions. In this case, socialists should support the demand for the oppressed group to defeat the colonial occupier and retake control of their region. But they should also be attuned to the limits of such an anti-colonial movement and, in the words of Lenin, make sure that they don't falsely give it a "communist colouring" by pretending that the overthrow of a colonial oppressor is necessarily the same thing as overthrowing capitalism.

Finally, a *national minority* is an oppressed section of society in a particular nation-state, or even multiple nation-states, which has formed a national consciousness, most often (but as we shall see later in this chapter, not exclusively) expressed by a demand for the creation of a new state controlled by members of the national minority group. In this situation, socialists should of course oppose the oppression faced by such a group. But how to relate to the demands of a national minority is a concrete question that will be explored in more detail below.

These categories of racial oppression, colonial oppression and national minority are not necessarily mutually exclusive, of course. National minorities can suffer racial or colonial oppression, colonially oppressed groups have often – although not always – been oppressed on the basis of their race, and so forth. In addition, the nature of a group's oppression can change over time; a people who are nationally or colonially oppressed in one era can be oppressed merely on the basis of race in another. So the Indigenous peoples of what is now called Mexico were historically oppressed as a national and colonial minority by the Spanish Empire, then later as a racially oppressed group in the República de Indios under the Spanish colonial system.

Despite such nuances, drawing out these three defintions is an attempt to drill down into some of the different ways different people can be oppressed – that is the point of distinguishing between them.

It is also worth noting that each of these categories is almost always cross-class; capitalists, the middle classes and workers can all be bound together due to their common racial, colonial or national oppression, even while such commonality is at the same time fractured by fundamental social and economic divisions within an oppressed group.

Indigenous people are undoubtedly a racially oppressed minority in Australia, and the majority are a racially oppressed section of the working class. As we have explored in many parts of this book, they do not constitute a colonially oppressed population. But when it comes to the national question, things are more complicated. Indigenous people have not cohered themselves into a nation which claims its own national territory or strives towards national liberation, in the way that the Algerians, Vietnamese, Indonesians or Indians did historically. However, the history of brutal oppression and their resistance to it has led Indigenous people to develop a national consciousness. This isn't a totally unique situation. A similar phenomenon has occurred among African Americans in the United States who, while not forming a nation, have developed various forms of Black nationalism. Russian revolutionary leader Leon Trotsky addressed this issue nearly 100 years ago:

> [T]he suppression of the Negroes pushes them towards a political and national unity... We of course do not obligate the Negroes to become a nation; whether they are is a question of their consciousness, that is what they desire and what they strive for... An abstract criterion is not decisive in this question; far more decisive is the historical consciousness of a group, their feelings, their impulses. But that too is not determined accidentally but rather by the situation and all the attendant circumstances.[330]

---

330. Trotsky 1967, p.31. Published after Trotsky's death based on discussions from the 1930s.

Demands for self-determination and sovereignty raised by the vast majority of Indigenous activists today are calls for greater autonomy within the Australian state, not the formation of a new Indigenous nation-state. While it is not theoretically impossible that the situation may change at some point in the future, only a tiny number of Indigenous people have ever advocated for national separation. This is a separate question from that of Indigenous nationalism, however; oppressed groups can develop a strong national identity without it being tied to a program for a new nation-state.

In Australia, there have been signs of the significant strengthening of Indigenous national identities. Aboriginal and Torres Strait Islanders have separate "national" flags, Indigenous people often describe themselves as belonging to particular Indigenous nations, there are projects to strengthen and regenerate Indigenous cultures and languages – even in places where these have been almost entirely destroyed by Australian capitalism – and the issue of land rights links at least some Indigenous identities to particular territories.[331]

This adds special dimensions to the Indigenous struggle in Australia which socialists can't ignore. However, it doesn't alter the fact that Indigenous people constitute an oppressed population *within* Australian society and that most Indigenous people are members of the working class.

A common objection to this framework is that it ignores Indigenous demands for self-determination. However, support for self-determination doesn't have to be linked to a conception of Indigenous people as a colonised people. After all, many oppressed groups have particular, specific aspects to their oppression which raise concrete and varied demands: migrant groups have demanded the right not just to be "accepted" into Australian society, but for their cultural heritage to be supported financially by state funding and by being given an autonomous space in mainstream culture; African Americans have raised a whole series of complex demands around both integration into society and resistance to assimilation; LGBTI+ groups have demanded that schools introduce educational programs around sexuality and sexual health which consider the broad spectrum of sexuality in modern society.

---

331. For an interesting examination of both class formation and national consciousness among Indigenous people in Australia, albeit from a Stalinised framework, see Middleton 2020.

The demand for Indigenous self-determination should be understood in this context, as a specific political demand raised by Indigenous people due to the particular aspects of their oppression which differ from those of other oppressed groups in Australia. Demands for self-determination must also be concretely assessed from a political perspective, particularly because "self-determination" can be used to mean anything from genuine land rights, to donating to Indigenous small businesses, to greater Indigenous representation in the media. It is also important to see how Indigenous identity and political demands have evolved over time, not only due to changes in Indigenous populations and in their relationship with broader society, but also due to political shifts taking place within that society. As Heidi Norman has explained regarding the demand for land rights:

> It is tempting to portray Aboriginal land activism in terms of a continuous primary political concern for Aboriginal people and a belated realisation by government of Aboriginal people's survival and resistance. However… the demands for land shifted and changed with changing ideas, political possibilities and local conditions, and continue to do so today.[332]

While demands for access to land have been a persistent feature of Indigenous struggles, these struggles have taken "different forms" and been "shaped by different circumstances, conditions and possibilities". Demands for land rights in the 1920s "were initially narrower and more practical, concerned with preserving and recovering those lands set aside from the mid-1850s 'for the use of Aborigines' as compared to those of the 1960s".[333] Different again were the urban land rights claims developed by Black Power activists of the 1970s. They embraced the demand for land rights not so much as a practical, material demand for themselves but more as an assertion of their Black identity; they strove for a regeneration of their culture, from which they were often more cut off than those living in Indigenous communities away from the cities, whom the urban radicals regarded as the "real Blacks".[334] This intersected with the

---
332. Norman 2015, p.2.
333. Norman 2015, pp.2–3.
334. See Gilbert 2013 [1977], pp.128–30.

anti-materialist, spiritual outlook of the 1960s student counterculture, which romanticised pre-capitalist life.

During this period, Black Power activists also articulated a form of nationalist consciousness that was quite different from today's common emphasis on belonging to specific Indigenous nations. This was a pan-Aboriginal Black nationalism which was conceived of as spanning the entire continent, deeply connected to the struggles of both African Americans and anti-colonial fighters throughout the third world. Gary Foley has linked this shift to the impact of native title legislation:

> One of the primary effects of Native Title was that it dispersed the pan-Aboriginal movement. People suddenly thought it was more important for them to think in terms of their own first and foremost, thus fracturing what had been a really strong national movement of resistance.[335]

Whether Indigenous people strive to assert themselves as a nationally cohered group, and exactly how they do so, is a question for them to decide democratically, in the face of future political and social developments; this differs from how the Communist Party historically approached the question. During the first half of the 1930s, the CPA simultaneously held the positions both that Indigenous people were a specially oppressed section of the working class and that they were a national minority. As we have seen, in the mid- to late 1930s Tom Wright attempted to clarify this contradiction. His argument was that each definition held true, but for different sections of the Indigenous population. So the Indigenous people living on remote communities and missions were a national minority, whereas the Indigenous people on the east coast living and working alongside whites were not essentially any different from other "coloured" or migrant workers. They were discriminated against, but they were not a national minority.

Wright's insistence on a strict separation between different Indigenous peoples was progressively abandoned by the CPA through the 1950s and early '60s. However, other bifurcations appeared. In the post-war years, the emphasis was on how Indigenous people were part of the working class and

---

335. "Can the Voice to Parliament deliver radical change? With Gary Foley", 7am Podcast, 4 January 2023.

their struggle was part of the broader fight of working-class and democratic forces against monopoly capitalism. At the same time, this was combined with a greater appreciation of the emergence of a pan-Aboriginal identity and a related but independent Torres Strait Islander identity.

The problem with the definition of Indigenous people as a national minority was that, for the CPA, it often became a substitute for developing a more rigorous Marxist analysis of Indigenous oppression and struggle. The term "national minority" was an umbrella concept with which Communists could argue that Indigenous people were fighting for basic civil rights, or for a separate nation-state (or states), or for self-determination within the framework of the Australian nation, or that they were engaged in a national liberation struggle against colonialism – or anything in between.

The CPA's theoretical shifts were responses to real developments in the dynamics of Indigenous identity and struggle, but the party's commitment to a Stalinist political outlook limited how far this could go. It was stuck within a narrow framework and a highly distorted understanding of class relations and capitalism. Meanwhile, the far left outside of the CPA has historically been both too weak a force and too politically confused to have developed much of an alternative framework for understanding Indigenous oppression.[336]

In summary, Indigenous people constitute a racially oppressed group within Australian capitalism. The group is made up of different socio-economic classes and has its own political particularities due to its Indigenous nature, as well as a nascent national consciousness. The next chapter will examine the development of the Aboriginal middle and capitalist classes, and their relationship to the capitalist system as a whole.

---

336. Partial exceptions to this can be found in Townsend 2009 and Fieldes 1997.

Chapter nine

The new Indigenous middle class and Australian capitalism

> [T]he ones who prominently say they are Aboriginal leaders are terribly wrong. There going backwards...and what's mesmerised our supposed leaders is the carrot of millions of dollars. It's not working class principles or raising our people up. In the meantime people get fooled because...we are well up in films, entertainment, football, all world class. Okay, but politically we've got nothing.
>
> — Ray Peckham, 2014.[337]

> I would argue that today the Black middle class are as great a problem as anything else that the Aboriginal community confronts. In the same way as the Black middle class in the African American situation has been the buffer between the ruling class establishment and the shitkickers.
>
> — Gary Foley, 2021.[338]

Over the Labour Day long weekend in October 1977, 200 Aboriginal activists and their supporters met at the Black Theatre in Redfern to discuss the launching of a new campaign for land rights. It was out of this meeting that the NSW Aboriginal Land Council was born. Its first convenor was Kevin Cook, a left-wing trade unionist and radical Aboriginal activist, and the committee was filled with activists who had been forged in the struggles of the '60s and '70s. The conference also established the Trade Union Committee on Aboriginal Rights (TUCAR) in order to link the land rights campaign with working-class organisations.

Forty-five years later, a very different meeting involving the Land Council took place in Redfern. On 2 August 2022, an emergency community meeting

---

337. From a NSWALC video interview "Legends of Land Rights – Ray Peckham" on YouTube.
338. From a video interview "Gary Foley the Godfather of Aboriginal activism speaking the truth" uploaded by melbournecalling on YouTube.

was held at the National Centre of Indigenous Excellence to protest against the closure of the centre and the summary dismissal of 50 staff members. The sacked workers, most of them Indigenous, had been offered a humiliating $700 if they would sign non-disclosure agreements with the owners of the centre – who just so happened to be the NSW Aboriginal Land Council.[339]

The co-founder and CEO of Redfern Youth Connect, Margaret Haumono, told the meeting that she and others had spoken to the Land Council and had been told that the closure was "not our [the Land Council's] problem". The meeting responded with cries of "gutless dogs" and "shame". Wiradjuri, Yuin and Gadigal woman Nadeena Dixon, granddaughter of the Aboriginal trade union activist Chicka Dixon, said that "too many of our community leaders have become dictators", while fired staff expressed disgust at being thrown out the door with little communication.

As if to confirm Dixon's words, two representatives from the Land Council then pushed their way to the front of the meeting and demanded the right to reply to their critics. One of the representatives berated the crowd, explaining that "we can't run this place on a loss" and that the only alternative to closing down the centre was to sell off the whole site to developers.

The other representative argued that there wasn't any money to be made out of swimming pools and gyms, and revealed that the Land Council was considering handing over the whole operation to the PCYC (Police and Community Youth Club). This was met with outrage from the crowd, most of whom were all too familiar with the history and culture of the police in Redfern. It certainly didn't help that Land Council representatives had been given a police escort to the meeting.

The Land Council had gone from an organisation run by a bunch of radicals and unionists to an organisation dominated by a group of Indigenous bureaucrats dedicated to fostering private enterprise and respectability. Its incorporation into the capitalist system is emblematic of a broader shift in many Indigenous organisations.

Originally, the NSW Land Council had been a voluntary grassroots activist group without any government funding. It relied on the resources of

---

339. The following description of the NCIE protest meeting is based on personal observations by the author, reported in Humphreys 2022a.

Tranby College, which had been established by the unions, for its land rights campaigning. In wake of the passage of the Aboriginal Land Rights Act (NSW) in 1983, the Land Council was formally constituted as a statutory corporation. At first, continuity seemed to outweigh change: Cook was made chairperson and the council still featured a number of prominent left-wing figures.[340]

However, by the 1990s the Land Council had undergone a significant transformation. From 1983 to 1998 it accumulated $281 million from land tax payments paid in compensation for stolen land. This money – far less than Indigenous people deserve in reparations – allowed the council to become a self-funding independent body. At the same time, it served as the basis for the strengthening and expansion of an increasingly conservative and capitalist-minded Indigenous bureaucracy. A key moment in this process took place in 1990, when a series of amendments were passed to the Land Rights Act which gave the NSW Land Council and its subsidiaries the ability to sell, mortgage or exchange the land they had gained through land rights claims. The same amendments also made the Land Council's elected seats into full-time salaried positions.

In 2012, the impact of these amendments became clear when the NSW Land Council applied for a coal seam gas permit covering 321,300 square kilometres in conjunction with an undisclosed business partner. This application came after three petroleum exploration licence applications earlier in the same year. It had been pushed by the full-time leaders of the Land Council, but the application was met with widespread opposition from Indigenous people and local land councils, particularly in the Northern Rivers and Illawarra regions where the coal seam gas projects were proposed. Fed up with the Land Council's schemes, a number of left-wing Indigenous activists set up the NSW Aboriginal Land Rights Association Inc in 2021. It was designed to be "a grassroots Aboriginal Community Controlled Organisation with a mandate centred around upholding the purpose of the NSW Aboriginal Land Rights Act 1983".[341]

The development of the NSW Aboriginal Land Council was not an anomaly. The Aboriginal Housing Company (AHC) was similarly established

---
340. See Norman 2015 for the history of the NSWALC.
341. Howden 2012.

out of the struggles to maintain Indigenous control over the Block in Redfern during the 1970s. In the 2000s, the AHC helped initiate the Pemulwuy Project to redevelop the Block, supposedly in order to regenerate this local Aboriginal community area. However, when designs became public in 2014, it became clear that the AHC was primarily interested in realising the untapped commercial value of the land, with space overwhelmingly allocated to retail, office space and expensive student housing. This led local Aboriginal activists to establish the Redfern Aboriginal Tent Embassy, which resisted the development for over a year. Eventually, federal Aboriginal Affairs Minister Nigel Scullion brokered a deal in which 62 homes would be built for Indigenous families at the same time as any commercial development of the Block.

Similarly, the Condobolin Local Aboriginal Land Council has come under sustained criticism for years from Aboriginal residents who say their housing has fallen into disrepair, with black mould, termites, electrical faults and broken sewerage pipes. "We've got our elders who are in their '70s and '80s that are living in houses with black mould, where the roofs are peeling off, the walls have deteriorated", Kira-Lea Dargin, a Wiradjuri woman and advocate for several of the residents, told ABC News. In July 2021, the Land Council signed 18 eviction notices after residents refused to pay rent. Writing for ABC News, Ella Archibald-Binge summed up the situation well, noting that this "crisis has become a microcosm of a broader issue across NSW, as relationships break down between Aboriginal communities and the local bodies set up to represent them".[342]

The new Indigenous middle class

There have always been political differences among Indigenous people in Australia, of course. In particular, there has long been a minority of Indigenous people who have found a place within the capitalist establishment. But until the later decades of the 20th century, this was confined to a tiny number of individuals who were easy to dismiss as sellouts rather than evidence of an established social phenomenon. The broadening of an Indigenous middle

---
342. Archibald-Binge 2021.

class, and the development of a small but growing Indigenous capitalist class, adds new dimensions to the differentiation within the Indigenous population.

Probably the most public expressions of these changes are the proposal for an Indigenous Voice to Parliament and the various state-based treaty processes currently underway, with the prospect for more in the future – including on a federal level. There have also been shifts in government and corporate policy – from economic partnerships to cultural recognition to an expansion in professional and managerial roles targeted at Indigenous people – as well as broader cultural shifts in how Indigenous culture and history are understood and discussed in the media, the education system and so forth.

Such shifts can be dismissed as mere tokenism. If by this it is meant they will not radically transform the oppressive conditions most Indigenous people lived under, then that is true. But it is wrong to think that they will have no impact at all. They will, and indeed already have, had a beneficial impact for a subsection of Indigenous people – what Indigenous activist Gary Foley calls the "Blak Bourgeoisie".[343]

Italian Marxist Antonio Gramsci describes this process well in his *Prison Notebooks*. He explains how ruling classes gradually absorb a layer of people from antagonistic oppressed or exploited groups in order to give greater legitimacy to their rule and widen the social base of those who have a material interest in its continuation.[344] This is particularly marked in oppressed groups that contain within themselves class divisions, such as women, migrants, and LGBTI+ people.

The emergence of a new Indigenous elite in Australia is the result of a number of concrete historical factors coming together. First of all, there is the creation of what academic Tim Rowse has called the "Indigenous Estate":

> In the last third of the 20th century, nearly one-fifth of the Australian land mass was transferred to Indigenous Australians' ownership. By 2013, Indigenous interests had been recognised over more than half of Australia – a combination of land rights, native title, and Indigenous Land Use Agreements enabled by the assertion of native title. To this estate, hectares will be added

---

343. Hall 2023.
344. Gramsci 1971, in particular pp.58–9 in his *Notes on Italian History*.

every year through purchases by the Indigenous Land Corporation (ILC), a statutory authority set up by the Keating government in June 1995. As long as the ILC's endowment yields an annual purchase fund, there is no limit to the acreage that can be, to some degree, Indigenous land.[345]

There are very stringent limits to this "Indigenous Estate" – mainly that it cannot infringe on commercial interests such as mining, tourism and farming. Nevertheless, in combination with myriad urban-based Indigenous businesses, consultancy firms, NGOs and community organisations, this estate has created "thousands of organisations making up the 'Indigenous sector', the joint product of Indigenous political mobilisation and state funding and legislation".[346] As well, there has been an expansion in the employment of Indigenous people in traditional middle-class academic, legal, media, governmental and cultural roles within institutions such as universities, law firms, media companies, state bureaucracies and cultural projects.

Any progress for Indigenous people entails some degree of bureaucratisation. If Indigenous people win greater control over their own affairs then organisations will be set up to facilitate and manage this, and in the context of capitalist society, such organisations will inevitably develop some degree of institutional conservatism. This isn't unique to Indigenous people – any oppressed or exploited group that manages to win some degree of acceptance in capitalist society encounters similar problems. In the wake of the US civil rights movement, there was a flowering of Black bureaucracies within government departments and private businesses. Even the workers' struggle has developed bureaucratised organisations within the trade union movement in response to its partial victories.

The problem is not necessarily in and of itself the emergence of these bureaucracies as a byproduct of social struggle, but when the dangers and challenges of this situation are ignored or downplayed, rather than criticised and understood.

Another factor in the development of an Indigenous elite has been the conscious intervention of the state and sections of private capital.

---

345. Rowse 2017, p.287.
346. Rowse 2017, p.380.

This factor has been particularly important in Australia because prior to the 1970s there was little class differentiation among the Indigenous population. Unlike Indigenous peoples in New Zealand or the Americas, pre-invasion Aboriginal societies here did not have class hierarchies, and after colonisation Indigenous groups were unable to develop any kind of independent economic base. Thus government and private capital have played a key role in creating opportunities for Indigenous businesses and bureaucracies to grow.

This approach has reflected a major shift in ruling-class thinking on Indigenous issues. An early sign was the Howard government's 1998 amendment to the Native Title Act, which both weakened and entrenched the legislation. Native title has gone from being one of the most controversial political issues in Australia to one on which there is now a large degree of consensus, as David Ritter has explained:

> On and off between 1992 and 1998, native title was staggeringly divisive and controversial; the subject of immense political storm and legal battles giving rise to numerous banner headlines, blockbuster parliamentary debates and marathon litigation in front of the High Court. At times, wilder opinion forecast the break-up of Australia, the collapse of the economy and outbreaks of violence... Students born in the last twenty years often look up from their desks in some puzzlement when one tries to evoke the hysteria and volume of debate that once existed over the recognition of native title... Native title is now just part of the furniture; or maybe, so dim is the collective awareness of the legal doctrine once dubbed a "revolution", that it can be thought of as no more than a design on the national wallpaper.[347]

This newfound acceptance by the ruling class is largely because the leaders of the mining, pastoral and tourism industries have come to see that they can get most of what they desire through the framework of native title. Whatever constraints or conflicts it might occasionally give rise to are offset by the ease with which their plans can be approved under the cover of "consultation". Clear victories for Indigenous communities are rare and hard fought for

---

347. Ritter 2009, p.xii.

under the existing native title system, and the spirit of "consensus" between Indigenous community leaders and mining bosses has largely benefitted the latter.

In general terms, Australia today is going down a path similar to that forged by Canada and New Zealand decades ago. As in those countries, the new policies of governments and corporations will not end or even significantly ameliorate Indigenous oppression. However, they will increase the scale and significance of the Indigenous upper and middle class in Australian society, and irreversibly change the contours of Indigenous politics.

Black capitalists

From the political establishment, there seems to have been a clear push towards "partnerships" with Indigenous leaders in the wake of Tony Abbott's 2015 campaign to close 150 Indigenous communities in Western Australia. While there was general agreement within government policy circles that "rationalising" the number of Indigenous communities was a worthy goal, Abbott's gung-ho attitude had generated more opposition than they were comfortable with – particularly as there was also growing public consciousness around issues such as racist policing and Australia Day. What these policy advisors proposed was greater engagement and partnerships with Indigenous leaders to try to avoid such opposition emerging in the future. The fruits of this can be seen on a number of fronts.

The Morrison government made a concerted effort to develop an Indigenous capitalist and middle class. From September 2020 to September 2021 the federal government's Indigenous Procurement Policy saw 10,920 government contracts, valued at $1.09 billion, awarded to 943 Indigenous businesses. This is set to increase in coming years, with Albanese maintaining the goal that 3 percent of the value of Commonwealth contracts be awarded to Indigenous businesses from 2022. It is notable that it is often government departments traditionally associated with the hard right of politics that have had some of the biggest contracts with Indigenous businesses. The largest number of contracts is with the Department of Defence, which signed 6,476 contracts (valued at $610 million) in 2020–21. State and territory governments have their own Indigenous procurement policies as well, similarly running into the hundreds of millions of dollars.[348]

To take just one example, the Department of Defence signed a $452 million contract with Indigenous-owned construction company Pacific Services Group Holdings (PSG) to work on redeveloping Garden Island dockyards. The director of PSG is Indigenous man Troy Rugless, a former rugby league player, who has been involved in the construction industry for years as a director of several companies. Through the government's procurement policy PSG has gone from a small cleaning service in a rundown warehouse to a multi-division construction company aspiring to registration on the Australian stock exchange.[349]

The Indigenous Procurement Policy has helped to facilitate the rapid growth in the number of Indigenous business owners, albeit from a very low starting point. Many start on more lucrative government jobs before competing in the private sector. Between 2006 and 2018, the number of Indigenous businesses jumped by almost 74 percent. The gross income for these businesses increased by 115 percent in the same period – by 2018 it had reached $4.88 billion. This probably underestimates the true figures, as it only includes businesses that are both at least 50 percent Indigenous-owned and are officially registered as Indigenous businesses. Other estimates put the number of Indigenous owner-managers at around 17,900 in 2016 (an increase of 30 percent compared to 2011), a figure that would be even higher today.[350]

While Indigenous businesses are still a very small section of capital, they are growing disproportionately. The proportion of non-indigenous people who are business owners is far greater than the proportion of the Indigenous population who are business owners, of course, but the gap is narrowing. Interestingly, registered Indigenous companies are larger on average than their non-indigenous counterparts, with a report published in 2018 finding they had an average gross income of $1.6 million and 14 employees, compared to $400,000 and two employees for the wider community.[351] A report by

---

348. National Indigenous Australians Agency 2021.
349. Australian Defence Force Magazine 2019.
350. Evans, Polidano, Moschion, Langton, Storey, Jensen and Kurland 2021 and Shirodkar, Hunter and Foley 2018.
351. Evans et al., 2021.

Supply Nation, an organisation that connects Indigenous and non-indigenous businesses, found that despite the impact of COVID-19 in the years 2019–21, "there was an increase in Indigenous businesses across all types of business ownership with the most growth observed in the number of registered sole traders and partnerships".[352]

Private capital has also played a role in promoting the formation of Indigenous businesses. In 2011, Fortescue Metals Group (FMG) awarded just $20 million in contracts to two Indigenous-owned companies. By 2021 FMG was awarding $3 billion to Indigenous businesses. One of these was Indigenous-owned mining maintenance contractor Warrikal Engineering, which recently signed a contract worth $350 million. Warrikal was only founded in 2017 and has already entered into major contracts with Rio Tinto and Pilbara Minerals. The company's workforce is around 20 percent Indigenous, and the chief executive is Amanda Healy, a Wonnarua Koori woman, who has run several different businesses and was recently appointed as an adjunct professor at Curtin University's business school.[353]

In 2019 the Business Council of Australia (BCA) launched the "Raise the Bar" initiative, which pledged businesses to collectively spend $3 billion on contracts with Indigenous businesses over five years. The businesses that signed up include Qantas, the Commonwealth Bank, Lendlease, BHP, BP, Rio Tinto, BAE Systems and Westpac. "Reconciliation Action Plans" have also become widespread in the business world, particularly at some of the largest companies in Australia including BHP, Lendlease and 44 others on the ASX200.[354]

Mining companies in particular have been keen to reset their relationships with the Indigenous community. This is particularly the case in the wake of Rio Tino's deliberate destruction of 46,000-year-old artifacts in Juukan Gorge and further revelations that they dumped heritage material from the Marandoo mine into a Darwin rubbish dump in the 1990s. The Wintawari Guruma Aboriginal Corporation, whose land the Marandoo mine is on, has cut ties with Rio Tinto and a moratorium has been placed on mining in the Juukan

---

352. Supply Nation 2022, p.8.
353. Smit 2021a and Smit 2021b.
354. BCA 2019.

Gorge. This has caused a reduction of about 2 million tonnes in Rio Tinto's production. In the aftermath of this disaster, their rivals BHP have taken the opportunity for some Black-washing, by pushing for the South Australian and Western Australian governments to introduce strict penalties for companies that damage heritage sites as well as giving Indigenous communities greater ability to appeal heritage decisions. This cynical campaign is being launched with the full knowledge that they will be less affected by such legislation than their competitors at Rio Tinto.[355]

The goal of these mining groups is to neutralise the morally powerful opposition to their projects posed by Aboriginal activism. The agreement that BHP signed in 2021 with the Barada Barna Aboriginal Corporation is a case in point. It is chock full of cheap symbolism, like giving a local airport an Indigenous name and painting Indigenous cultural murals at the airport and the mining site. At the same time, it prioritises building up Indigenous corporations and consciously seeks to enmesh them in the mining industry in order to undermine potential criticisms. This includes a historic level of investment, training and contracts for local Indigenous businesses, which will last for multiple generations. Both BHP and the Barada Barna Aboriginal Corporation frame this project as one of "self-determination", which shows the extent to which this term has become detached from any radical, let alone anti-capitalist, association. Barada Barna Aboriginal Corporation chairperson Luarna Walsh celebrated the agreement as one that "sets Barada Barna on a path of self-determination":

> It will ensure BBAC is sustainable into the future and help our next generation of descendants achieve their goals through schooling and university, and employment and training. This Agreement also provides BBAC with the ability to diversify our income streams, by creating Traditional Owner business that can tender for a variety of contracts on Country.[356]

---

355. Knowles 2021.
356. BHP & BBAC 2021.

Black bureaucrats

The promotion of a layer of Indigenous people with a material interest in Australian capitalism isn't confined to a few thousand business owners. Alongside this has developed a broader layer of middle-class Indigenous people, involving tens of thousands of managers, bureaucrats and professionals.

In the 10 years from 2011 to 2021, the number of Indigenous managers grew from 9,406 to 21,218. This is an increase of 125.5 percent, the largest increase in any Indigenous occupation outside of sales assistants. There has also been a modest increase in the percentage of Indigenous people who are managers compared to other occupations. In 2006, only 3.8 percent of employed Indigenous people were managers; in 2021, it was around 8.2 percent.[357]

Similar changes can be seen in the number of Indigenous professionals. From 2011 to 2021 the size of this layer almost doubled, from 19,358 to 36,013. ABS data is too imprecise for a a clear line to be drawn between middle-class and working-class people in that category, but presumably some thousands more middle-class people were created in this period of growth. These figures do not include the significant number of Indigenous writers, artists, musicians and political commentators who play an increasing role in shaping political discussion and popular culture, with a prominence far beyond their numerical size. While income levels aren't an exact guide to class differences, the widening levels of economic inequality within the Indigenous population are also a sign of growing class differentiation, as Ross Gittins has explained:

> If you take the weekly disposable personal incomes of all Indigenous people aged 15 or older, adjust them for inflation, rank them from lowest to highest, then divide them all into 10 groups of 10 percent each, you discover some disturbing things.
>
> Between 2011 and 2016, the average income of those in the top decile rose by $75 a week, compared with $32 a week for those in the middle decile.

---
357. The following statistics are all from ABS 2022.

Individuals in the bottom decile had no income (possibly because they were students or home minding kids), while those in the second and third lowest deciles saw their incomes fall.[358]

Similarly, the 2021 census recorded that while 52.2 percent of Indigenous households had an average weekly income of less than $1000, only 36.7 percent of households earned above this threshold.[359]

The Voice to Parliament: representation or co-option?

The emergence of an Indigenous elite and shifting attitudes in the Australian ruling class have combined to produce calls for new institutions that can navigate this new situation. A range of options have been proposal, the most notable of which is the Voice to Parliament.

Opposition to the Voice has been dominated by right-wingers but there is a minority of figures who have raised criticisms of the Voice from a progressive position. This was on display at the 2023 Invasion Day rallies, which in most cities stridently attacked the Voice, as well as in the actions of former Greens senator Lidia Thorpe, who resigned from her party over the issue. Concern over the Voice goes back as far as the 2017 Constitutional Convention; a breakaway group of seven delegates and their supporters from Victoria, Canberra and New South Wales, including long-time Indigenous activists Jenny Munro and Lyall Munro Jr, as well as Lidia Thorpe, walked out in protest at what they saw as a charade stitched up by conservative Indigenous leaders such as Noel Pearson. A statement by Les Coe, Nioka Coe and Ruth Gilbert condemned the convention as a "scandalous, deceitful process" dominated by the "Conservative Black Political elite" in which any genuine discussion about sovereignty and self-determination was marginalised in favour of surface-level changes.[360]

So there is at least some awareness of the growing role of Indigenous elites, although the debates around the Voice also reveal the difficulties in

---

358. Gittins 2018.
359. ABS 2022.
360. See the "Walkout Statement: Aboriginal Embassy Statement from the Sacred Fire" at https://nationalunitygovernment.org/content/walkout-statement-aboriginal-embassy-statement-sacred-fire.

developing concrete alternatives. For instance, treaties are often presented as a more left-wing alternative to moderate proposals like the Voice. But while there has been relatively greater reluctance about the granting of treaties from the Australian establishment, there have been shifts on this front too.

The Victorian state government is involved in an already quite developed treaty process, which has led to the establishment of the First Peoples' Assembly of Victoria. This institution, in conjunction with the state government, has created a nominally independent Treaty Authority to oversee treaty negotiations and a Treaty Negotiation Framework to set the parameters of these negotiations, as well as a Self-Determination Fund which is supposed to provide financial resources to Indigenous people in Victoria so they can participate in these negotiations on a more equal footing with the state government.

Socialists should be sceptical about the likely outcome of treaty processes such as that being pursued in Victoria. After all, governments in New Zealand and Canada have not allowed Indigenous political bodies, truth and reconciliation commissions, or even treaties to stop them violating land rights in the pursuit of profit. In 2020, the Canadian government persevered with a multibillion-dollar gas pipeline project despite fervent opposition from representatives of the Wet'suwet'en First Nation. In New Zealand, successive governments have repeatedly rejected the Waitangi Tribunal's recommendation that Māori be given foreshore and seabed rights.

Whether it is an Indigenous Voice to Parliament or a treaty, or some combination of both, there is significant and growing support for some kind of Indigenous political representative body. Of course, the left cannot be against such a body in principle. But for it to have a real impact it needs to be a step towards self-determination and justice, involving real funding and control. The alternative is just another committee like the many we've seen before, which enriches and empowers the minority who are lucky enough to be part of it, while doing nothing for Indigenous people more broadly.

One example of such a body is the Coalition of Peaks. This is a grouping formed in 2019 by over 50 Indigenous organisations. Within a few months it had established an agreement with the Council of Australian Governments (COAG). In 2020, the National Agreement on Closing the Gap was signed between the Coalition of Peaks, the prime minister, state premiers, chief ministers of the territories and the president of the Australian Local Government Association. The National Agreement was ostensibly motivated by the lack of Indigenous input into Closing the Gap programs. While this is a valid critique, the inclusion of the Coalition of Peaks doesn't appear to have made much of a difference. The problem is not to be found in the colour of the skin of the bureaucrats implementing the program, but in its fundamentally neoliberal nature. As the National Agreement states:

> This Agreement builds on, and replaces, the NIRA. It continues the successful elements of the NIRA, strengthens others and addresses foundational areas previously excluded from consideration. The most significant of those was that NIRA was only an Agreement between Australian governments whereas in this Agreement, for the first time, representatives of Aboriginal and Torres Strait Islander people are also parties.[361]

Despite this supposedly landmark agreement, the 2022 Closing the Gap report stated that the program's targets were either "not on track" or worsening – that is, there were more adults in prison, more deaths by suicide, more children in out-of-home care, fewer children who were school-ready and increased income inequality.[362]

Case study #1:
Inuit – from talking chiefs to a native corporate elite

We can also look at the development of Indigenous elites in other countries with minority Indigenous populations to see where the emergence of such class divisions leads.

The Inuit are an Indigenous group of around 100,000 people who primarily live in the Arctic and subarctic regions of Alaska, northern Canada and Greenland. They are distinct from other Indigenous groups in the region like First Nations and the Métis.[363]

---
361. Closing the Gap 2020.
362. Closing the Gap 2022.
363. The following analysis of the Inuit is largely drawn from Mitchell 1996.

Prior to European colonisation, there was no separate ruling layer within Inuit societies. There were only informal leaders known as the *isumaitoq*, who were usually older males whose authority rested on their hunting ability, and religious figures called *angakoq*, who could be male or female and lived primarily by getting their own food, supplemented with gifts in return for spiritual services.

Due to their geographical isolation, the impact of colonisation on the Inuit was initially limited to trade with whalers; the whalers attracted some of the Inuit to the trading posts they had established and introduced new commodities into their societies. However, it was the arrival of fur traders, missionaries and police in the early 20th century that really began the process of bringing capitalist social relations into Inuit communities.

Traders were driven to establish permanent settlements in the Inuit areas due to international demand for white fox fur. By the 1920s there were almost 70 posts in 48 locations around the Arctic. As competition between trading companies, individual traders and the declining whaling industry heated up, there was a fierce struggle over control of trading posts, land and water use, as well as relations with the Inuit who had started trading white fox fur in exchange for weapons and whaling boats.

As traders penetrated into Inuit communities, the missionaries and then the police followed. From the start of the 20th century Anglican, Catholic and Moravian missionaries spread across Inuit communities, establishing "a powerful intellectual influence" and fighting to undermine and destroy the authority of the *angakoq*.[364] As the economic value of the Arctic and subarctic regions became clear, police also established a foothold in the region to help regulate the exploitation of its resources and ensure territorial sovereignty over the area for their respective governments.

By the 1930s, the combined impact of traders, missionaries and police had radically altered Inuit societies. While many Inuit still produced some of their own food, they increasingly depended for survival on either selling furs or casual employment in the trading settlements. The ideological authority of the *angakoq* was defeated and while traditional spiritual practices endured, Christianity rapidly became the dominant formal religious affiliation for the

---

364. Mitchell 1996, p.93.

Inuit. These economic and ideological processes resulted in rapid centralisation of the Inuit as their traditional patterns of seasonal migration were disrupted and replaced with a focus on the economic, social and religious opportunities in the trading settlements. This was reinforced as welfare, schooling and medical care spread into the north; access to these services was primarily located in the settlements. Thousands of Inuit moved from their traditional homes to live in camps on the outskirts of the settlements in an attempt to access these benefits. Once in the camps, they became even more dependent upon their integration into the capitalist economy.

As thousands of Inuit gathered around the settlements, the economic basis of their societies started to collapse, as the demand for their services wasn't enough to provide the necessary resources for so many people to live a sedentary life in centralised communities. As they tried to supplement this with hunting, the local wildlife was devastated, leading to widespread starvation. Diseases then tore through the camps, killing hundreds of Inuit. In response the police and government officials moved to push the Inuit back into more remote areas, causing further chaos.

It was in this context that the first instruments which would lead to the creation of an Inuit elite were introduced. Realising that something had to be done to resolve the situation, the Canadian government increasingly intervened into Inuit communities from the 1950s onwards. It secularised the education system, introduced welfare payments and organised medical services. However, this did little to resolve the underlying economic problems of the Inuit; welfare payments exceeded the combined income that Inuit made from fur trapping and casual employment during the 1950s and '60s. In order to promote greater economic development the Canadian state began to reorganise Inuit communities into a co-operative system, starting with the George River Co-operative in 1959.

The co-operative system facilitated the development of an Inuit elite in a range of ways. Firstly it institutionalised a small layer of Inuit who were made into managers, bosses and directors of the co-ops with authority over the vast majority who were simply employees and customers, drastically polarising class relations in Inuit society. While the highest positions within the co-ops were almost always in the hands of non-Inuit, the creation of a layer of

Inuit managers whose power and authority derived from their class position reshaped class relations among the Inuit.

In order for the co-ops to be successful they needed to move towards the mass production of goods such as traditional stone carvings which had become popular in Canada. This meant importing more sophisticated machinery – but in order to get this technology they needed capital. This further enmeshed them in the capitalist market; as Mitchell explains, "the more manufactured goods they needed, the more cash they had to have, and in order to get more cash, they needed more manufactured goods".[365] This cycle furthered the need for a differentiation between those Inuit employed as wage labourers and those in charge of organising investment, management of labour and importation of tools.

This led to two simultaneous developments. On the one hand, the subordinate position of the Inuit in capitalist society was further institutionalised and, at the same time, the class differentiation within Inuit societies was crystallised. These two developments also prompted the emergence of an incipient Inuit national identity which had previously been limited by the decentralised nature of Inuit communities.

The development of an Inuit capitalist class was furthered by the emergence of Inuit development corporations in the 1970s. These corporations were established through funds derived from land claim settlements that started to be negotiated during the '70s. The Canadian state was motivated to negotiate these settlements in order to facilitate the mass exploitation of profitable resources in Canada. For instance, the James Bay and Northern Quebec Agreement of 1975 was signed after the Supreme Court of Canada stopped a large-scale hydroelectric project from proceeding, due to a pre-existing Indigenous title to the territory held by Inuit and Cree peoples. Land claim settlements like this did not give the Inuit actual ownership over the land. Instead, they legitimised the dispossession of these groups by granting the Inuit conditional access and use of the land in return for lump sum cash payments from the Canadian government – payments which were given to the newly established native development corporations.[366]

---

365. Mitchell 1996, p.xiv.
366. Nowlin 2020, pp.77–8.

On paper, these corporations are supposed to use the funds to pursue economic projects that benefit all Inuit, and they are supposed to be democratically accountable to the Inuit communities they supposedly represent. However, they have come under sustained criticism for instead pursuing the interests of a narrow elite of Inuit.

The Makivik Corporation in Nunavik was established as a result of the James Bay and Northern Quebec Agreement and has received over CA$120 million in compensation funds. The bulk of this money has been used for business investments, either in Canada or internationally, and in profit-driven economic projects in Nunavik. Makivik owns two airline services – Air Inuit and Canadian North – as well as Nunavik Geomatics (a geographic data consulting agency) and Halutik Enterprises (a fuel and heavy equipment firm). It also has joint ventures with other Inuit corporations in the air traffic radar, sea shipping, shrimp trawling and seal harvesting industries.

The Inuit directors of Makivik, while elected, have been criticised for their six-figure salaries, self-interested business activities, subservience to the government and indifference to the lives of ordinary Inuit. However, much of the opposition to the directors of native development corporations like Makivik comes from Inuit managers in the declining co-operative sector who, despite sometimes framing the conflict as a struggle between the apparently "socialist" objectives of the co-ops and the capitalism of the development corporations, are more motivated by their own narrow interest in defending their role in Inuit communities – a role which laid the basis for the native development corporations in the first place.

Despite the obvious self-interest underlying criticism by co-op leaders, the native development corporations have indeed led to greater inequality among the Inuit, with the gap between rich and poor Inuit communities and individuals increasing since their emergence. It is no wonder that the directors of these corporations have come under criticism, when they have hundreds of millions of dollars at their disposal yet, for the majority of Inuit, nothing seems to have changed for the better.

A similar process of class differentiation has occurred among the Indigenous population in Alaska following the passage of the Alaska Native Claims Settlement Act (ANCSA) in 1971. After the passage of ANCSA "a cadre of

Alaska Natives became the first generation of Native capitalist leaders holding monopoly control over corporate decisions concerning natural resource development and monetary investment in Alaska". By 1978, nearly one billion dollars had been given to this Native capitalist class for investment in over 44 million acres of territory.[367]

Many of these Alaska Native capitalists already had a degree of cultural and political influence before the ANCSA provided them with the opportunity to control significant amounts of capital.

The Native capitalists who emerged from the Alutiiq people on Kodiak Island were often from mixed-race, middle-class families with an American education, whose fathers were generally European traders; frequently they also had non-Native wives. Many had converted to the Baptists from the Russian Orthodox church of their trader fathers, and most could not speak the Alutiiq language fluently. They were highly "westernised" and identified themselves with America culturally, as one academic study explains:

> The cohort's racial and cultural affiliation with "white" America integrated them in ways that would not distinguish them from the American lawyers in the state and national capitals with whom they had to deal during the reconstruction years following the tidal wave of 1964 and the land claims movement thereafter. Many of the cohort interviewed had identified themselves in other parts of the United States prior to the settlement act as "simply Americans."[368]

In the aftermath of the 1964 earthquake which devastated Kodiak Island, this layer of young Alutiiq emerged as community leaders, able to more easily negotiate with American government officials and business leaders involved in the reconstruction process.

With the emergence of the land claims movement across North America in the late 1960s, this layer of younger Alutiiq leaders began to strongly identify themselves with their Alutiiq heritage and traditions. Within a few years, they emerged as the established leadership of the Alutiiq on Kodiak

---
367. Mason 2002, p.6.
368. Mason 2002, pp.8–9.

Island. They acquired considerable economic power from their position as managers of the newly created native development corporations, while the majority of Alutiiq were transformed into rank-and-file "shareholders". The class differentiation among the Alutiiq was felt strongly, as one Native corporate leader has explained:

> After [the settlement act] we're Native people, but we have individual assets, in some cases disproportionate assets. Some folks have more land, some folks had more money, and there was a period of time where you had these various factions among Native corporations, between intra-Native corporations... People had different interests. In some cases those interests were selfish, in some cases they were not. But in large part...there was a considerable loss of equity brought on by themselves.[369]

The Indigenous directors of the native development corporations in Canada and Alaska have emerged as a distinct capitalist class, with the Inuit co-op managers in Canada forming a rival but secondary elite layer. Unsurprisingly, this elite, particularly the corporate directors, have interests which are strongly intertwined with the Canadian, Québécois and American bourgeoisie and their capitalist states, whom they rely on for capital and access to markets.

One result of crystallised class distinctions within Inuit communities has been greater articulation of a national consciousness among the Inuit, as well as divisions between Inuit groups. Among the Alutiiq elite, for instance, a concern that their society was fragmenting in the late 1970s led the next generation of Alutiiq capitalists to place a greater emphasis on the need to reclaim and regenerate Alutiiq Native culture. In the 1980s, this cultural project was advanced through an alliance between the Alutiiq capitalists and liberal Alaskan academic intellectuals, who promoted Native culture, established museums and archaeological sites, and produced studies and oral histories of the area. This also led to the emergence of what some have called an "identity industry" due to the fact that the Native capitalists have transformed Native cultural symbols into private commodities marketed to non-Native Alaskans. The result of this has been to further entrench the

---
369. Mason 2002, p.12.

domination of the Native capitalists over Alutiiq society by strongly tying Alutiiq culture to the production of commodities, which is controlled by the Native capitalists.[370]

This process of class formation is not confined to the Inuit, but has been replicated across all of the Indigenous groups in Canada. Across Canada, there are now more than 250 First Nations, Métis and Inuit development corporations with several billion dollars in assets collectively. Strong ties have been built between the Indigenous capitalist class in Canada and the resource extraction industry, which is now the largest private employer of Indigenous people in Canada.

The Haisla Nation, for instance, has formed strong links with the liquefied gas natural (LNG) industry, in 2010 establishing a working group made up of industry executives and Haisla Nation councillors. This working group boasted that Suncor Energy spent more than $4 million with Haisla-owned businesses in 2013 and that there are now 19 Petro-Canada stations owned and operated by First Nations companies. In 2016, the Haisla Nation-owned Cedar LNG obtained a 25-year LNG export licence from the Canadian government. The most controversial decision of the Indigenous capitalists who run the Haisla Nation has been its participation in the $40 billion LNG Coastal GasLink pipeline. The project has been endorsed by elected chiefs and councils from 20 Indigenous nations but has been rejected by some of the Wet'suwet'en people, including a number of hereditary chiefs. In 2020, this clash led to a substantial movement across Canada of both Indigenous and non-indigenous protesters, who drew attention to the environmentally destructive and profit-driven nature of the Coastal GasLink pipeline.[371]

Another expression of the convergence of interests that has arisen between First Nations elites and fossil fuel capitalists is the alliance between Western Australian mining billionaire Gina Rinehart and the leaders of the Piikani Nation in the Rocky Mountains of Canada. They are seeking to overturn a court-ruled environmental ban on a proposed coal mine.[372]

---

370. Mason 2002, pp.13–15.
371. Nowlin 2020.
372. de Kruijff 2021.

Case study #2:
Māori bureaucrats and tribal capitalists

Māori are the Indigenous people of mainland New Zealand, who originated from East Polynesia but developed their own distinctive culture after settling in New Zealand sometime between the 1320s and 1350s. There has always been a section of Māori elites willing to play an intermediate role within capitalism, as expressed in the system of tribal councils and reserved Māori parliamentary seats during the 19th and 20th centuries. But the adoption of a policy of "bi-culturalism" by the Labour Party government during the 1980s ushered in a new era, allowing for the greater development of both a conservative Māori bureaucracy in the state sector and a Māori capitalist class.

The Labour government did this in two ways. First, programs and services formerly delivered by the NZ central government were devolved (i.e. semi-privatised) to local tribal authorities. Secondly, it expanded the role of the Waitangi Council which had been first established in 1975 in response to the Māori protest movements of that time. The plan was to co-opt Māori activists from these movements by giving them state jobs to oversee programs for the Māori community. This strategy was significantly expanded during the 1980s and 1990s; by the late '90s "Māori units, divisions or secretariats had been established in Ministries of Education, Environment, Health, Inland Revenue, Justice, Labour, Social Welfare and Women's Affairs".[373]

These state jobs were complemented by the creation of another section of the Māori state bureaucracy. This was to staff the specialist Māori advisory and liaison bodies, set up from the late '70s onwards to oversee new consultative arrangements and treaty discussions between the NZ government and local and pan-tribal Māori bodies.

At the same time, there was an explosion in the Māori private capitalist class. This was centred on Māori-owned consultancy companies which were contracted to "help government to incorporate Māori values and perspectives into the operating procedures and management styles of mainstream

---
373. Poata-Smith 2001, p.261.

government departments and to identify and remove discriminatory and culturally prejudicial practice".[374]

The Marxist Māori writer ES Te Ahu Poata-Smith has explored how the career paths of two prominent Māori activists from the 1970s and early 1980s, Donna Awatere and Ripeka Evans, highlights the role of these consultancy companies:

> Awatere established Ihi Communications Consultancy in 1985, which developed into a million dollar annual enterprise providing expert Māori advice to government agencies and the private sector organisations delivering programmes and services to the public. Meanwhile, Ripeka Evans became the "Cultural and Planning Assistant" to the chief executive of State owned Television New Zealand, which under the influence of biculturalism, increased its Māori staff by seventy percent over three years by 1989.[375]

The Labour government helped create a Māori "tribal capitalist" class by concentrating Māori community assets in the hands of a small number of "tribal executives".[376] A key role was played, as in other countries, by new bodies set up to administer compensation funds which had been granted in response to the land struggles of the '60s and '70s. At first, these Trust Boards simply administered these funds, but by the 1980s their role had expanded into overseeing the economic development of Māori communities, pursuing commercial ventures, and settling land disputes.

The Labour government's move to substantially expand a Māori ruling class was made easier by developments in Māori politics during the 1980s, as Poata-Smith explains:

> Unfortunately, the fourth Labour Government's attempt to appease Māori discontent was made easier by a qualitative change in the direction of the Māori protest movement itself with the proliferation of "identity politics". In the absence of mass struggles against oppression with the decline of the working

---
374. Poata-Smith 2001, p.261.
375. Poata-Smith 2001, pp.261–2.
376. Poata-Smith 2001, p.261.

class movement internationally and the rise of the New Right, many of the assumptions of identity politics were reflected in the New Zealand context with an emphasis on cultural identity as the determining factor in Māori oppression. The inherent traits of Pakeha were seen as the basic causes of an oppressive and unequal society, while the traditional and egalitarian virtues of the Māori community were critical for their resolution. Such a "cultural" explanation for Māori inequality was easily accommodated by the state because unlike the demands of the earlier movement, cultural nationalism did not represent a fundamental threat to the underlying social relations of capitalism. In fact, the partial adoption of bicultural rhetoric by the state and the co-optation of elites into state institutions gave the illusion of a "partnership" as espoused under the Treaty of Waitangi, while marginalising the more radical demands.[377]

During the 1990s there was a revival of Māori protest movements. An important factor shaping this resurgence was that the "commercial interests of Māori tribal executives, Māori corporate enterprises, and the Māori bureaucracy" were "increasingly at odds with the interests of the vast majority of working class Māori families".[378]

These divergent class interests were highlighted by a push for greater neoliberal reforms led by the government of the the conservative National Party, elected in 1990, and the capitalist class, and their attempts to limit the fiscal impact of unresolved Treaty claims. In order to achieve this, the National government started secret negotiations with a select group of Māori capitalists who agreed with the free market economic model being promoted by the government and capital. When the content of these deals became public, it led to widespread anger among the Māori population. This was notable in negotiations between the National government, commercial Māori fishing interests and tribal executives over the purchase of Sealords, at the time the largest fishing company in New Zealand. The National government agreed to provide $150 million so that Māori fishing interests could buy half of Sealords' shares. In return, this deal was to be recognised as a full and final settlement of all Māori claims over sea, coastal and inland fisheries. This was

---

377. Poata-Smith 2001, p.276.
378. Poata-Smith 2001, p.276.

the first step in the National Party's plan to resolve all treaty claims with a NZ$1 billion fiscal cap. While the Sealords deal generated substantial Māori opposition, activists were unable to stop the deal from being signed, nor from subsequently being endorsed by the courts. In the aftermath of the deal, there was a further push to cement free market ideas as the economic model for Māori development, and a growing corporate "militancy of Māori commercial interests both at the tribal and individual level" during the 1990s:

> [T]here was a consistent advertising expose on the success of certain Māori businesses and the emphasis on Māori commercial development in both individual and tribal forms as the key to successful Māori economic and social development. The Māori owned press, radio and television repeatedly saturated the Māori community with the idea that Māori business was the way forward for Māori and the "corporate warrior" philosophy emerged as the catch-cry for Māori development in the 1990s. It was convenient for a government faced with the fiscal pressures of a recession, that advocates of Māori capitalist development argued, like the New Right ideologues in treasury and the Business Roundtable, that the welfare system had held Māori back and that real self-determination and liberation for Māori can only be achieved under unrestrained, free market capitalism.[379]

The National government's broader aim of a final settlement for all treaty claims faced sustained opposition, however. Hundreds of protesters dramatically disrupted the official Waitangi Day celebration in 1995,[380] booing conservative Māori leaders and scuffling with the police. Then on 28 February 1995, Whanganui Māori occupied Moutoa Gardens, initiating the country's largest act of collective civil disobedience in decades. This protest sparked a wave of occupations throughout 1995, involving thousands of protesters.

While these protests revealed the gulf that had opened up between the majority of working-class Māori and the Māori elite, the activists who led the protests had a limited awareness of the political implications of class

---

379. Poata-Smith 2001, p.293.
380. Waitangi Day (6 February) is the national day of New Zealand, marking the anniversary of the signing of the Treaty of Waitangi between Māori chiefs and representatives of the British empire —*Ed.*

divisions among the Māori. The vast majority of activists were still strongly influenced by cultural nationalist politics and the fundamental idea "that all Māori, despite class or gender differences, are bound to each other by their overriding common interests as Māori".[381] The conservative Māori leaders and business interests were seen as breaking with Māori culture – selling out their people and adopting a white European mindset – rather than expressing the class interests of their own social layer within the Māori population. This cultural nationalist outlook continues to shape Māori politics in New Zealand to the present day. Poata-Smith argues:

> [I]t has become increasingly difficult to sustain the notion that all Māori share the same sets of experiences of inequality, and that Māori, irrespective of their place in production relations, are united as a community of resistance. While it is certainly the case that successive governments have been responsible for establishing a settlement framework that locks Māori self-determination into a free-market, capitalist economic framework, it is also *a notorious fact* that the political ideologies and practices that have dominated Māori protest politics since the early 1980s have left the majority of Māori ill-equipped to resist the repressive and anti-working class policies that successive governments have introduced to restore the economic conditions for profitable capital accumulation. In particular, the insistence that Māori are a culture united in their resistance against Pakeha has failed dramatically as a strategy for the majority of working class Māori whanau.[382]

Class analysis and Indigenous politics

Indigenous people are often understood, even by people on the socialist left, in a sympathetic yet ultimately romantic, ahistorical and stereotyping fashion. A noble desire to reject the long-standing racist assumptions about Indigenous people, propagated for decades by many of the key institutions of capitalist society, can easily lead anti-racists to portray Indigenous peoples as

---

381. Poata-Smith 2001, p.6.
382. Poata-Smith 2001, p.11.

homogeneous, exotic and incapable of change. Preconceived and moralistic notions of Indigenous people then get in the way of trying to unpack the actual class relations within Indigenous groups and their contradictory and often complex economic and political developments.

It is notable that writers on the socialist left have been far more hesitant to discuss questions of class within Indigenous groups than they have within other oppressed peoples under capitalism. This is in large part because of the dominance of identity politics among academic and left-wing political circles. As Samuel W Rose has explained, in the context of debates in North American anthropology:

> The Marxist turn in the 1970s saw the proliferation of anthropological work about Native North America, including the expansion of the historical critique of indigenous articulations with capitalism as well as the beginning of the critique of contemporary Native American political economy… An indigenist critique emerged in the 1980s, which was in reaction to this proliferation of Marxist thought. The critique, while having unique characteristics, should be viewed as part of the postmodern turn in theorizing in academia and within the political Left itself. In this postmodern vein, it is part of the larger turn where class politics give way to identity politics as the central organizing concept. The indigenist critique focuses on Marxism's Western and modernist origins and theoretical connections, using this foreignness as a means to discredit Marxism. As such, they denounce Marxism as another face of the colonial project.[383]

Even when writers on the left have acknowledged the emergence of Indigenous elites, they have often understood them not in class terms but with what is still an essentially cultural identity framework. So the activist-academic Nandita Sharma can recognise the limitations of confining the idea of Indigenous liberation to a nationalist and ultimately pro-capitalist perspective, but she does not link this to the emergence of class divisions within Indigenous societies.[384] Partly this reflects the elasticity of class relations inside Indigenous

---

383. Rose 2015.
384. See Humphreys 2022b.

communities for whole periods of history. It can appear that other differences between Indigenous people – such as divides between "assimilated" and traditional, so-called "half-caste" and "full blooded", reservation and urbanised, militants and moderates, or between different Indigenous nations – are more decisive than those between the social classes within Indigenous groups. Certainly, in some historical periods they actually were more important.

However as Indigenous people have been drawn into capitalist development a sharper differentiation of class within Indigenous groups, replicating that within capitalist society as a whole, is inevitable. The exact way in which this differentiation has occurred is shaped both by the particular history of socio-economic development within the Indigenous group in question, as well as the particular interests and concerns of non-indigenous capital and the state. The development of class divisions within Indigenous groups, to the point at which an Indigenous elite emerges from within, doesn't inherently lead to a generalised advance for the majority of Indigenous people in that group. Instead, such a development tends to entrench inequality within Indigenous groups as the elite gain greater material advantages, political influence and cultural legitimacy.

Indigenous elites are often criticised for "selling out" to non-indigenous interests, and contemporary Indigenous institutions such as the proposed Voice to Parliament are condemned because they apparently represent non-indigenous settler politics. This ignores the fact that Indigenous capitalists have a shared material interest, together with their non-indigenous counterparts, in exploiting all workers in the production process – whether Indigenous or not.

Indigenous bosses and bureaucrats are not hapless victims of non-indigenous capital and states. They are eager collaborators with them, always pursuing their own class interests, which are increasingly distinct from and antagonistic to the interests of the Indigenous working class and poor. This doesn't mean that the interests of Indigenous elites and the non-indigenous ruling class are totally harmonious; their interests can clash to a greater or lesser extent. After all, the primary concern of non-indigenous capitalists and states is the accumulation of profits and the continuation of the exploitative class relations that make those profits possible, not the creation of Indigenous elites. But often these goals are compatible and mutually reinforcing, as is the case in the mining industry.

The emergence of an Indigenous elite thus becomes a barrier for the future advance of the interests of the majority of working-class Indigenous people, due to the differing class interests between the two and the way in which those conflicting interests are often obscured by a shared Indigenous heritage. This necessitates a more political engagement with Indigenous struggles, in which the socialist left should be sensitive to the differing class interests among Indigenous peoples, how those interests are shaped by their broader relationship to the non-indigenous capitalist class and the state, and how those class forces shape the political debates that arise around Indigenous issues. The rejection of any serious discussion about the relationship between class, capitalism and Indigenous people by most contemporary progressive writers on Indigenous issues only obscures the vital issues involved and makes it harder to set out on the path to true liberation.

The Indigenous working class and capitalism

Of course, the flipside to the emergence of an Indigenous elite is the growth of the Indigenous working class. The Indigenous population in Australia is becoming increasingly proletarianised and urbanised. During the 19th and most of the 20th century, the vast majority of the Indigenous population was confined to the fringes of capitalist society, whether on the missions, in urban slums or in remote communities. Today the majority of the Indigenous population is made up of workers; a significant section is more integrated into the urbanised blue- and white-collar working class than ever before. Greater Western Sydney is emblematic of this trend. The Indigenous population doubled between 2006 and 2021, from 26,467 to 55,128 people. This population is overwhelmingly working-class: only 7.1 percent in the region are managers; 10.7 percent are professionals, with most working in manual labour, manufacturing, transport, or social and community services. This compares to the 11.1 percent of non-indigenous people who are managers and 23.9 percent who are professionals.[385]

---
385. Lawton 2016.

The same pattern can be found in Queensland, the state with the second largest Indigenous population. More than one-third of Indigenous people live in what statisticians call the Brisbane Indigenous Region (which includes Brisbane, the Sunshine Coast and the Gold Coast). The Indigenous population in this area now includes over 100,000 people – roughly one-ninth of the entire Indigenous population in Australia.[386] As in western Sydney, Indigenous people living in the Brisbane Indigenous Region are overwhelmingly working-class. Out of the 80 percent in either full- or part-time work, 35.7 percent are employed as labourers, tradespeople or transport workers, a further 38.1 percent as retail, social or office workers – only 22.1 percent are either professionals or managers.[387]

Importantly, this proletarianisation of Indigenous people has not led to assimilation, with all the negative connotations that carries, but to a new cultural fusion and new social facts. Positive references to Indigenous culture and politics are increasingly part of public life in the major cities, particularly in working-class institutions like trade unions. As well, the number of people identifying as Indigenous is growing, as more discover and celebrate their previously repressed heritage. This partly explains why support for Indigenous rights is so hegemonic among younger generations.

These shifts have implications for the future of Indigenous struggle. Issues such as land rights will remain an important part of Indigenous politics, even for those Indigenous people living in urban environments, due to their historic significance. But the central site of exploitation for the vast majority of Indigenous people is in the heart of the capitalist economy. The greater integration of Indigenous people into the working class significantly strengthens both their potential power to advance their interests and the possibility – though it is not guaranteed – that such action could win support from non-indigenous workers. At the same time, the ongoing racism faced by Indigenous workers gives the lie to the idea that such racism will be overcome simply through greater integration into the mainstream of capitalist society.

These facts are often downplayed by commentators on the international left. So Glen Coulthard, a Yellowknives Dene writer, while acknowledging

---

386. ABS 2022.
387. ABS 2022.

that most Indigenous people in Canada today are wage earners living in urban areas, still insists that "dispossession, not proletarianization, has been the dominant background structure shaping the character of the historical relationship between Indigenous peoples and the Canadian state". From this he draws the necessary conclusion that Indigenous anti-capitalist resistance "is best understood as a struggle primarily inspired by and oriented around the question of land".[388]

Similarly, the Vancouver-based Indigenous socialist activist Mike Krebs argues that it is wrong for the socialist left "to frame the Indigenous struggle in Canada as one of an oppressed minority without taking up the question of land and the question of Indigenous people as nations". Krebs argues that this "approach unscientifically separates the discrimination that Indigenous people face from its material base".[389] However, as Roxanne Dunbar-Ortiz has argued, "all capitalism starts with expropriation of land from the producers, and not just in the Americas but as the prerequisite for the development of capitalism in Europe". The dispossession of the European peasantry of control over land, often achieved via state force, was necessary to create an industrial proletariat during the Industrial Revolution.[390]

Socialists of course support the demand for land rights and reparations. But the insistence that land dispossession remains the central element of Indigenous oppression today is totally unscientific.

Such a framework has serious political implications. For example, Tom Keefer's work on Indigenous reserves in Canada wildly exaggerates their anti-capitalist potential:

> As counterintuitive as it may seem in an advanced capitalist country like Canada, the transition to capitalism remains incomplete on Indigenous reserves, and the Indian Act – designed as a means to control and disenfranchise Indigenous populations destined for extinction – now acts as the primary blockage to the full penetration of capitalist social relations into these reserves.[391]

---

388. Coulthard 2014, p.13.
389. Krebs 2008, pp.3–4.
390. Dunbar-Ortiz 2016.
391. Keefer 2010.

This argument is not merely counterintuitive, it is utter rubbish. The reserves themselves are a product of capitalism, and were incorporated into the broader Canadian economy long ago. Societies do not need to look like Toronto or Melbourne to be categorised as capitalist.

This leads to two other problems with this analysis. Firstly, because it conceives of Indigenous society and capitalism as two distinct and separate categories, it struggles to grapple with how capitalism has fundamentally shaped and reshaped Indigenous politics, culture and consciousness in myriad complex and contradictory ways. Secondly, this analysis fails to see that the primary fault line in capitalist societies – including those with Indigenous populations – is the cleavage between a multi-racial working class, with the potential to unite within itself all oppressed and exploited people, and those social classes that have a stake in the continuation of capitalism, including those of Black and Brown heritage.

As Poata-Smith has argued, the key weakness of Māori cultural nationalist politics in New Zealand is that it ignores "the significance of the location of the majority of Māori in the working class within New Zealand's class structure and therefore in their objective interest, along with other members of the working class, in collectively transforming and ultimately transcending the exploitative and oppressive foundations of capitalist society".[392]

This same weakness plagues Indigenous identity politics, and the left more broadly, in Australia today.

Conclusion

The emergence of an Indigenous middle class is an expression of the fact that Indigenous people have been able to win greater acceptance for themselves from Australian society in recent years. The natural consequence of this is that sections of the Indigenous population have been able to integrate themselves into the broader middle class, even while most Indigenous people struggle at the bottom of our class-divided society.

Recognising the development of this elite Indigenous layer is vital for understanding some of the dynamics of modern Indigenous politics. The

---
392. Poata-Smith 2001, p.319.

political horizons of the Indigneous elite are narrowly focused on the classic middle-class themes of political and cultural representation, integration into institutions of power and the accumulation of private wealth as the key to personal fulfilment.

The narrow self-interest of this elite is often obscured by the verbose language of identity politics. The establishment of more Indigenous-owned businesses is presented as a step towards self-determination, the creation of yet another Indigenous advisory body hailed as the dawn of true reconciliation, the career progression of an influential Indigenous figure interpreted as an unqualified advance for all Indigenous people.

Invocation of identity politics also suits the Indigenous middle class and the small layer of Indigenous capitalists because of the particular position they have within capitalist society in Australia. While their expansion over the last two decades has been significant, they are still a fairly narrow social layer which is highly dependent upon the capitalist state, and to a lesser degree private capital, for jobs and social advancement. They lack any real independent economic base, unlike Māori in New Zealand or Indigenous groups in Canada who have been able to create a much larger private Indigenous business sector, Indigenous financial institutions and even Indigenous political parties. The Indigenous middle class in Australia is strongly dependent upon promotion within the capitalist state, media, cultural or educational institutions, and to a lesser degree private business in order to gain greater wealth, influence and power in society. The fact that they have gained this to a greater extent than ever before, but are still mostly locked out of the core centres of capitalist power, encourages a focus on the challenges of lived experiences with oppression understood through the lens of individual advancement and self-promotion.

This approach is presented as being in the interests of Indigenous people as a whole, similar to the way in which middle-class women, migrants or African Americans have presented their advancement as synonymous with progress for whole oppressed groups. This has negatively impacted contemporary discussions around questions of Indigenous self-determination. Historical calls for Aboriginal control of Aboriginal affairs, self-determination and sovereignty were grounded in the fact that Indigenous people have suffered under the undemocratic control of extremely racist government management. Today however the same slogans are often put forward in defence of a dramatically narrowed conception of liberation which reflects the self-interest of the Indigenous middle class.

Instead of accepting the agenda of the Indigenous middle class as the upper limit of what is possible, we need to look to a strategy centred on mass grassroots campaigns that seek to empower ordinary people, disrupt the status quo, and build united action from below to win meaningful reforms. Throughout the 20th century, it was precisely movements of this kind that led to the greatest advances for the largest numbers of Indigenous people: the post-war campaigns to end racial segregation involving both Indigenous and non-indigenous left-wing trade unionists, and the land rights and Black Power movements of the 1960s and '70s.

Special attention by working-class movements and the sociast left to the particular demands of sections of society oppressed in specific ways, such as Indigenous people, is crucial for developing such movements. However, support for such demands – genuine land rights, stopping Black deaths in custody, ending structural racism – needs to be linked to a broader project of uniting the working class in a struggle to ultimately dismantle the capitalist system.

This is essential, because the capitalist system is the root cause of the oppression and exploitation of Indigneous people in particular, and the majority of the population as a whole in general. It is capitalism – with its racism, inequality and inexhaustible desire for greater profits – which stands in the way of true liberation. The sooner this is recognised, the quicker we can begin to build a movement to challenge it.

Chapter ten
Indigenous liberation, class struggle and socialist revolution

> The only sort of Australia that I think Aboriginal Australia can ultimately live alongside in true harmony is some form of socialist republic Australia where racism, sexism and exploitation have been eliminated.
>
> — Gary Foley, 1988.[393]

> The real education of the masses can never be separated from their independent political, and especially revolutionary, struggle. Only struggle educates the exploited class. Only struggle discloses to it the magnitude of its own power, widens its horizon, enhances its abilities, clarifies its mind, forges its will.
>
> — Lenin, 1917.[394]

THE ANALYSIS OF INDIGENOUS OPPRESSION as rooted in the nature of Australian capitalism and the history of anti-racist working-class action which have been outlined in this book lay the basis for the elaboration of a revolutionary strategy to combat racism. The united struggles that both Indigenous and non-indigenous workers were able to forge show that solidarity isn't some utopian dream. Despite this working-class culture of solidarity being beaten back during the decades of the neoliberal offensive, it remains a broken thread to be remade on a deeper, broader and stronger basis.

There are significant obstacles to the creation of such a united movement. These obstacles are reflected in the trajectories of Indigenous politics over the last four decades. The forging of solidarity between sections of non-indigenous and Indigenous workers, from the post-war years to the heights of the late 1960s and early '70s, was rooted in the strength of the working-class

---

393. Speech to the 1988 Rainbow Alliance conference.
394. Lenin 1917.

movement. The connection between working-class struggle and Indigenous politics continued into the late '70s and 1980s. In 1981, 1,500 dockworkers at Williamstown Naval Dockyard walked off the job when an Aboriginal worker was unceremoniously sacked by management over a previous police record. In 1983, Aboriginal miners employed at the Mitsubishi silica mine in North Queensland launched a two-week strike over racist discrimination in pay and conditions. There were also repeated strikes throughout the '80s by Aboriginal members of the Public Service Association (PSA) – which had over 1,000 Aboriginal members by 1989 – over staffing levels and the lack of government resources for Aboriginal services.[395]

From the mid-1980s, there was a revived level of activism within the Aboriginal movement around the issues of land rights and Black deaths in custody, particularly leading up to the bicentenary in 1988, which saw a demonstration of tens of thousands organised by the National Coalition of Aboriginal Organisations.

The Trade Union Committee on Aboriginal Rights (TUCAR) was founded in 1977 by a range of Indigenous and non-indigenous activists and trade unionists. At the time, there was a growth in Indigenous public sector employment and so TUCAR put some effort into building links with the unions that covered these jobs. Through newsletters and meetings, TUCAR argued that trade unions should support the campaigns around Black deaths in custody and land rights, and that the development of the union movement was vital for the success of these campaigns. As one TUCAR newsletter put it:

> If Aborigines are to get the rights they are fighting for, they need the power and support of the trade unions behind them. Aboriginal workers also need the support and protection that comes from being a member of a union.[396]

A "Migrants for Aboriginal Rights" group was formed by working-class activists from the Greek, Chilean, Turkish, and many other communities. The leftist Federation of Italian Migrants and Their Families played an

---
395. *Tribune*, 22 July 1981, p.4; 26 October 1983, p.4; 16 May 1984, p.15. On the PSA more generally see the report by Peter Murphy in *Tribune*, 5 April 1989, p.11.
396. *TUCAR Newsletter*, November 1984, p.1.

important role; its publication *Nuovo Paese* carried articles by the Black Power activist Gary Foley encouraging migrant participation in the protest against the bicentenary:

> Aboriginal people are keenly conscious and very aware of the fact that in many instants migrants have come from situations of extreme adversity, of great political oppression, of torture of both body and soul. We understand. We empathise. We have experienced that ourselves for over two hundred years so there is a natural empathy on both sides in that respect. In some instances there are peoples among the migrants, such as the Palestinian people, who come from an identical situation to us. People who have been dispossessed. People who we feel a great empathy with. We understand their struggle from the bottom of our hearts because we know the experience of dispossession. We know the experience of oppression – It's a bond that is common to us all.[397]

Organisations like TUCAR and Migrants for Aboriginal Rights made the correct political points about the need for united working-class action to take on racism. Unfortunately, though they emerged at a time when the workers' movement, while still a significant force in society, was undergoing an important transformation that would undermine it in the long run.

The rank-and-file union organisation which had flourished during the high point of the '70s had significantly declined by the 1980s. Despite there still being a relatively high number of strikes, these were not accompanied by any sense of a broader political radicalisation in Australian society. These weaknesses were exacerbated by the impact of the Prices and Incomes Accord, which saw trade union leaders trade away the wages and conditions of workers for the illusory goal of social peace. The failures of the Accord strategy laid the basis for a catastrophic decline in union membership, which sank from a high point of 51 percent in 1976 to 12.5 percent in 2022.

The retreat of the workers' movement severed the connections that had been built between the struggles of Indigenous people and the working class. While the gains of that period couldn't be entirely obliterated, either in the

---
397. *Nuovo Paese*, February 1988, p.3.

consciousness of working people or in society more generally, and important struggles continued to attract significant levels of sympathy from unionised workers, they typically were unable to mobilise the kind of social power necessary to win.

This decoupling of the workers' movement and Indigenous activism reinforced a growing sense of pessimism among much of the left and a retreat into the beginnings of what we would today call identity politics. Separatist arguments emphasising the autonomy of different struggles gained a stronger foothold. This kind of destructive politics only served to further fragment the solidarity and unity which had emerged in the '60s and '70s, as Tom O'Lincoln, a socialist activist during these years, describes:

> At the start of the 1970s, the various movements against oppression tended to see themselves as part of a wider struggle to change society as a whole. This was partly because of the existence of a mass antiwar movement, to which everyone felt they belonged. It was also partly due to the high levels of industrial struggle, which gave people confidence in the labour movement as a force capable of seriously challenging capitalism. Even when the antiwar campaigns had ended and the class struggle was in decline, the various movements continued to cross-fertilise...

> ...[B]ut the 1970s was also the decade that entrenched the idea of *independent movements* of the oppressed. At the start of the decade, radical activists had emphasised the importance of understanding the specific oppression of Indigenous people or women or of mobilising specific movements for the rights of each. These initiatives were valuable in opening up new fronts in the struggle against capitalism and developing critiques of the prevailing social order – so valuable, perhaps, that it was easy to lose sight of their limitations. By the early 1980s, the belief that "autonomous" movements were needed for every oppressed sector had become an article of faith on the left.[398]

Struggles didn't just disappear; from the 1988 anti-bicentennial marches to the Invasion Day rallies today, people have continued to mobilise around the

---
398. O'Lincoln 2023 [1993], pp.259–60.

issue of Indigenous justice in Australia. However, these campaigns generally suffer from some of the same weaknesses as those of the late '70s and '80s – in particular, a lack of any real economic or political power allowing them to begin to challenge the roots of Indigenous oppression. This is the context in which superficial political frameworks like settler colonial theory have flourished, with their pessimistic attitude towards the possibilities of working-class anti-racist action.

It would be misleading, however, to think that it is as simple as returning to the struggles of the past and recreating the same organisations and movements over again. We can learn a lot from the history of struggles outlined in part two of this book; they are solid evidence against the claims that working-class politics and Indigenous rights have nothing to do with each other. However, as we have also seen, there were important limitations to many of these movements. Some of these limits were imposed on activists and their organisations by the objective situation of the times. The fact that the shearers of the late 1800s showed any sympathy for Aboriginal people at all is fairly astonishing, considering the virulent nature of racism at the time. Even more surprising is that they began to discuss how the Indigenous issue fitted into the broader movement for working-class emancipation, despite having no real tradition or pre-existing political framework with which they could approach this question.

Other limitations were produced by the movements themselves and the politics which guided them. The Communist left's understanding of Indigenous struggles was seriously disorientated by its commitment to Stalinism. This meant that when such struggles reached their high point, it only resulted in further confusion about the issue for the Communist left, instead of clarity. More broadly, the Communist Party played a terrible role in the workers' movement and the left, laying the basis for the significant defeats both suffered from the late 1970s onwards. Those outside of the mainstream Communist tradition struggled to break through the historical dominance of the left by reformist and liberal approaches to fighting oppression. Indigenous activists themselves have not struggled in isolation from these broader debates and developments, and clarity over the questions of anti-racist strategy has often been lacking despite the best efforts of many who have heroically resisted the pervasive racism in our society. Many of the themes of identity politics, as O'Lincoln alludes to above, first came onto the scene at the beginning of the 1960s radicalisation, when the ultimate limitations of such ideas were not clear; they were therefore rarely challenged.

What we need, then, is to critically engage with the histories and politics of past struggles, so that we can create new organisations with quite different politics, strategies and leadership. Such organisations will be built in the real world through the hard work and dedication of activists, not just in the realm of ideas. Clarity about the political basis on which such organisations can be built is nonetheless important. That is the topic of the rest of this chapter.

Class struggle and social movements

The fact that solidarity is even possible is because of the particular nature of the working class as compared to other social classes that have existed in the past and today. The working-class movement, as the *Communist Manifesto* explained, "is the self-conscious, independent movement of the immense majority, in the interest of the immense majority".[399]

Unlike all preceding and contemporary social classes which have fought for change, the working class "cannot stir, cannot raise itself up, without the whole superincumbent strata of official society being sprung into the air".[400] This is particularly the case since the modern working class is made up of people from many different oppressed groups – women, migrants, Indigenous and LGBTI+ people – who will necessarily be a part of any mass working-class movement to challenge the capitalist system.

Middle-class liberals might have genuine sympathy for the oppressed of the world, but only the working class can end their oppression. All preceding classes which managed to come to power – the feudal lords, the capitalist bourgeoisie, etc. – could only do so by subjecting society to their own narrow interests. The working class, by contrast, is the only social force in history that cannot come to power without destroying the basis for all oppression

---
399. Marx and Engels 1848.
400. Marx and Engels 1848.

and exploitation, instead of simply modifying the nature of it. As Marx and Engels once wrote, "they have nothing of their own to secure and to fortify; their mission is to destroy all previous securities for, and insurances of, individual property".[401]

Today the relative weakness of the workers' movement in Australia and across the advanced capitalist world has encouraged many on the left to abandon any notion of working-class struggle, instead looking towards movements of oppressed groups, or an alliance of such movements, as the primary means of achieving social change.

There are two significant problems with this approach. First of all, there is no necessary or immediate unity between different oppressed groups, which are by their nature riven by conflicting class differences.

Secondly, movements of the oppressed have no real social power to fundamentally transform the system unless they are allied with or become part of a workers' movement that can champion the demands of all the exploited and oppressed. A strategy based on autonomous movements of the oppressed, or even an alliance of different independent movements, is bound to lurch from left to right because it has no material force which can achieve its goal of ending oppression. There is also no guarantee that movements of the oppressed will produce the best political strategies for liberation. Often, the interests of middle-class elements have dominated movements and discussions about political strategy which take place within them.

Even a more directly confrontational Indigenous movement would not be able to avoid the questions of political power and social class. In Chile, the Mapuche militant organisation Coordinadora Arauco-Malleco (CAM) has organised direct occupations of lands stolen from the Indigenous population, even calling for armed struggle to defend these actions. Despite the heroism of CAM in the face of considerable state repression, it has not been able to achieve its goals and has become increasingly isolated as its leadership has been imprisoned. A key reason for this is the weaknesses of the political strategy adopted by CAM, which is based on the "accumulation of forces" through the gradual spread of autonomous Indigenous territory by means of land seizures, and which rejects the notion of any revolutionary upheaval

---
401. Marx and Engels 1848.

allied with the urban working class. However, as the Chilean Marxist Juan Valenzuela argues:

> By opposing the "accumulation of forces" to the "insurrectionary and revolutionary path", the problem of how to conquer the volumes of force necessary to deal a defeat to the oppressive capitalist State is avoided, something which is only possible through the power of the workers who put into operation the mainsprings of the economy together with the poor of the city and the countryside.[402]

Valenzuela also points out that CAM's strategy lacks "a more concrete conception of capitalist power, which is based on the exploitation of the working class, to which Mapuche workers also belong, many of whom work in the cities or the countryside, sometimes for miserable wages". He draws attention to the fact the main power of the capitalist state lies in the metropolitan cities, and so any strategy to defeat them must look towards an alliance with urban social forces. For "that reason, not counting on the strength of millions of workers who live and produce in this city and who are exploited by these same capitalist groups constitutes an important strategic deficit".[403]

Chile presents a very different situation from that in Australia. However, the example reveals that even if Indigenous people were able to organise themselves into a militant movement of remote communities engaged in direct action, or even armed struggle to take back their lands, the question of political strategy could not be avoided.

Instead of amalgamating separate, autonomous movements of the oppressed, we need to build a revolutionary working-class movement that can unite the working class across its different oppressed sections. This doesn't mean ignoring questions of oppression in order to "unite" the working class on the basis of a purely economistic program which appeals to the most backward sections of the class without challenging their ideas. This is how "united" working-class movements are often conceptualised by moderate

---
402. Valenzuela 2022.
403. Valenzuela 2022.

social democratic theorists. Through a complex interaction of working-class struggle, the development of an anti-capitalist layer of workers in the course of that struggle, and the creation of strong revolutionary working-class organisations, the possibility of a sustained working-class movement in solidarity with the fight for Indigenous liberation can emerge. Such a movement, while rooted in the industrial power of the working class, would not be counterposed to mass street protests or militant actions by minorities; these actions can play a vital role in giving confidence to the oppressed, in publicising their issues and in politicising the working class.

Real working-class unity can only be built from below, on the basis of a common class struggle against the capitalist system and an understanding of the unique social power wielded by the working class due to its structural position within capitalist society. Throughout this book, we have seen how periods in which the working class was on the offensive were also those in which Indigenous people were most easily able to advance the fight for their own particular interests. Today the working-class movement in Australia is at a low ebb; its resurgence could do much to aid the struggle for Indigenous rights. It could fight for significant increases in funding for Aboriginal housing, health, education and welfare, changes to criminal law, and the disarming and defunding of the police force. Such demands could be raised alongside those for greater democratic control by Indigenous people over their communities and resources. Such a fight would be able to forge a stronger connection between the workers' movement and Indigenous people.

Socialism and revolution

Ultimately, however, only the establishment of a socialist society can guarantee the complete abolition of Indigenous oppression. In the minds of many people today, socialism is equated either with social democratic welfare governments, like those in Northern Europe, or with Stalinist dictatorships. But a genuine socialist society would be one in which the working class, who make up the vast majority of the world's population, would have total democratic control over all aspects of society: economic, political and social.

Under socialism both Indigenous and non-indigenous people would, for the first time in history, have real control over their lives – over how and when they work, the resources which they produce and consume, and the world in which they live. Economic development would be planned on a rational basis according to the interests of the vast majority and under their democratic control, rather than according to the whims of a parasitic minority of capitalists. Political, social and cultural issues could be resolved fairly, because the structural basis for oppression would be dismantled; social equality wouldn't constantly be weighed up against what is profitable for the small, powerful elite. Rather than paternalistic consultations and hollow advisory bodies, a socialist system based on workers' democracy would ensure that the vast majority of humanity, including Indigenous people, would have a direct say in all aspects of society. Only with socialism, then, will Indigenous people finally have what capitalism has long promised but never delivered: the ability to determine their own fate. Remote communities would not have to face the bind of choosing between either exploitative economic development or living in grinding poverty without the hope of even minor improvements. The police force would be dismantled; a socialist society would have no need for a body of armed thugs harassing historically oppressed minorities. Most of all, the enormous resources created by hundreds of millions of workers around the world would finally be under the democratic control of the working class itself, and could be used to raise everyone's living standards to previously undreamt-of heights.

This might seem utopian, but we have seen glimpses of such a society in the historical high points of working-class struggle. In 1917, workers seized power in the major industrial cities of Russia and established workers' councils, while the peasantry overthrew their landlords and created similar bodies. These organisations coordinated the economic activity of the Russian working class and peasantry, and as the labouring majority took direct control of the economy, it in turn stripped the capitalists of their control over society's resources.

The full development of this revolution was cut short by the new socialist government's international isolation in the 1920s and the consequent victory of the Stalinist counter-revolution. However, the idea that workers could run their own lives without capitalism has continued to inspire struggles across the world.

The Russian revolutionaries and those who have looked to their example also sought to uproot and destroy the particular oppressions that plagued the capitalist societies in which their revolutions began. In Russia, Jews and other national and religious minorities had been mercilessly oppressed by the tsarist regime. During the Russian Revolution, there were huge upheavals among the oppressed nationalities of the Russian empire. When the working class took power in October, they abolished the 650 laws discriminating against Jews and many prominent Jewish Bolsheviks took leading positions in the new Soviet government – most famously Leon Trotsky, who would become the leader of the Red Army.

Many of those who made up the oppressed nationalities, including the Finns, the Ukrainians and others, demanded more than just equality – they wanted independence from Russia, even a socialist Russia. The new workers' state supported that right, despite the risk that it would sap resources from the revolution and leave it open to attack from counter-revolutionary forces. This was in line with the long tradition of opposition to oppression in the revolutionary wing of the Russian socialist movement. Lenin wrote extensively on the various nationalities oppressed in Russia, as Trotsky explained:

> Lenin early learned the inevitability of this development of centrifugal national movements in Russia, and for many years stubbornly fought – most particularly against Rosa Luxemburg – for that famous paragraph 9 of the old party programme which formulated the right of nations to self-determination – that is, to complete separation as states. In this the Bolshevik Party did not by any means undertake an evangel of separation. It merely assumed an obligation to struggle implacably against every form of national oppression, including the forcible retention of this or that nationality within the boundaries of the general state. Only in this way could the Russian proletariat gradually win the confidence of the oppressed nationalities.[404]

This strategy's spirit was incorporated into the Communist International,

---
404. Trotsky 1992 [1932], p.38.

established by the Bolsheviks to fan the flames of global revolution in the wake of 1917 and help the formation of mass revolutionary parties across the world. The International declared in 1920:

> [T]he Communist International's entire policy on the national and the colonial questions should rest primarily on a closer union of the proletarians and the working masses of all nations and countries for a joint revolutionary struggle to overthrow the landowners and the bourgeoisie. This union alone will guarantee victory over capitalism, without which the abolition of national oppression and inequality is impossible.[405]

This meant not just support for anti-colonial struggles but also opposition to racist immigration controls, solidarity with oppressed migrant populations and support for racially oppressed groups such as African Americans. At the Fourth Congress of the Communist International in 1922 there was an extensive discussion, which included the Black activists Otto Huiswoud and Claude McKay, about the role of the Communist Party in fighting against Black oppression in the United States.

The Congress adopted a series of theses on the struggle of Africans which explained that the "Communist International views with satisfaction the resistance of exploited Blacks to the attacks of their exploiters, since the enemy of their race and of the white worker is identical: capitalism and imperialism".

Under the influence of these discussions, the British and French Communist parties began to organise African and Caribbean migrant workers and activists during the 1920s. In 1924, French Communists helped found the Union Intercoloniale, composed of members living in France who hailed from the French colonies in Asia, Africa and the Caribbean. It included the important Senegalese working-class activist Lamine Senghor, who would join the Communist Party and run as the party candidate in the Paris local elections in 1925. British Communists organised Black workers within the trade unions by means of the National Minority Movement – in particular the Seamen's Minority Movement, which organised militant Black seamen.[406]

---
405. Lenin 1920.
406. Adi 2010.

In each case, the revolutionary left strove to analyse the particular characteristics of specific oppressed groups, and to develop tactics and strategies for combatting their oppression in line with the general principles of the revolutionary socialist movement. While Lenin and the revolutionary left of the early 20th century supported the struggles of the oppressed, they were not ignorant of the divergent interests of the various social classes within oppressed groups – this was the case at least until the degeneration of the Communist movement under Stalin. In his draft theses on the national and colonial question, Lenin argued "for a determined struggle against attempts to give a communist colouring to bourgeois-democratic liberation trends in the backward countries":

> [T]he Communist International should support bourgeois-democratic national movements in colonial and backward countries only on condition that, in these countries, the elements of future proletarian parties, which will be communist not only in name, are brought together and trained to understand their special tasks, i.e. those of the struggle against the bourgeois-democratic movements within their own nations. The Communist International must enter into a temporary alliance with bourgeois democracy in the colonial and backward countries, but should not merge with it, and should under all circumstances uphold the independence of the proletarian movement even if it is in its most embryonic form.[407]

One of the major motivations for supporting the right to self-determination in Russia was that it was the only way that Russian workers could hope to win the working-class members of the nationalities away from the influence of middle-class and bourgeois-nationalist leaders. There were extensive discussions among the Bolsheviks about the various social forces within the different oppressed nationalities, which ranged from the relatively Europeanised Finns to the pre-capitalist peoples of far-eastern Russia.

Similarly, there were important debates about the class divisions within the African American population, and how communists in the US should relate to political movements ranging from the Black nationalist Garveyites

---
407. Lenin 1920.

to the more respectable National Association for the Advancement of Colored People.

The revolutionary left also strongly opposed trends towards separatism or the autonomous organisation of oppressed groups *within* the socialist movement, as Trotsky explained:

> The policy of Bolshevism in the national sphere had also another side, apparently contradictory to the first but in reality supplementing it. Within the framework of the party, and of the workers' organisations in general, Bolshevism insisted upon a rigid centralism, implacably warring against every taint of nationalism which might set the workers one against the other or disunite them. While flatly refusing to the bourgeois states the right to impose compulsory citizenship, or even a state language, upon a national minority, Bolshevism at the same time made it a verily sacred task to unite as closely as possible, by means of voluntary class discipline, the workers of different nationalities. Thus it flatly rejected the national-federation principle in building the party. A revolutionary organisation is not the prototype of the future state, but merely the instrument for its creation. An instrument ought to be adapted to fashioning the product; it ought not to include the product. Thus a centralised organisation can guarantee the success of revolutionary struggle – even where the task is to destroy the centralised oppression of nationalities.[408]

Lenin criticised those who wanted to form separate socialist parties and organisations based on the different oppressed groups of Russia. In a debate with those who wished to create a Jewish socialist party that would be independent from the Russian socialist movement, he argued that the socialist movement should organise "propaganda and agitation in Yiddish, its own literature and congresses...to satisfy local needs and requirements arising out of the special features of Jewish life" – but he continued:

> [In] the struggle against the autocracy, the struggle against the bourgeoisie of Russia as a whole, we must act as a single and centralised militant organisation,

---
408. Trotsky 1992 [1932], p.38.

have behind us the whole of the proletariat, without distinction of language or nationality, a proletariat whose unity is cemented by the continual joint solution of problems of theory and practice, of tactics and organisation; and we must not set up organisations that would march separately, each along its own track; we must not weaken the force of our offensive by breaking up into numerous independent political parties; we must not introduce estrangement and isolation…[409]

These revolutionaries approached the question of the specific oppression of particular groups under capitalism from the point of view of the struggle for working-class power and socialism.

Building revolutionary class politics today

In order to end Indigenous oppression, the capitalist system must be overthrown and replaced with a socialist society. For this to happen the working class must reach a level of organisational and political maturity that will allow it to both see the necessity for a socialist revolution and be capable of taking the concrete steps necessary to carry it out. Essential to developing this level of organisational and political maturity is the creation of a significant layer of working-class militants, organised in a revolutionary Marxist party.

If you accept that it is capitalism that oppresses Indigenous people, then that means you need an explicitly anti-capitalist revolutionary organisation in order to defeat this oppression. Grassroots campaign groups taking up Indigenous demands can be very important for politicising Indigenous issues, but even the best will not be sufficient to end Indigenous oppression for good. Only an organisation of militant working-class activists, trained in the politics of socialism, will be capable of contributing effectively to a working-class seizure of power.

A political argument must be made among the Indigenous population – and all sections of the oppressed and exploited – for a working-class socialist perspective on the causes of and solutions to oppression. This requires an understanding of how the question of Indigenous liberation fits

---
409. Lenin 1903.

into the broader struggle against capitalism as a whole, and into the task of winning both Indigenous and non-indigenous activists to revolutionary Marxist politics.

Identity politics, with its narrow self-obsession with lived experience and elitist cynicism about the progressive potential of the working class, must be decisively rejected. Socialist support for Indigenous rights isn't based on the idea that Indigenous struggles are inherently more revolutionary than other struggles, but on the fact that it is in the interests of the working class to combat all forms of oppression and exploitation, as part of the fight to unite workers into a cohesive force that can destroy capitalism.

Any serious revival of struggle around Indigenous issues would raise a whole series of political debates, including some of those left unresolved by the movements of the '60s and '70s. What the exact terrain of such debates will be and which issues they will involve can't be predetermined, shaped as they will be by innumerable factors. However, a better understanding of both the strengths and weaknesses of how socialists in the past have tried to understand Indigenous politics can definitely help to clarify issues in the future. This is precisely what has been lacking on the Australian left.

This book is hardly the final word on these issues; many topics have only been touched upon, or dealt with inadequately, or require further research. Hopefully some of the ideas and arguments in this book can be the jumping off point for further research – into questions such as the contemporary class nature of the Indigenous population, the evolution of Indigenous political identity, the place of Indigenous-run organisations in the broader dynamics of the capitalist system, and the outcome of treaty processes. Despite these limitations, I hope this book can contribute to building the kind of socialist anti-racist movement we desperately need.

References

Writing this book was made substantially easier by the National Library of Australia's Trove project, which has digitised a huge amount of left-wing and trade union publications. The thousands and thousands of articles by the Australian left on Indigenous politics included in the Trove project were essential for a book on a topic that has so far been vastly underdocumented. As a part of the research for this book, I have also created a substantial guide to the writings of the Australian left on Indigenous issues which can be accessed at: https://medium.com/@jorhumphreys/a-guide-to-some-primary-resources-on-indigenous-struggle-the-workers-movement-and-the-socialist-40918703a0f7

ABS 2021, *Prisoners in Australia*, https://www.abs.gov.au/statistics/people/crime-and-justice/prisoners-australia/latest-release

ABS 2022, *National, state and territory population*, ABS website.

Adi, Hakim 2010, "The Comintern and Black Workers in Britain and France 1919–37", *Immigrants & Minorities: Historical Studies in Ethnicity, Migration and Diaspora*, 28 (2/3).

AIHW (Australian Institute of Health and Welfare) 2020, *Youth detention population in Australia 2019*, Bulletin 148, cat. no. JUV 131, Canberra.

Allam, Lorena and Nick Evershed 2022, "Almost half the massacres of Aboriginal people were by police or other government forces, research finds", *Guardian Australia*, 16 March.

Allen, Theodor 2012, *The Invention of the White Race: Volume 1. Racial Oppression and Social Control*, Verso Books.

Archibald-Binge, Ella 2021, "Black mould, termites and no electricity or hot water: Inside the Aboriginal housing divide", ABC News, 13 October 2021.

Armstrong, Mick 2007, *1,2,3 What are we fighting for? The Australian Student Movement from its Origins to the 1970s*, Socialist Alternative.

Armstrong, Mick 2020, "The NSW BLF: The battle to tame the concrete jungle", *Marxist Left Review*, 20, Winter.

Attwood, Bain 2020, *Empire and the Making of Native Title: Sovereignty, Property and Indigenous People*, Cambridge University Press.

Attwood, Bain 2021, *William Cooper: An Aboriginal Life*, The Miegunyah Press, Melbourne University.

Attwood, Bain, and Andrew Markus 2007, *The 1967 referendum : race, power and the Australian Constitution*, Aboriginal Studies Press.

Australian Defence Force Magazine 2019, "Garden Island project drives Indigenous engagement", 31 January. https://www.australiandefence.com.au/business/garden-island-project-drives-indigenous-engagement.

Banaji, Jairus 2010, *Theory as History: Essays on Modes of Production and Exploitation*, Haymarket Books.

BCA 2018, *Submission to the Joint Select Committee on Constitutional Recognition Relating to Aboriginal and Torres Strait Islander Peoples*, June.

BCA 2019, *Indigenous Engagement Survey*, 1 December. https://www.bca.com.au/2019_indigenous_engagement_survey1

Becker, Marc 2006, "Mariátegui, the Comintern, and the Indigenous Question in Latin America", *Science and Society*, 70 (4), October.

Beckett, Jeremy 1977, "The Torres Strait Islanders and the pearling industry: a case of internal colonialism", *Aboriginal History*, 1 (1/2).

Best, Ysola 2022, "O'Shane, Gladys Dorothy (1919–1965)", *Australian Dictionary of Biography*, National Centre of Biography, Australian National University.

BHP & BBCA 2021, *Joint statement Historic Agreement to provide intergenerational benefits to the Barada Barna people*, 13 August. https://www.bhp.com/news/media-centre/releases/2021/08/joint-statement-historic-agreement-to-provide-intergenerational-benefits-to-the-barada-barna-people

Black Peoples Union 2023, *Statement on anti-imperialism*. https://www.blackpeoplesunion.org/statements/statement-on-anti-imperialism

Bloodworth, Sandra 2006, "Aboriginal rights & trade unions in the 1950s and 1960s", *Marxist Interventions*. https://sa.org.au/interventions/

Boughton, Bob 2001, "The Communist Party of Australia's involvement in the struggle for Aboriginal and Torres Strait Islander Peoples' Rights 1920–1970", *Labour and Community: Historical Essays*, Raymond Markey (ed.), University of Wollongong Press. https://ro.uow.edu.au/cgi/viewcontent.cgi?article=1012&context=labour1999

Boughton, Bob 2005, "Assimilationism and anti-communism. A Reflection on Gerald Peel's 'Isles of the Torres Strait'", *Contesting Assimilation: Histories of Colonial and Indigenous Initiatives*, Perth: API-Network.

Bramble, Tom 2008, *Trade Unionism in Australia: A history from flood to ebb tide*, Cambridge University Press.

Bramble, Tom 2012, "Is there a labour aristocracy in Australia?", *Marxist Left Review*, 4, Winter.

Brian, Bernie 2001, *The Northern Territory's One Big Union. The Rise and Fall of the North Australian Workers' Union, 1911–1972*, PhD thesis, Northern Territory University.

Broome, Richard 2019, *Aboriginal Australians : 5th Edition*, Allen and Unwin.

Burgmann, Meredith and Verity Burgmann 2017, *Green Bans, Red Union: The Saving of a City*, NewSouth Publishing.

Carboni, Raffaello 2004 [1855], *The Eureka Stockade*, Melbourne University Publishing.

Cavanagh, Edward and Lorenzo Veracini (eds.) 2017, *The Routledge Handbook of the History of Settler Colonialism*, Routledge.

Clark, Ian 2005, *Another Side of Eureka – the Aboriginal presence on the Ballarat goldfields in 1854 – Were Aboriginal people involved in the Eureka rebellion?*, Working Paper, University of Ballarat Business School.

Clark, Jennifer 2008, *Aborigines & Activism: Race, Aborigines & the coming of the Sixties in Australia*, UWA Press.

Clayton-Dixon, Callum 2019, *Surviving New England: a history of Aboriginal resistance & resilience through the first forty years of the colonial apocalypse*, Anaiwan Language Revival Program.

Cleary, Paul 2021, *Title Fight: How the Yindjibarndi Battled and Defeated a Mining Giant*, Black Inc.

Closing the Gap 2020, *National Agreement on Closing the Gap*, July. https://www.closingthegap.gov.au/national-agreement/national-agreement-closing-the-gap

Closing the Gap 2022, *Commonwealth Closing the Gap Annual Report*, 30 November. https://www.niaa.gov.au/resource-centre/indigenous-affairs/commonwealth-closing-gap-annual-report-2022

Colonial Frontier Massacres Digital Map Project 2022. https://c21ch.newcastle.edu.au/colonialmassacres/map.php

Commonwealth of Australia 1937, *Aboriginal Welfare: Initial conference of Commonwealth and State Aboriginal Authorities*. https://nla.gov.au/nla.obj-52771316/

Communist Party of Australia (CPA) 1930, *Australia's Part in the World Revolution: Theses of the Central Committee Plenum, Communist Party of Australia, June 28th and 29th*. https://www.reasoninrevolt.net.au/objects/pdf/d0885.pdf

CPA 1967, *Full Human Rights for Aborigines and Torres Strait Islanders, A program adopted by the 21st Congress of the Communist Party of Australia June 1967*. https://www.marxists.org/history/international/comintern/sections/australia/1967/aborigines.htm

Connell, RW and TH Irving 1980, *Class Structure in Australian History: Documents, Narrative and Argument*, Longman Cheshire.

Cook, Kevin and Heather Goodall 2013, *Making Change Happen: Black and White Activists talk to Kevin Cook about Aboriginal, Union and Liberation Politics*, Aboriginal History Monographs.

Cosoleto, Tara 2022, "Vic treaty negotiations a step closer", *Canberra Times*, 11 March.

Coulthard, Glen 2014, *Red Skin, White Masks: Rejecting the Colonial Politics of Recognition*, University of Minnesota Press.

Cunneen, Chris 2022, "Stepney, Andrew Stuart (Andy) (1851–1914)", *People Australia*, National Centre of Biography, Australian National University. https://ia.anu.edu.au/biography/stepney-andrew-stuart-andy-32470

d'Avigdor, Lewis 2019, "Black Power and white solidarity: The Action Conference on Racism and Education, Brisbane 1972", in *The Far Left in Australia Since 1945*, Jon Piccini, Evan Smith and Matthew Worley (eds.), Routledge.

Davies, Jack 2023, "The world turned outside in: Settler colonial studies and political economy", *Historical Materialism* Issue 32 (2&3): Race and Capital.

Day, Rowan and Drew Cottle 2015, "Wobblies on the Wallaby", *Labour History*, 109, November.

Day, William 2019, *A brief history of the strikes by Aboriginal workers in Darwin, 1947–1951*. https://www.drbilldayanthropologist.com/resources/NadpurAKAFredWaters&PrinceofWales1951BD.pdf

de Kruijff, Peter 2021, "Australian billionaires face steep challenge to mine coal in Canada's Rocky Mountains", *Sydney Morning Herald*, 27 July.

Docker, Comrade 1934, "Work in Districts 5 & 6", *Communist Review*, 1 (3), June.

Donaldson, Mike, Lee Bursill and Mary Jacobs 2017, *A History of Aboriginal Illawarra, Volume 2: Colonisation*, Dharawal Publications.

Donaldson, Mike 2020, "Ray Peckham 1929–", in *Comrades! Lives of Australian Communists*, Bob Boughton, Danny Blackman, Mike Donaldson, Carmel Shute and Beverly Symons (eds.), SEARCH Foundation, Sydney.

Drachewych, Oleksa 2017, *The Comintern and the Communist Parties of South Africa, Canada, and Australia on the questions of Imperialism, Nationality and Race, 1919–1943*, PhD thesis, McMasters University. https://macsphere.mcmaster.ca/bitstream/11375/22007/2/drachewych_oleksa_m_2017september_PhD.pdf

Drachewych, Oleksa 2021, "Settler Colonialism and the Communist International", *The Palgrave Encyclopedia of Imperialism and Anti-Imperialism*, second edition, Palgrave MacMillan.

Dunbar-Ortiz, Roxanne 2016, "'A sense of hope and the possibility of solidarity': Colonialism, capitalism, and Native liberation", *International Socialist Review*, 103. https://isreview.org/issue/103/

Englert, Sai 2020, "Settlers, Workers, and the Logic of Accumulation by Dispossession", *Antipode: A Radical Journal of Geography*, 52 (3). https://www.researchgate.net/publication/343085801_Settlers_Workers_and_the_Logic_of_Accumulation_by_Dispossession

Evans, M, C Polidano, J Moschion, M Langton, M Storey, P Jensen and S Kurland 2021, *Indigenous Businesses Sector Snapshot Study, Insights from I-BLADE 1.0*, The University of Melbourne. https://fbe.unimelb.edu.au/cibl/assets/snapshot/RFQ03898-M-and-M-Snapshot-Study.pdf

Fieldes, Diane 1997, *Land Rights Now!*, Socialist Alternative.

Foley, Gary 1997, *Native Title is not Land Rights*. http://www.kooriweb.org/foley/essays/pdf_essays/native title is not land rights.pdf

Foley, Gary 2001, *Black power in Redfern 1968–1972*. http://gooriweb.org/history/233.pdf

Gapps, Stephen 2021, *Gudyarra: The first Wiradyuri war of resistance – The Bathurst War 1822–1824*, NewSouth Publishing.

Gibson, Padraic 2020, *"Stop the war on Aborigines": The Communist Party of Australia and the fight for Aboriginal rights 1920–1934*, unpublished PhD thesis, University of Newcastle.

Gilbert, Kevin 2013 [1977], *Because a white man'll never do it*, Angus and Robertson.

Gittins, Ross 2018, "Finally, an Indigenous middle class emerges", *Sydney Morning Herald*, 9 February.

Goodall, Heather 2008, *Invasion to embassy: land in Aboriginal politics in New South Wales, 1770–1972*, Sydney University Press.

Gramsci, Antonio 1971, *Selections from the Prison Notebooks*, International Publishers, New York.

Gray, Geoffrey 2007, *A Cautious Silence: The Politics of Australian Anthropology*, Aboriginal Studies Press.

Hall, Bianca 2023, "Division over Voice as huge crowd turns out for Invasion Day rally", *Sydney Morning Herald*, 26 January.

Hirson, Baruch 1990, "The Black Republic Slogan – Part II: The Response of the Trotskyists", *Searchlight South Africa*, 1 (4), February.

Holt, Stephen 1988, *A Veritable Dynamo: Lloyd Ross, the Australian Railways Union and left-wing politics in inter-war Australia*, PhD thesis, Australian National University.

Horner, Jack 1974, *Vote for Ferguson for Aboriginal freedom: a biography*, Australia and New Zealand Book Co.

Horner, Jack 2012, "Leon, Lester (Charlie) (1900–1982)", *Australian Dictionary of Biography*, National Centre of Biography, Australian National University,

Howden, Saffron 2012, "Plan to explore for gas under 40% of state", *Sydney Morning Herald*, 8 December.

Howitt, William 2011 [1855], *Land, Labour and Gold: Two Years in Victoria: with Visits to Sydney and Van Diemen's Land*, Cambridge University Press.

Humphreys, Jordan 2021, "Aboriginal unionists in the 1890s shearers' strikes: a forgotten history", *Marxist Left Review*, 22, Winter.

Humphreys, Jordan 2022a, "Fury over Indigenous centre closure", *Red Flag*, 2 August.

Humphreys, Jordan 2022b, "When Black Power came to Wee Waa: the 1973 cotton chippers' strike", *Red Flag*, 5 April.

James, CLR 2018, *C.L.R. James and Revolutionary Marxism: Selected Writings of C.L.R. James 1939–1949*, Haymarket Books.

Keefer, Tom 2010, "Marxism, Indigenous Struggles, and the Tragedy of 'Stagism'", *Upping the Anti: a journal of theory and action*, 10, 18 May. https://uppingtheanti.org/journal/article/10-marxism-indigenous-struggles-and-the-tragedy-of-stagism

Knowles, Rachel 2021, "BHP pulls out in front as Rio Tinto flounders", *National Indigenous Times*, 22 July.

Krebs, Mike 2008, *For the Land! Roots and Revolutionary Dynamics of Indigenous Struggles in Canada*, Socialist Voice.

Lawton, Amy 2016, *Census 2016 Topic Paper: Indigenous population of Greater Western Sydney*, WESTIR Ltd.

Lenin, VI 1903, "Does the Jewish Proletariat Need an 'Independent Political Party'?", *Iskra*, no. 34, 15 February. https://www.marxists.org/archive/lenin/works/1903/feb/15.htm

Lenin, VI 1925 [1917], "Lecture on the 1905 Revolution", *Pravda*, no. 18, 22 January.

Lenin, VI 1920, *Draft Theses on National and Colonial Questions For The Second Congress Of The Communist International*. https://marxists.org/archive/lenin/works/1920/jun/05.htm

Macintyre, Stuart 1998, *The Reds: The Communist Party of Australia from origins to illegality*, Allen & Unwin.

Maddison, Sarah 2019, *The Colonial Fantasy: Why white Australia can't solve black problems*, Allen & Unwin.

Mansell, Ken 1980, *The Marxism and Strategic Concepts of the Communist Party of Australia 1963–1972*, honours thesis, La Trobe University.

Mariátegui, José Carlos 2021, *Selected Works of José Carlos Mariátegui*, Iskra Books.

Marks, Russell 2022, *Black Lives, White Law: Locked Up and Locked Out in Australia*, La Trobe University Press.

Martínez, Julia 1999, *Plural Australia: Aboriginal and Asian labour in tropical white Australia, Darwin, 1911–1940*, PhD thesis, University of Wollongong.

Marx, Karl 1990 [1867], *Capital: A Critique of Political Economy. Volume I*, Penguin Books.

Marx, Karl and Frederick Engels 1848, *Manifesto of the Communist Party*. https://marxists.org/archive/marx/works/1848/communist-manifesto/

Mason, Arthur 2002, "The rise of an Alaskan Native bourgeoisie", *Études/Inuit/Studies*, 26 (2), Populations et migrations / Populations and Migrations.

Maynard, John 2007, *Fight for liberty and freedom: the origins of Australian Aboriginal activism*, Aboriginal Studies Press.

McKinnon, Crystal 2008, "Duplicity and deceit: Gary Foley's take on Rudd's apology to the stolen generations", *Melbourne Historical Journal*, Issue 36, University of Melbourne Postgraduate Association.

McNeill, Dougal 2015, "Māori and Communism in the 1930s", *ISO Aotearoa*, 9 July. https://iso.org.nz/2015/07/09/maori-and-communism-in-the-1930s/

McQueen, Humphrey 1976, *A New Britannia: An argument concerning the social origins of Australian radicalism and nationalism*, Penguin Books.

Menghetti, Diane 2018, *The Red North: The Popular Front in North Queensland*, Resistance Books.

Merritt, John 1986, *The Making of the AWU*, Oxford University Press.

Middleton, Hannah 1977, *But now we want the land back: A history of the Australian Aboriginal People*, New Age Publishers.

Middleton, Hannah 2008, "Reflections on the Aboriginal Movement", *Australian Marxist Review*, 47, January.

Middleton, Hannah 2020, "The Aboriginal National Minority: Class and National Formation", *Australian Marxist Review*, Issue 70, December.

Mitchell, Marybelle 1996, *From Talking Chiefs to Native Corporate Elite: The Birth of Class and Nationalism among Canadian Inuit*, McGill-Queen's University Press.

Morgan, George 2006, *Unsettled Places: Aboriginal people and urbanisation in New South Wales*, Wakefield Press.

Morris, Barry 2014, *Protest, land rights and riots : postcolonial struggles in Australia in the 1980s*, Berghahn Books.

Morrissey, Michael 2006, "The Australian state and Indigenous people 1990–2006", *Journal of Sociology*, 42 (4), December.

National Indigenous Australians Agency 2021, *Indigenous Procurement Policy*. https://www.niaa.gov.au/indigenous-affairs/economic-development/indigenous-procurement-policy-ipp

Norman, Heidi 2015, *What do we want? A political history of Aboriginal land rights in New South Wales*, Aboriginal Studies Press.

Norris, Murray 2003 [1982], "Rebuilding the North Australian Workers Union, 1942–1951", in *A few rough reds: Stories of rank and file organising*, Hal Alexander and Phil Griffiths (eds.), Australian Society for the Study of Labour History.

Nowlin, Christopher 2020, "Indigenous Capitalism and Resource Development in an Age of Climate Change: A Timely Dance with the Devil?", *McGill Journal of Sustainable Development Law*, 17 (1).

O'Lincoln, Tom 1985, *Into the Mainstream: The Decline of Australian Communism*, Stained Wattle Press.

O'Lincoln, Tom 2023 [1993], *Years of Rage: social conflicts in the Fraser era*, Interventions.

Owen, Chris 2016, *"Every Mother's Son is Guilty": Policing the Kimberley Frontier of Western Australia 1882–1905*, UWA Publishing.

Paisley, Fiona 2012, *The Lone Protestor: A M Fernando in Australia and Europe*, Aboriginal Studies Press.

Palmer, Bryan 2004, "Review: Race and Revolution", *Labour / Le Travail*, 54, Fall.

Peckham, Ray and Rob Willis 2012, *Ray Peckham interviewed by Rob Willis in the Activists for Indigenous rights in the mid 20th century oral history project* [sound recording]. https://nla.gov.au/nla.obj-213880846/listen

Pedersen, Howard and Banjo Woorunmurra 1995, *Jandamarra and the Bunuba resistance*, Magabala Books.

Peel, Gerald 1947, *Isles of the Torres Straits: an Australian responsibility*, Current Book Distributors.

Perheentupa, Johanna 2020, *Redfern: Aboriginal activism in the 1970s*, Aboriginal Studies Press.

Philips, Gregory and Tanja Hirvonen 2021, "Decolonisation of the workplace! Is more important than ever", *IndigenousX*, 17 November. https://indigenousx.com.au/decolonisation-of-the-workplace-is-more-important-than-ever/

Pittock, A Barrie 1970, *Easter 1970 and the origins of the National Tribal Council: A Personal View*. http://www.kooriweb.org/foley/resources/pdfs/142.pdf

Poata-Smith, ES Te Ahu 2001, *The political economy of Māori protest politics, 1968–1995 : a Marxist analysis of the roots of Māori oppression and the politics of resistance*, unpublished PhD thesis, University of Otago, Dunedin, New Zealand.

Reynolds, Henry 1983, "Aborigines and European social hierarchy", *Aboriginal History*, 7 (1/2).

Riddell, John (ed.) 2012, *Toward the United Front: Proceedings of the Fourth Congress of the Communist International, 1922*, Haymarket Books.

Ritter, David 2009, *Contesting Native Title: From Controversy to Consensus*, Allen & Uwin.

Robinson, Fergus and Barry York 1977, *The Black resistance : an introduction to the history of the Aborigines' struggle against British Colonialism*, Widescope.

Rose, Samuel W 2015, "Marxism and mode of production in the anthropology of native North America", *FocaalBlog*, 17 November. www.focaalblog.com/2015/11/17/samuel-w-rose-marxism-and-mode-of-production-in-the-anthropology-of-native-north-america.

Rowse, Tim 2017, *Indigenous and other Australians since 1901*, UNSW Press.

S Shirodkar, B Hunter and D Foley 2018, "Ongoing growth in the number of Indigenous Australians in Business", Working Paper, *Centre for Aboriginal Economic Policy Research*, ANU College of Arts & Social Sciences.

Sakai, J 2014 [1983], *Settlers: The Mythology of the White Proletariat from Mayflower to Modern*, Kersplebedeb Publishing.

Scrimgeour, Anne 2020, *On Red Earth Walking: The Pilbara Aboriginal Strike, Western Australia 1946–49*, Monash University Publishing.

Shachtman, Max 2003, *Race and Revolution*, Verso Books.

Sharma, Nandita 2020, *Home Rule: National Sovereignty and the Separation of Natives and Migrants*, Duke University Press.

Smee, Ben 2023a, "Mob surrounding Rockhampton home blocked by police amid tensions over youth crime", *Guardian Australia*, 8 May.

Smee, Ben 2023b, "Vigilante fears: Queensland man accused of chasing stolen car had 'edged weapons', police say", *Guardian Australia*, 11 May.

Smit, Sarah 2021a, "Empowerment is the key to FMG's joint ventures", *National Indigenous Times*, 16 June.

Smit, Sarah 2021b, "Warrikal earns landmark deal with FMG", *National Indigenous Times*, 3 August.

Stanbrook, Gavin and Diane Fieldes 2019, "William Ferguson: The life of an Aboriginal rebel", *Marxist Left Review*, 18, Winter.

Sullivan, AJ 2005 [1916], "Retrospect of a Labourer's Life, 1872 to 1916", *Hummer*, Australian Society for the Study of Labour History, 4 (4), Winter.

Sustar, Lee 2012, "Self-Determination and the 'Black Belt'", *Socialist Worker* (US), 15 June.

Supply Nation 2022, *State of Indigenous Business: An analysis of procurement spending patterns with Indigenous businesses 2019–2021*. https://supplynation.org.au/research-paper/an-analysis-of-procurement-spending-patterns-with-indigenous-businesses-2019-2021/

Sykes, Roberta 1989, *Black Majority*, Hudson Publishing.

Taffe, Sue 2005, *Black and White Together: FCAATSI: The Federal Council for the Advancement of Aborigines and Torres Straight Islanders 1958–1972*, University of Queensland Press.

Taffe, Sue 2009, "The Cairns Aborigines and Torres Strait Islander Advancement League and the Community of the Left", *Labour History*, 97, November.

Townsend, Terry 2009, *The Aboriginal Struggle & the Left*, Resistance Books.

Trotsky, Leon 1967, *Leon Trotsky on Black Nationalism & Self-Determination*, Pathfinder Press.

Trotsky, Leon 1992 [1932], *History of the Russian Revolution*, Pathfinder Press.

Valenzuela, Juan 2022, "La lucha mapuche después del rechazo: ¿ahora qué?", *Ideas Socialistas*, September.

Ward, Charlie 2016, *A Handful of Dust: The Gurindji Struggle, After the Walk-Off*, Monash University Publishing.

Wolfe, Patrick 1999, *Settler colonialism and the transformation of anthropology*, Bloomsbury Publishing.

Wolfe, Patrick 2001, "Land, Labor, and Difference: Elementary Structures of Race", *The American Historical Review*, 106 (3), June.

Wolfe, Patrick 2006, "Settler colonialism and the elimination of the native", *Journal of Genocide Research*, 8 (4), December.

Wolfe, Patrick 2016, *Traces of History: Elementary Structures of Race*, Verso.

Wright, Tom 1944 [1939], *New Deal for the Aborigines*, Current Book Distributors, Sydney.

Wright, Tom 1947, "Fight for Aborigines", *Communist Review*, April.

Zumoff, Jacob 2014, *The Communist International and US Communism, 1919–1929*, Haymarket Books.

REDFLAG

Socialist Alternative publishes Red Flag, to provide an unashamedly anti-capitalist voice in Australian politics.

Our paper also serves as an educational resource — we cover the hidden history of class struggle as well as core concepts in Marxist theory. We raise awareness of international struggles and contribute to global debates on the socialist left.

We don't receive corporate donations — to continue our work we need your support.

Read Red Flag and subscribe at redflag.org.au

REDFLAG

Socialist Alternative publishes *Red Flag* to provide an unashamedly anti-capitalist voice in Australian politics.

Our paper also serves as an educational resource – we cover the hidden history of class struggle as well as core concepts in Marxist theory. We raise awareness of international struggles and contribute to global debates on the socialist left.

We don't receive corporate donations – to continue our work, we need your support.

Read *Red Flag* and subscribe at **redflag.org.au**

mlr
Marxist Left Review

A peer-reviewed theoretical journal published twice yearly by Socialist Alternative.

- Serious Marxist analysis of our changing world
- Historical, political and economic research
- Engagement with debates on the Australian and international left

Read now & subscribe:
marxistleftreview.org

mlr

Marxist Left Review

A peer-reviewed theoretical journal published twice yearly by Socialist Alternative.

- Serious Marxist analysis of our changing world
- Historical political and economic research
- Engagement with debates on the Australian and international left

Read now & subscribe:
marxistleftreview